WHY EUROPE?
PROBLEMS OF CULTURE AND IDENTITY

VOLUME 1: Political and Historical Dimensions

From the same publishers

Joe Andrew, Malcolm Crook, Diana Holmes and Eva Kolinsky (*editors*)
WHY EUROPE? PROBLEMS OF CULTURE AND IDENTITY
Volume 2: Media, Film, Gender, Youth and Education

Why Europe? Problems of Culture and Identity

Volume 1: Political and Historical Dimensions

Edited by

Joe Andrew
Professor of Russian
Keele University

Malcolm Crook
Professor of History
Keele University

and

Michael Waller
Professor of Politics and
Director of European Studies
Keele University

First published in Great Britain 2000 by
MACMILLAN PRESS LTD
Houndmills, Basingstoke, Hampshire RG21 6XS and London
Companies and representatives throughout the world

A catalogue record for this book is available from the British Library.

ISBN 0–333–72443–7

First published in the United States of America 2000 by
ST. MARTIN'S PRESS, INC.,
Scholarly and Reference Division,
175 Fifth Avenue, New York, N.Y. 10010

ISBN 0–312–22793–0

Library of Congress Cataloging-in-Publication Data
Why Europe? : problems of culture and identity / edited by Joe Andrew,
Malcolm Crook and Michael Waller.
p. cm.
Based on papers presented at a conference held at Keele
University, Sept. 6–9, 1996.
Includes bibliographical references and index.
Contents: v. 1. Political and historical dimensions — v.
2. Media, film, gender, youth and education.
ISBN 0–312–22793–0 (v. 1 : cloth). — ISBN 0–312–22794–9 (v. 2 :
cloth).
1. Europe—Politics and government Congresses.   2. Nationalism–
–Europe Congresses.   3. Ethnicity—Europe Congresses.   I. Andrew,
Joe.   II. Crook, Malcolm, 1948–   .   III. Waller, Michael, 1934–   .
D217.W49   1999
940 — dc21   99–36945
                                                              CIP

This book is printed on paper suitable for recycling and made from fully managed and
sustained forest sources.

10   9   8   7   6   5   4   3   2   1
09   08   07   06   05   04   03   02   01   00

Printed and bound in Great Britain by Antony Rowe Ltd, Chippenham, Wiltshire

Contents

List of Figures

Preface

The chapters in this volume, like those in the companion volume, *Media, Film, Gender, Youth and Education*, arise from a conference, 'Why Europe? Problems of Culture and Identity,' which was held at Keele University, on 6–9 September 1996. While the scope of the conference, and of both volumes, was by no means limited by or to the European Union, it had as its impulse the Intergovernmental Conference which took place in that year. Following on from Maastricht, this event was envisaged as helping to determine the future direction, shape and size of Europe as a whole, and the European Union in particular.

The conference adopted a distinctive approach to these issues. Concentrating on questions of history, origins, culture and citizenship, it sought to evaluate the extent to which a specifically European identity had begun to emerge, and what profile this identity was beginning to take. The conference, and this volume alongside its 'twin', addressed a range of issues which underlie the notions of European identity. Among them are: What does it mean to be a European? What ideologies have shaped the political debate over the last two centuries? What place will minorities find in the Europe of the twenty-first century? What roles will women play in the future communities? Will Europe become more open to diversity, or become increasingly introspective, a 'fortress Europe'?

The orientation of the conference was organized by the work of the Department of Modern Languages and the Keele European Research Centre, and focused primarily, but not exclusively, on cultural issues, as the chapters in this volume will illustrate.

A number of individuals and organizations were instrumental in making the conference a success, and I would like to take this opportunity to thank both them and those who have helped me with the preparation of this volume. In particular, I wish to thank La Délégation Culturelle Française, the ESRC and the Goethe Institut; my fellow organizers and editors, Malcolm Crook, Diana Holmes, Eva Kolinsky and Michael Waller, as well as Pat Borsky, Joan Hope, Shirley Stubbs; and Angela Merryweather who has provided invaluable assistance in preparing this volume for publication.

JOE ANDREW

Notes on the Contributors

Edward Acton is Professor of Modern European History at the University of East Anglia. His previous posts have been at the universities of Liverpool and Manchester. He is the author of *Alexander Herzen and the Role of the Intellectual Revolutionary* (1979), *Rethinking the Russian Revolution* (1990), *Russia: the Tsarist and Soviet Legacy* (1995), *Stalinism and Nazism: a Suitable Case for Comparison?* (1998), and co-editor of *Critical Companion to the Russian Revolution, 1914–1921* (1997). He is currently writing, with two co-authors, a history of Europe from Napoleon to the Millennium for Penguin, taking as the central theme the rise, fall and remaking of the nation-state.

Joe Andrew is Professor of Russian at Keele University. He has published four monographs on Russian literature and society and women in Russian literature, and has edited a number of works devoted to structural analysis and formalism. He is co-chair of the Neo-Formalist Circle and co-edits its journal, *Essays in Poetics*.

Christopher Brewin is Lecturer in International Relations at Keele University. He has written extensively on the institutions and policies of the European Union, and its relations with non-member states. He is the author of *The European Union and Cyprus* (1999).

Margaret Canovan is Professor of Political Thought at Keele University, having previously taught at the University of Lancaster. She has published books and articles on many areas of political thought, including *Hannah Arendt: a Reinterpretation of her Political Thought* (1992) and *Nationhood and Political Theory* (1996).

Malcolm Crook is Reader in History at Keele University. He has published *Toulon in War and Revolution, from the Ancien Régime to the Restoration, 1750–1820* (1991), *Elections in the French Revolution: an Apprenticeship in Democracy, 1789–1799* (1996) and *Napoleon Comes to Power: Democracy and Dictatorship in Revolutionary France, 1795–1804* (1998). He continues to work on the history of Revolutionary and Napoleonic France, while preparing a study of electoral culture in nineteenth-century France.

Jolyon Howorth is Professor of French Civilization and Jean Monnet Professor of European Political Union at the University of Bath. He has held previous appointments at the Sorbonne, and Wisconsin, Madison, Aston and Harvard universities. He has published extensively on French and European foreign and security policy, including *Europeans on Europe: Transnational Visions of a New Continent*, co-edited with Mairi Maclean (1992), and *The European Union and National Defence Policy*, co-edited with Anand Menon (1998).

Robert Hudson is Senior Lecturer in European History and Politics and Head of European Studies at the University of Derby. He is a member of the European Union-funded Thematic Network on Ethnic Conflict and also a fellow of the Royal Society of Arts and has recently worked for the OSCE in Serbia and Bosnia-Herzegovina. His principal area of research is focused upon Yugoslavia and the Yugoslav Successor States and issues of identity and belonging. His fourth book, *Politics of Identity: Migrations and Minorities in Multi-Cultural States* has recently been published by Macmillan.

Brian Jenkins is Professor of French Area Studies at the University of Portsmouth. He is the author of *Nationalism in France: Class and Nation since 1789* (1990) and editor (with S. Sofos) of *Nation and Identity in Contemporary Europe* (1996). He is also co-editor of the *Journal of European Area Studies: an Interdisciplinary Review.*

Aleksandar Pavković is Associate Professor in Politics at Macquarie University, Sydney. He is the author of *The Fragmentation of Yugoslavia: Nationalism in a Multinational State* (1997) and *Slobodan Jovanovic: an Unsentimental Approach to Politics* (1993) and an editor of *Nationalism and Postcommunism* (1995) and *The Serbs and their Leaders in the Twentieth Century* (1997). He has also written on utopian thought.

Nicole Questiaux studied at the Institut d'Etudes politiques and the Ecole nationale d'administration, before fulfilling a variety of posts at the French Conseil d'Etat, culminating as Section President in that body. She is now Honorary Section President at the Conseil d'Etat. She has taught social policy in the Institut d'Etudes politiques and has published *Le Traité du social* with J. Fournier and J. M. Delarue.

Robert Reid lectured in Slavonic Studies at Queen's University, Belfast, before moving, in 1989, to Keele University where he is now Reader in Russian. His research interests centre on Russian Romanticism and his publications include monographs on works by Pushkin and Lermontov. He is also co-editor of the journal *Essays in Poetics* and translates Russian poetry.

Bego de la Serna-López graduated from the Universidad Complutense in Madrid, before undertaking postgraduate study in Public Policy at QMWC in London. Her current research interests are in the field of citizenship in nineteenth-century Europe, with particular reference to Germany.

Michael Tappin has been the Member of the European Parliament for Staffordshire West and Congleton since 1994. In this capacity he is European Parliamentary Labour Party Secretary, President of the European Parliament Ceramic Intergroup, Member of the European Parliament Budget and Budget Control Committees, and substitute member of the Economic, Monetary and Industrial Policy Committee. He has also been Lecturer in American Politics since 1974 at Keele University.

Wolfgang Ullmann studied theology and philosophy in Berlin and Göttingen, before taking his doctorate and working in the church in Saxony. He then went on to be Professor in Church History at the Church University in Naumburg. After holding an equivalent position in Berlin-Brandenburg, he was a co-founder in 1989 of the Citizens' Movement 'Democracy Now'. He has since held various positions on the Joint Constitutional Committee, and has been an MEP for the Greens since 1994.

Hans-Joachim Veen is Professor of Comparative Government at the University of Trier. He has published widely in the fields of voting behaviour, political attitudes and party systems in Germany and Western Europe more broadly. His main publications include *Opposition in the German Bundestag* (1976), *Christian-Democratic and Conservative Parties in Western Europe* (5 vols, ed., 1984–98), *The Greens in the Early Nineties* (1992), *Transformation and Change in Western European Party Systems* (ed., 1995).

Michael Waller is Professor of Politics and Director of European Studies at Keele University. The main focus of his work has been communism, on which he has published a trilogy of books: *The Language of Communism* (1972), *Democratic Centralism: an Historical Commentary* (1981) and *The End of the Communist Power Monopoly* (1993). His interest since the fall of communism in Europe has been on the process of party formation, and on loyalty and the post-national state, which has brought his work into a broader European framework. He is Joint editor and co-founder of *The Journal of Communist Politics and Transition Politics*.

Introduction:
the Remaking of Europe
Michael Waller, Malcolm Crook and
Joe Andrew

Had it been in today's discussions about Europe that Klemens Metternich, through some time-warp, made his celebrated tongue-in-cheek remark that Asia begins in the Landstrasse district of Vienna he would have been given very bad marks for political correctness, but there are aspects of his remark that still evoke the difficulties of today's discussions on Europe's identity, and above all their open-endedness. For one thing, this Austrian Chancellor had a political axe to grind in the context of the relations between Austria and its subject peoples at the time when he made the remark, and in any case his image of what lay beyond Vienna may have been influenced by his Rhineland origins. Statements about what constitutes Europe clearly have to be evaluated in terms of the social and political position of their author in time and space, which makes generalization hazardous. Secondly, his supposedly geographical statement cloaked rather thinly a judgement about cultural distinctions, with marked political overtones, and in current discussions about Europe and its identity difficulties are still encountered in relating cultural, geographical and political factors to one another – a problem that comes about largely because of the obdurately open-endedness of definitions of Europe. On cultural criteria there is hardly a corner of the globe that is not in a sense European. As for the geography, few today would find much value in a distinction that puts Europe to one side of a stone in the Ural hills and Asia to the other.

Politics is another matter. Had Metternich phrased his remark in a way slightly less offensive to his Hungarian neighbours by locating in the suburbs of Vienna not the beginning of Asia but the end of Europe his words would have evoked today's circumstances in yet another way. At the time of writing, in 1998, the Austrian frontier, some 50 kilometres east of Vienna, constitutes the frontier also, in that part of the world, of the European Union. Today, the 15 member states of the Union have come to constitute Europe in a very sharp organizational sense. However intense the anguish among members of that Union about what their relationship should be to one another, and however credible the claims of at least some of the peoples outside that boundary to be no less European than those within it,

1

in this case there is no doubt about who is in and who is out. That said, despite the sharpness of the definition, Europe in these terms is expandable. There is a substantial antechamber of states, including Turkey, whose accession to the Union is officially a matter of time, just as at its origins this organizational Europe comprised just six states.

IDENTITY AND IDENTIFICATION

It is not the main concern of this book to attempt to winnow out a precise and comprehensive description of a general European identity. Although considerable attention will be accorded to the vital eastern periphery, the focus falls on the European Union, the process of integration within it, and the impact of that process on neighbouring countries. It deals with the way in which the organizational logic of integration contrasts with the unbounded nature of European culture and with the numerous and conflicting loyalties, shaped by history, that the Union's component members display. It adopts an approach that favours a view of European history in terms of the making and remaking of a complex and mobile epicentre, the formation of this epicentre and the links with its periphery being determined in different ways in different historical periods. Europe has had a geographical core to the extent that a contiguous group of countries in a particular location have shared a dynamic process of economic and social development which inevitably created a periphery in developmental terms. But a core has developed also in terms of ideas and values which have shown a propensity to travel while remaining related in an organic way with the countries of their origin. To this should be added the crucial consideration, which comes out strongly in the pages that follow, that it is flesh-and-blood people who have driven the development of this composite epicentre and its periphery, as beneficiaries or victims in either case. That is, European development has been a matter of geopolitics (Brewin, Chapter 5), in which physical boundaries and the reach of influential ideas have varied, depending on the political relationships obtaining at any given time.

This geopolitical view of Europe casts a particular light on the notion of the 'Other', in relation to which Europe in many presentations has been seen to have developed, since the specification of that Other has likewise depended on the political forces in play and cannot be seen as immutable. Interactions with Others – notably Islam and Russia – have indeed marked the development of a European identity. But this view distracts attention from the contribution that has been made to the formation of a European identity by interactions among the peoples and states of a European epicentre themselves and – by definition to a diminishing extent – its periphery. Empire, religion, dynastic marriages, intellectual movements, industrial development, trade, perhaps above all wars and their subsequent treaties have all played their part. In fact, war between the denizens of the epicentre acting in concert and an Other have been very rare, even the Cold War representing an invasion of the periphery into a part of the epicentre. On the other hand, wars within the epicentre have been constitutive of that epicentre, if the attendant processes of treaty-making are taken into account. With the treaty-making relating to war have gone all the multifarious councils, diets, conferences – religious and secular – through which the components of the epicentre and its periphery have got to know one another and to take the measure of one another. It hardly needs pointing out that it was this epicentre itself that was the locus for both the occurrence of the Second World War and for the treaty-making designed to prevent its repetition – including the Treaty of Rome.

Furthermore, changes in what constitutes the Other for Europe illustrate well the open-endedness of the general European identity, and also the way in which that identity has been shaped by the intensity of contacts in and around the European epicentre. They illustrate also another theme that occurs in this book – the lag between conceptions of Europe and what is actually going on. The clearest case of an Other, dating from the seventh century and creating a powerful myth about where the boundaries of Europe lie, is Islam. That Europe has for a long time assimilated without demur Muslim communities in territories once ruled by Turkey, and notably in Bosnia, may be held not to qualify to any great extent the perceived incompatibility between Europe and Islam. But what certainly must qualify it is the presence in a number of countries of the European epicentre of substantial immigrant Muslim communities, enjoying – though not in all cases – the same political and social rights as other citizens of those countries. Islam can no longer be seen as integrally Other, and those Europeans who hold to the historical incompatibility must now presumably make distinctions within Islam in order to align their conceptions with a changing reality. Even for those European states that do not accord rights of citizenship to immigrant workers and their families, the Other – in the case of Muslim immigrants – is now within, and the contacts, conflicts and deals that have created the general European identity through the centuries may be expected to do their work here too.

While the European epicentre is today grappling with this incursion of Islam into its heartlands, it is at the same time confronted with change in areas that have also represented an Other, but this time much more equivocally. Russia has frequently been presented as Janus-faced, as looking partly westwards to Europe and partly eastwards to Asia. So massive is Russia, in terms of both territory and its population, that to view it as a part of Europe's periphery is bound to be a distortion. The Cold War itself was enough to demonstrate Russia's ability to impose itself as a rival to Europe and to that extent a political and economic, if not totally a cultural, Other. That rivalry has made the countries that lie between Russia and Europe's epicentre peripheral to both. They have indeed been known historically as 'the lands in-between'. However fervently the Poles lean culturally towards the West, history has repeatedly asserted their peripheral position in geographical terms, the likely resolution of this through membership of the European Union coming little more than a decade after the end of a period when Poland was incorporated in a post-war sphere of Russian domination.

Lastly, this dual peripheral status was replicated in the history of southeastern Europe, where for centuries Christian populations lived under Turkish rule. With the passing of Turkish imperial power the duality was sharply diminished. But, as noted, the presence of Muslim populations in Albania, Bosnia, Bulgaria, Macedonia, Yugoslavia, Moldova and Romania means that while these countries lie on the periphery of Europe, they are still central to Europe's relations with an Other. The very fact that the chief emphasis of this book is placed on the European Union demands that consideration be given to those peoples and territories that at present fall outside it, but which can claim to share in a European identity in the broader sense. Poland, Serbia and Russia each have a chapter devoted to them below.

Although it makes no attempt to present a comprehensive description of a general European identity, identity in other areas and in other senses is of central concern to this book. First, the very fluidity of the general definition of Europe can lead to an ignoring of the extent to which the European Union itself has been acquiring an identity of its own. How could it not? This thing exists, and has been developing for forty years in a process that can be slowed down, but is hard to imagine to be anything but irreversible. Second, this very process brings a problem of *identification* into prominence. Groups and communities within the member states, including member states themselves as communities expressing themselves through referenda and the like, have been called on to react to the reality of European integration through either identifying themselves with it or rejecting it. A large part of the material presented in this book is devoted to that problem, as the book's subtitle suggests.

Finally, despite the fluidity and open-endedness of general definitions of Europe it can be held that Europe has developed certain shared values and traditions that are worth defending and promoting. 'Can be held', because this consideration leads us into difficult problems of ideology which unfortunately must be confronted. The strength of this view will vary, it is open to question, and it again involves the notion of a core – this time in the realm of ideas. The claim that there is such a core of traditions and values is a strong theme in this book, but it is treated critically. None of the authors contests it; some are concerned to assert it forcefully; all are concerned to examine its derivation and the questions that it raises at the contemporary stage.

A TRANSFER OF LOYALTY

It is within this general perspective that this book asks the question 'Why Europe?' The aim is not primarily to discuss the pros and cons of undertaking a process of integration in Western Europe since, as noted, that process is already under way. That said, the original justifications for moving towards economic and political union remain as valid today as they were in the immediate aftermath of the Second World War, and they are presented here in straightforward terms in a number of chapters (Questiaux, Veen, Ullmann, Tappin and Brewin). First, the possibilities of rivalries among European states leading to a repetition of the wars that have done so much damage to the continent in the past should be eliminated. Second, opportunities for improving the well-being of the peoples of the Union through economic integration should be exploited. Third, this improved well-being should have a political dimension which builds upon conceptions of democracy and social welfare that are an essential legacy of European history. Finally, stability on the territory of the Union should serve to stabilize the Union's neighbours in the east and south-east of Europe and in the Mediterranean. No treatment of the 'why?' of the European Union can omit these basic – and very geopolitical – considerations.

But the intention is to pose also a somewhat different question, which arises once the process of integration is under way and its implications are making themselves felt. It concerns the reasons that individuals, groups and nations might have for according loyalty to the institutions of the EU or for withholding it. The problems that are analysed are those that stem from the multiple identities and loyalties that have to be accommodated in one way or another if the construction of the EU is to proceed. Culture and identity only become problems in relation to a goal that calls them into question. The goal that lies behind the title *Why Europe?* is that which underlies the Treaty of Rome and the later accession treaties, committing a number of European states to an economic association with one another and to progress towards political union. But if the strength of advocacy varies, all the contributors to the collection are critically aware of the problems of culture and identity that attend any move towards union among the peoples of Europe, however Europe is defined. These problems necessarily bring any such moves if not into question, then at least under scrutiny.

The book's focus is therefore on the present predicament of Europe at the end of the twentieth century and at the dawn of a new one, at a moment when a process of integration in the west of the continent has reached a critical stage and when the EU has been called on to react to a contrary process of disintegration of the political and economic bonds that have held the east of Europe together since the end of the Second World War.

CREATING THE STATE: LESSONS FROM THE PAST

Those who are concerned to build up the European Union as an object of loyalty face an uphill task. The power and the variety of the factors that operate against them are quite remarkable, and show little sign of abating. Globalizing pressures have to some extent reduced the accumulation of competences that Brussels might expect to enjoy, but they are as nothing compared with the constant confirmation of the fact that the dominant focus of loyalty in Europe is still the nation-state. The daily presentation of news and commentary by the media ensures that the reference to the nation-state remains constant and strong. It is not only the tabloid papers that play this role. The quality press written and read by élites of the various nations presents the world daily in national terms, although the extent to which this is the case does differ quite widely. Most marked of all are the spectacular events that arouse real passions and are organized actively around nation-states as rivals. If the Eurovision Song Contest is only at the margin of this phenomenon, football is at the centre of it.[1] Competition of this kind is certainly an acceptable alternative to war, but it equally certainly has a powerful effect on where the focus of loyalty is to lie.

In striving to understand what is involved in a transfer of loyalty from smaller communities to a new integrating centre it is possible that there are lessons to be learned from the European experience itself, and this is another theme that is dealt with at a number of places in this book. The cases that are treated directly by Serna-López and Jenkins, and tangentially by Howorth, are Italy, Germany and France. Those treatments bring out the variety in the three cases – itself usefully reminding us that the European experience is not uniform but constitutes a range of responses to challenges which were to a great extent common to the building of states and nations in Europe. If it was post-revolutionary France that has offered the clearest example of the nation as a political association of individual citizens coterminous with the state, the striving to develop nation and state in tandem was common to all three cases, and success in this enterprise can be claimed in all the cases, despite the vagaries of their individual experiences.

How much of that experience is relevant to today's enterprise of European integration? The answer in all three cases is necessarily mixed, given the fact that the experiences have been so varied. Clearly, however, there are difficulties in transposing to the level of the European Union at the close of the twentieth century the nineteenth-century concept of the nation, the term itself having become the centre of debates that render its very use hazardous. What those debates have suggested (Serna-López quotes John Breuilly here) is that historically it is states that have created nations, and not the reverse. If there is a lesson in this it is perhaps that if there is to be a shift in the focus of loyalty from the member states to the European Union it will not come spontaneously from a generalized 'we-feeling' among Europeans, but will be the result of mobilization in some form – either through the political activity of people committed to an idea of a united Europe, or through the more diffuse workings of economic factors that demonstrate an advantage in collective action or collective support.

The case of Italy is somewhat special. 'Now that Italy has been made we have to make Italians', said Massimo d'Azeglio in a celebrated remark after the unification of Italy in 1861, and the difficulties of building an Italian nation after the creation of the state provide lessons of a not necessarily pessimistic kind. It is not so much that a lack of trust in the Italian state leads Italians today to be stronger than other Europeans in their support for a European Union that appears to them as a bulwark of efficiency. The idea that European unity can be achieved through the inefficiencies of European states would not run very far, though in conjunction with the now familiar tendencies towards larger markets and more integrated economies it could be made to play a role. But there are two other aspects of the Italian state that are of greater analytical interest. The first is that the structure of loyalties in it is more clearly three-tiered than in any other member state of the EU. In addition to the willingness to support the process of integration in the EU, noted above, Italians show sufficient loyalty to their hundred-year-old state to keep support for separatist movements such as the Northern League at bay. And yet the identification of Italians with their local roots remains unusually strong. The European Union is studded with minority languages and local *patois*, but nowhere other than in Italy is there a complete patchwork of languages in current use covering the entire territory. What is to count as a language and what as a *patois* is admittedly to a degree a matter of stipulation, but there is an important distinction between the strong dialectal variations of spoken German and the regional languages of Italy.

Second, this three-tiered structure of loyalties in Italy must be seen against Italy's experience in struggling with regional pressures, demands – and problems. The accommodation of the demand for autonomy in the South Tirol, coping with the Liga's call for 'Padanian' independence, the massive problem of developing a relatively deprived south necessarily at the expense of a more favoured north (itself so important a factor in the emergence of the Northern League) and attempting to bring the Mafia under control, all suggest that what the architects of the European Union have taken on is perhaps being rehearsed in one of its component states.

In sum, the practical and analytical value that the history of the formation of European states offers is mixed. Concepts of 'nation' and 'state' have undergone a century of evolution, and there is no *a priori* reason to assume that what is being created with the European Union is state-like, nor that the kind of loyalty that nation-states have historically demanded of their citizens is appropriate to that exercise. On the other hand the history of the European states has provided models and concepts whose value has survived shifts in the contexts in which they have been invoked. If the term 'nation' is today problematic, that other child of the French revolution – citizenship – is at the heart of current debates that have an intimate bearing on the evolution of Europe, as is brought out in many of the contributions that follow, the actual French connection being dealt with in particular by Jolyon Howorth and Brian Jenkins. But above all, the parallels from history show how the creation of a new political entity is a matter of crafting, the deliberate work of architects, involving an idea and the mobilization of support for it – not in a vacuum, but in a complex context of opportunities, fears and the assertion of group and individual interests.

BEING AND DOING

The chapters of the book mark a clear distinction, inherent in the book's original conception, between the past and the future, between the cultural patchwork from which a Europe is being created and the forward-looking project of that creating. The distinction is articulated in what follows by Christopher Brewin as one between *Kultur* and *Bildung*, and by Jolyon Howorth as one simply between being and doing, but in one version or another it in fact informs the whole text. In short, the question 'Why Europe?' shifts the discussion from identity to purpose, while the subtitle of the book serves as a reminder that the two ultimately cannot be separated.

This distinction between being and doing prompts a number of reflections. First and foremost, it raises the question of the extent to which the process of integration in Western Europe is being driven by purposive action and to what extent it is simply happening, the result of economic and political developments in the region which have followed a logic of their own and which it falls to governments merely to steer and ideologists merely to rationalize. There is the associated question of the extent to which this logic has already transcended the bounds of the European region (Howorth). Many of the constraints on governments, such as those concerning the environment, are now global, as are many of the opportunities, and the financial and business frameworks that encadre those opportunities. Similarly the discussion on democracy and on citizenship, so vital to any view of the political future of the European Union, has developed a global dimension.[2] 'Doing' in Europe may be more akin to riding in a tram than driving a car; and may turn out to be directed towards goals that lie beyond Europe as much as within it.

To a certain extent the question of agency has been fully addressed in the long-running discussion between 'federalist' and 'functional' views of European integration, the former maintaining that integration is a matter of political will and treaty-making, the latter suggesting that it can be made to come about through a succession of steps, each step following pragmatically from the last and justifying, equally on pragmatic grounds, the taking of the next step. But both approaches to integration are clearly on the 'project' side of any distinction between political project and cultural context. More expressive of that distinction is the relationship between culture and ideology developed, for example, by Karl Mannheim in his seminal work *Ideology and Utopia*, concerning the promotion of new ideas and their routinization, but also the conflict between the new ideas and the historically shaped cultural context from which – and against which – they have emerged.[3] This conflict is particularly prominent at points of revolution and their aftermath, both the French and the Russian revolutions having generated a rich literature on the topic.[4]

The creation of the European Union is difficult to conceive in revolutionary terms. It would be hard to locate among the forces in play a *tiers état* or an authoritarian modernizing élite of the Bolshevik stamp.

No guillotine or *gulag* is giving a grisly profile to the demand of loyalty to a new order. The process of European integration nonetheless involves a conflict between ideology and culture, or in this case between ideology and the cultures of the communities that are being called upon to form the new order. There is an impulse for integration in the European Union which is being actively articulated and promoted, and there is the consequential tension between this impulse and existing ways of being. Howorth uses the French experience to illustrate how, in that particular European society, the product of such a tension was a political culture which brought a degree of harmony between the conflicting elements, even – it might be added – if that political culture still today bears traces of the conflict that gave it birth.

While the distinction between doing and being has this merit of relating a political project to its cultural context, it has one particular demerit, still concerning the crucial question of agency. To isolate doing from being quite rightly draws attention to the particular role of the 'doers' – those who have framed the project and attempt the mobilization necessary to bring the project to fruition and who, in the present case, may loosely be termed the architects of Europe. This, again quite rightly, invites discussion about who these proponents of the idea are, to what extent they speak with one voice, how they set about the task of mobilization and with what resources – matters that have been treated in the now substantial literature on collective action. But political action in support of a given project can expect to meet political action opposed to it. If the project involves change, opposition can be expected from groups that contest that change. Leaders will emerge from these groups, and mobilization on this side of the equation will match that in favour of the project, but it is likely to make an appeal to those poles of loyalty that are associated with 'being' – notably nationality, ethnicity, and confessional and regional appurtenance. It is therefore important to be clear on the work that the distinction between being and doing is made to do. The idea developed in a number of places in this book (Howorth; Brewin; Serna-López) is that the creation of a European union is a political task akin to the state-building of an earlier age. Like that earlier task it involves the active formation of a community of affect. It is acknowledged that the differences in time and in scale between the two exercises are of the first importance, but then as now, in the creation of the nation-state as in the attempt to create a framework of legitimacy for the European Union, what is involved is a political project that must use, or channel – and if necessary confront – existing poles of loyalty. The distinction between doing and being must not be pushed beyond this simple point to suggest, for example, that in the construction of the European Union a politically active élite group of 'doers' confronts an inert mass whose political role is limited to living out cultural values. First, the proponents of change cannot but themselves carry the cultural values of their society. Second, it is normally easier to mobilize people against change than in favour of it – a point that is made forcefully below by Margaret Canovan.

WHY EUROPE?

And so to the question that many would regard as the crucial, and in many ways the most important, theme that this book addresses. How can the problems of culture and identity that are dealt with in this collection be prevented from frustrating the further development of the ideas and practices that Europe has produced in its history, and how can the process of integration in the European Union be made to pick up and develop those ideas and practices in a new context? These are themes that are touched on at many points in the pages that follow, but two particular views may be presented in this introductory chapter.

The first is put forward by Nicole Questiaux. Since it was not possible in the early days of the construction of the European Union to move directly to the political constitution of a federal or confederal Europe, economics was given the lead by developing the common market. This led to a preoccupation with the dismantling of obstacles to competition – a perspective that weighed heavily on achievements that European societies have made over the years in the sphere of welfare and the practices and policies that have guaranteed it. Those practices and policies were in turn associated with a certain view of what democracy entails. If we are to take the enterprise of creating a European union seriously, we need, first, 'to give a positive meaning to citizenship', and this requires new thinking about the fundamental rights that citizenship should involve in this new context. Second, considerations of social security and welfare should be submitted to the same critical but positive treatment. And third, the opportunity should be taken to ask what are the appropriate functions of government and administration in modern, educated societies. Questiaux makes it clear that her views are influenced by a long-standing subscription to a socialist tradition, but whatever the derivation of those views, the point that is being made is that the current process of integration is in danger of missing the opportunity to build on characteristically European values and practices which could be used to attract the loyalties of the denizens of Europe and to make of them European citizens.

For his part, Brian Jenkins points out that the vertical intergovernmental processes that at present characterize the politics of the European Union lead away from such an outcome and threaten to create subjects rather than citizens. A practical step that might be taken to promote the creation of a democratic European space is, in his view, to develop the horizontal integration of many social identities, linked by their interests across current national boundaries. It is a recommendation that enables the diversity of European cultures to be valued. Thus, while culture and identity may be problems from certain perspectives, from this horizontal perspective they can be perceived as a 'rich resource'.

These are just two of the views put forward in this book that answer the question 'Why Europe?' by being prepared to advocate that loyalty to a European Union can best be promoted by investing the Union's structures with practices and ideas that can be drawn from the rich repository of the experience of European societies, in such a way that, by combining doing with being, European citizens can recognize themselves both in their local settings and in the broader enterprise of the remaking of Europe. To do this is to strengthen Europe and to confirm some important values that European societies have contributed to democracy and social progress. Not to do it is not only to miss an opportunity but, by giving market globalism its head, to make national and regional identities turn in on themselves and become islands of parochial resistance.

BEYOND THE EUROPEAN UNION: HISTORICAL AND CULTURAL PERSPECTIVES

Three chapters in this book are devoted to historical case studies of territories that lie outside the European Union: Russia, Poland and Serbia. Such terrain is all too seldom the location for discussions of national identity, though these are areas where newly awakened nationalism has erupted with particular force. One of the great merits of Norman Davies's magisterial *Europe: a History*, which rightly reminds us that Slavs are the largest of Europe's ethnic families, lies precisely in its recognition of the prominence of Eastern Europe.[5] These areas are included to provide perspectives on what being European signifies beyond – at the time of writing in 1998 – the restricted discourse of the consolidation of a group of European states in a European Union. That dealing with Russia analyses the complexities of the cultural relationship between Russia and a Europe which many Russians regard as external to their country. The chapters on Poland and Serbia illustrate how nationalism, while causing problems for a transfer of loyalty in a European Union that is seeking unity, have an entirely different logic outside the European Union. It is a logic that illustrates remarkably well both the importance of geopolitics in the history of European nations, and also the implications of being located in a peripheral position in relation to the European epicentre.

Paradoxically, while nascent nationalism stressed differences in identity, as opposed to the cosmopolitanism of the Enlightenment, it was itself a universal phenomenon, an integral part of the modern European experience. Lord Acton, one of the first British historians to address the matter, traced the theory of nationality back to the partition of Poland in the late eighteenth century and correctly predicted that it would continue to exert a fundamental influence over history. A hundred years later the Treaty of Versailles, which resurrected the Polish state, appeared to herald the victorious dawn of liberal nationalism. Yet, like so many of its central European counterparts, Poland was rapidly crushed by its overmighty neighbours, this time in the shape of the German Reich and the Soviet Union, both declared enemies of self-determination for smaller nations. It has taken the recent downfall of Communism to usher in the real triumph of nationalism, reinforced by the completion of the decolonizing process in other parts of the world.

In this volume Edward Acton, a descendant of the famous nineteenth-century historian, suggests that the recovery of genuine Polish independence at the end of the twentieth century should be seen as the supreme vindication of the nationalist idea. The re-emergence of Poland represents a romantic tale of transformation from Soviet satellite to sovereign state, without the barbarism that has accompanied similar transitions elsewhere in Europe. Acton argues that Poland is a rare example of a true nation-state, culturally, ethnically and religiously homogeneous, unlike so many nationalist states which are based on the denial of significant minorities. Unfortunately, not all processes of national liberation have proved so harmonious.

The example of Serbia raises some uncomfortable issues, for the aggressive nationalism that has erupted in the Balkans represents a virulent strain of racism that many observers believed had disappeared from Europe with the defeat of Nazism. In hindsight it seems much harder to explain the existence of Yugoslavia than to understand its demise. On his deathbed in 1980 Tito, who was a Croat, proclaimed that he was the only remaining Yugoslav. Yet there were collaborative traditions on which to build a broader Yugoslavian identity and, in the past, consensus as well as conflict has characterized the region. Though narrower definitions based on different religious and ethnic traditions have always been in evidence, linguistic similarities between Serbs and Croats, for instance, have encouraged notions of Slavic unity, summed up in Illyrianism and Yugoslavism.[6] The potential for fostering a wider sense of loyalty was, however, seriously undermined within the confines of a one-party state dominated by Serbia. It proved impossible to contain internal tensions within a less authoritarian framework and the recent disintegration of Yugoslavia has unleashed an orgy of destruction. In regions where different communities cohabited uneasily, the result has been burned-down villages, a tide of refugees and human suffering on a massive scale.

The Serbs, who have so often been cast as the villains of the piece in the Balkans, have been sinned against as well as sinning. Nationalism thrives in adversity, in opposition to the 'Other' and to some extent the severity of the Serbs' reaction to the breakdown of Yugoslavia reflects their siege mentality. Robert Hudson's study of their contemporary music and poetry reveals a people who regard themselves as victims rather than victors. Folksongs and ballads have always played a key role in the creation and maintenance of national consciousness among the so-called 'submerged' or 'unhistoric' peoples of south-eastern Europe. Since the late eighteenth century this cultural heritage has been rescued and kept alive by intellectuals and academics; Hudson demonstrates how Serbian writers and singers continue to fulfil the same function today. Contemporary popular music in Serbia resonates with hatreds from the past, which serve as an atavistic refuge for the insecure. Only, perhaps, by leaving their historical ghetto can the Serbs prevent the pursuit of a Greater Serbia ironically culminating in a small Serbia, reduced to its borders of 1878.

Literature has also played an important part in the creation of national identity, but rarely to the degree experienced in nineteenth-century Russia, where the 'public sphere' was constricted by a notoriously repressive tsarist political system. The famous philosophical debate between the Slavophiles and Westernizers which began in the 1830s reflected a crisis of national consciousness which had no simple solution, and the East/West dichotomy has proved an enduring theme of Russian intellectual thought to the present day. Robert Reid explores the richness and ambiguities of the Russian quest for nationality via the concept of the ethnotope. One's own people in its own place is not particularly conducive to reflection upon identity and, though the presence of foreigners in Russia offered a good deal of stimulation, it was travel that broadened the mind most of all. Russians defined themselves abroad, Westernizers often rediscovering their Slavic roots as a consequence of closer contact with Western Europeans. As Reid suggests, contact with non-Russian groups on the Empire's southern boundaries also assisted in the construction of national identity, this time as a result of encounters with apparently primitive, as opposed to advanced, 'Others'.

On account of their peripheral geography, Eastern Orthodox religious tradition and specific historical experience, the Russians' relationship with Europe has remained profoundly ambivalent. Indeed, at the turn of the twentieth century, a unique Eurasian identity emerged from these ambiguities and enjoyed considerable popularity.[7] For his part, Reid analyses Pushkin's famous poem, *The Bronze Horseman*, and other artistic images of St Petersburg – two aspects of the disputed heritage of the westernizing tsar Peter the Great – as classic symbols of ethnotopic confusion. Yet, as Russians became more aware of their own particular identity in the nineteenth century, they were actually conforming to the development which occurred all over Europe in the wake of the French Revolution. An intense debate on the Russian character has naturally revived in the post-Soviet era, though isolationism is an even less viable option today than it was in the tsarist era.

As Robert Reid demonstrates, the question of national identity is an extremely complex matter, endlessly refracted through varied experiences. To this extent there is no single or fixed consciousness. While allegiance to the nation may have become the primary claim upon individuals whose first loyalty previously lay elsewhere, it has supplemented as much as supplanted the claims of dynasty or region. People have always maintained multiple identities and there is no reason why nationalism cannot coexist with some sort of supranational allegiance. It was Elias Canetti, the famous essayist from the multi-national Habsburg Empire, who asserted that: 'Nationalism cannot be overcome by internationalism ... The answer is plurinationalism'.[8] To this extent, Lord Acton's optimistic prediction of different races living together in freedom and harmony may not prove as utopian as some contemporary events would suggest. The development of a European identity can offer a shared sense of community and purpose for all its peoples. Norman Davies ends his *Europe: a History* by asserting that: 'Europe is not going to be fully united in the near future. But it has a chance to be less divided than for generations past' (p. 1136).

Twice in this book Václav Havel's statement that all the countries of Europe are in the same boat is cited. He himself was President of a state that lay outside the European Union at the time he expressed that thought. The idea that he was articulating constituted an answer to the question 'Why Europe?' which cannot be restricted to the European Union alone. In terms of its culture, its achievements and its geopolitics Europe extends beyond the confines of that Union. If it is possible to speak of a European destiny it cannot be so bounded. That, it might be said, goes without saying. But in the words of a fellow-diplomat of Metternich from another European country, 'Ca ira encore mieux en le disant'.

NOTES

1.   For a fuller discussion of this phenomenon, see the 'Introduction' to the companion volume *Why Europe? Problems of Culture and Identity: Film, Media, Gender, Youth and Education* and, especially, the chapter 'The European "Goal" and the Popular Press' by Pamela Moores.
2.   Held, D., 'Democracy: From City States to a Cosmopolitan Order?', and other essays in his edited collection entitled *Prospects for Democracy, Political Studies*, 40 (Cambridge, Polity Press, 1993).
3.   Mannheim, K., *Ideology and Utopia: an Introduction to the Sociology of Knowledge* (London, Kegan, Paul, Trench and Trubner, 1936).
4.   Furet, F. *et al.* (eds), *The French Revolution and the Creation of Modern Political Culture*, 4 vols (Oxford, Oxford University Press, 1987–94) and Brown, A. and Gray, J. (eds), *Political Culture and Political Change in Communist States* (London, Macmillan, 1977).
5.   Davies, N., *Europe: a History* (Oxford, Oxford University Press, 1996), p. viii.
6.   Bracewell, W., 'National Histories and National Identities among the Serbs and Croats', in Fulbrook, M. (ed.), *National Histories and European History* (London, UCL Press, 1993), pp. 141–60.
7.   See, for example, Weststeijn, W., 'Aspects of Eurasianism', in Reid, R., Andrew, J. and Polukhina, V. (eds), *Structure and Tradition in Russian Society* (Slavica Helsingiensia 14, Helsinki, Department of Slavonic Languages, Helsinki University, 1994), pp. 171–86. (A paper, entitled 'The Russians and Eurasia', was read by Simon Dixon at the conference 'Why Europe?')
8.   Canetti, E., cited in Bloomfield, J., 'The New Europe: a New Agenda for Research?', in Fulbrook, M. (ed.), *National Histories*, p. 255.

Part I
The Political Debate

1 Why Europe? From Contradiction to Refoundation

Nicole Questiaux

I start by thanking the editors of this volume, the organizers of the conference which underlies it, for giving me the opportunity of answering a challenge.

The challenge is in the question. Is it not extraordinary that in countries that for more than a generation have committed themselves to Europe by binding treaties and by the incorporation of common references in the rule of law should, 40 years later, ask why? And when a conference is convened to address this question, it covers such a wide field of interests that the question breaks up into a kaleidoscope of questions.

And, of course, as soon as I perused the list of topics, I realized that, as this was not a conference of French administrative lawyers, of socialist ex-ministers or of persons born of Franco-Scottish ancestry, I had no obvious qualification to introduce such discussions. But I do believe that, as if from Mars, I may have a message for you. It is very simple: you are European. Why can I be so sure of this? Because, for many years, I have been involved in the process of screening all important laws and regulations which come into force in one of the member states. This provides the possibility of evaluating the impact of the obligations related to the treaty on the rules binding the citizens of one of our countries. And although our perception of the workings of administration may be different, I know the same forces are at work in all the member states.

The political discussion about Europe more usually focuses on Europe as a construction. It underplays the fact that Europe is functioning and when the public is taken by surprise and has to sit back and let Brussels decide on the meat-course in the menu, it ignores the fact that the same thing is continually happening in numerous fields. In France, practically every week, the wheels of administration turn to introduce some rule discussed in common, and may well have been influenced by, among others, a British administration which may at the same time have been making a show of Euroscepticism. And, of course, in parallel, the British are taking steps which will have been thought out in discussions with the French.

Now, given that this is the real state of affairs, it is high time, if we are asking why, to have the answers ready.

There are very good reasons for the six, then the 12, then the 15 countries concerned with Europe to conceive a common destiny, such very good reasons that they could be termed valid in an even wider circle. Yet, as time goes by, there seems to be a grumbling dissatisfaction about Europe, all the more interesting because it does not seem to give voice to a strong alternative view. So, time and again, the relatively narrow and privileged circles which, in all our countries, are definitely committed to Europe rely on the obscurity of the debate and the narrow majorities rallied around each further commitment to invest in the future. Apparently, they are less sure of the outcome, as is clearly shown in the periodical bouts of embarrassment in France, on the right and on the left of the political spectrum, about this subject.

It seems it might be a good start to our discussions to try and understand the reasons for this state of dissatisfaction. Are they not related to the contradictions which have been built into the European process itself, contradictions which may appear vivid enough to make our common enterprise a provocation for history? Is there a way out of the maze for whoever is convinced enough, if not to solve the contradictions, at least to bypass them by tackling some new issues which could interest a new generation in all our countries? Might there not be some form of cultural deficit in the method chosen to build Europe? Might there not be some form of contribution to be made by culture in the refounding of Europe?

1   THE UNCERTAINTY OF BEING EUROPEAN

As a starting point, I shall make the case that, while there are very good reasons to be European, they are plagued by a form of invisibility. Either they are so good and so well proven that people have become too used to them; or else, our old sophisticated societies have become too subtle and have gone too far in the techniques which seem to allow consensus without allaying contradiction.

As suggested in a very interesting book, which I shall recommend for an illustration of our subject, *Généalogie de l'Europe*, Lamaison and Vidal-Naquet's geography has been kind to Europe. Fertile plains and protective mountains, plenty of water, the rich variety of the seasons, the sea and ocean hugging a beautiful coastline, vineyards and fisheries and enough resources to meet energy needs: no wonder our lands attracted the great variety of populations who have made us what we are.

Our confluent histories, however, have not been peaceful and this explains one very good reason to be European. We have in common the experience of war. The meaning of this may not be immediate for the large percentage of our people who were born after the Second World War. For many of our contemporaries, peace is like electricity in the house or running water; we take it all for granted. War is for others, and may eventually be watched on television. I am old enough to remember the war, although I did not belong to those who were terrified, humiliated or just suffered. And I have had contact with those who tried and failed to prevent war. One of those was a Frenchman, René Cassin, whose destiny was to lead him to draft the Universal Declaration of Human Rights; but between the two wars he was among those who had tried desperately to build some system of international security. And from the experience of this type of people, it appears clear that real peacemakers nourish their convictions in the realism of war. If they are not here to say so themselves, someone has to relay the message.

This is why it is so important that the European enterprise involves countries and people who have made war and peace. The people of the United Kingdom, who did not within recent memory and indeed well back into their history know the humiliation of being occupied, may view this theme with caution and comment on the relation between France and Germany as the modern expression of a balance of powers on the continent they have been taught to mistrust. This is a narrow-minded attitude, because it is fundamental for all Europeans that war becomes impossible between those two countries, or along the Oder-Neisse line, or that Spain has turned the page on a civil war which engaged much more than its national interests. All our people have paid in the past the price of war; they know the value of peace. And that is why we must understand that a long-term consolidation of peace in Europe is the bedrock motive for all the energy spent over the last forty years within the European process.

All our countries have in common the experience of democracy. This also should not be taken for granted. What is really important is that democracy has matured in a fascinating process of interactive influences. Our political theorists and leaders took a long time to bring this about, a time which was used for rivalry, strife, revolutions and setbacks. But the result is there for all to see. The Europeans are fascinated by democracy, whether it be of their own formula or that of their neighbour. There is no more exciting account of the French Revolution than that of Carlyle, who more than disapproved of it. And here again, in defiance of all past and present-day sceptics, democracy is alive in all our countries, alive, successful, modern and messianic.

Successful, certainly, if one thinks of recent developments in Spain or Greece, and, of course, in post-war Germany and, just yesterday, as it were, under the conditions of its reunification. Modern, as it has adapted to the birth of the modern nations or, within the boundaries of these nations and under the pressures of urban concentration, to the necessities of decentralization. Sophisticated, with its tools: universal suffrage, and for all of us the saga of the women's vote; the checks and balance built into the constitution, written or unwritten; the rule of law or principle of legality under the supervision of an independent system of justice. Messianic, as much of this reference to democracy is built into binding treaties and proposed to the world at large through a universal conception of human rights. Successful again, when by the Helsinki process such principles show sufficient vitality to influence profoundly the evolution of Eastern Europe.

So far, this analysis of our common heritage will probably not seem particularly controversial. I propose to argue that our common experience of the labour movement and the welfare state has also played a determining role in knitting our destinies together. Europe as a whole has been shaped by its industrial revolutions and their consequent effects on the concentration of the population in vast urban conglomerations, as well as on the birth rate. Of course, many other regions in the world have known the upheaval of development. But why is it that the reaction of the labour movement has been in our case so positive? Was it an after-effect of the Age of Enlightenment? Why was it that modernization coincided with the will to educate the masses? Was this deemed necessary for the best utilization of new technologies? Or was it coincidence in the drive of economic and democratic forces? In any event, we must admit as a fact that organized labour showed a remarkable capacity to influence events. First, it made good use of the modes of communication available in the nineteenth and early twentieth centuries to bring together individual complaints, structure them into motives for solidarity and mobilize a collective energy to promote such aims. One of the attainments of this movement has been the symbolic value attached to work, and few of us, whatever our political creed, will deny that this is part of our common heritage. The right to strike, the techniques of collective bargaining and the challenge to society to procure security and freedom from want collected into what appears now, for most of us, an essential aspect of the social contract.

Realism obliges us to recognize that by its very nature this part of our heritage is conflictual. In fact, it consists in recognizing the role of social conflict in development and accepting that such conflicts do oppose legitimate interests and involve, if they are to be solved, something else than a combination of economic laws. But I would like us to look back with sufficient respect to the intellectual and physical contribution made by those who were able, for the first time, to formulate reasons for solidarity, as well as methods which reached over distance and time to answer the needs which had been identified. Accidents, illness, old age, the bearing and bringing up of children were not to be the individual and often dramatic lottery of life, but events to be provided for. What is even more admirable is that those who had little, built generosity into the techniques of insurance and held, without initially being obligated by law, that the richer could contribute more to support those on lower incomes. It is in this perspective not abnormal that solidarity should become in the wake of great upheavals an issue for democratic governments. In all our countries, the state was called upon to organize the transfer of income and dispense services deemed necessary to protect from want and achieve a more egalitarian way of life.

The welfare state, which is now being described as an archaic web of constraints, was founded on the extension of the concept of solidarity to the global population of our nations. This must not be obscured in the technical debates of the present times. In our European sphere, it is unethical and against our fundamental rights not to provide free or cheap education to all, not to allow some form of income to those who are legitimately in a situation of non-work, or to exclude the sick from some form of health-care on financial grounds. And whatever is said about reforming the methods, no democratic government in any of our countries would attempt, on principle, to deny a collective responsibility in providing such services.

2 CONTRADICTION WITHIN THE PROCESS OF EUROPEANIZATION

If one tries to formulate an appreciation of the ties that now bind us in successive treaties, they appear as a vivid illustration of what happens when very experienced and over-intelligent minds come together. They were, of course, fully conscious of all the difficulties involved in drawing up a common frame for evolution. So the matter was put in the hands of the drafters and we agreed, at different intervals, to negotiate on the respective jurisdiction of the Community or Union and of the member states, and on the powers vested in the new organs.

The result could only be a very sophisticated organization. And we seem, if we look back or if we face the implications of the extension of the

Union, to have envisaged a very complex power structure. Of course, it was inevitable that power should be shared. But this is a reality that means much more than the relations between the European level and the member states; or between the Council, the Commission and the European Parliament. Power is shared in all ways: the matters dealt with at community level are sectorially defined, according to divisions which may cut across traditional responsibilities in member states; some acts are immediately binding, some require implementation at national level; and more often than not, the latter are expressed in great detail and do not in fact leave a margin for national interpretation. A parliament selected through direct election has none of the trappings of the supremacy of parliament and it is for independent and, as critics do not fail to say, politically irresponsible judges to have a last word in matters of great significance for the citizens of Europe.

This is where time has consolidated contradiction. These institutions have been run by the most remarkable men and women. They made them work and they are at the forefront of all the proposals to adapt the treaties. The system has become complex enough to be a legal and political world in itself; but this only became apparent to the national political and administrative circles very gradually, and not necessarily in a manner affecting all their sectors of responsibility equally. So here we have a system of decisions which has only recently made itself felt in the realities of our lives, and it can easily be understood that public opinion is many years later taken aback by what has been decided, all the more so if it becomes an easy way out for national decision-makers to attribute some unpopular decision to our European commitments. Whatever happens, reform will intervene, if only to accommodate our new partners. But it is more than a matter of finely honed majorities, and to shake ourselves out of complacency we will need all the skills of what all our countries know in the field of administrative reform, and with a vengeance.

To sum things up, it has become a common saying that we should look to compensate a deficit in democracy in Europe; but this comes at a time when public opinion is drifting towards a negative appraisal of certain aspects of Europeanization and where some of the national parliaments, in a world which has made it increasingly difficult for them to carry sufficient weight, resent the powers now vested in the organs of the Union.

This, I believe, leads us to the crux of our interrogations. As it was not politically conceivable to put politics first and to agree on a federal or confederal perspective, we gave precedence to the creation of a common market. Now, who can deny that this is one of the more evident reasons to bring together countries which want to adapt to the modern conditions of competition; which have lost their traditional realms of supremacy but retain the skills and energy necessary for a new era of development? We have already benefited from the widening scope of our agricultural, industrial and commercial interests and we can fairly expect much from this readaptation of our economic assets. But by agreeing to put this objective first, we underestimated the ideological impact of this dissociation of responsibilities. Free trade is part of a general world system. It has two characteristics in that it is led by a capitalistic organization – this is only a statement of fact and involves no critical intent – and that it does not recognize protection for the European common market.

Let us take the second point first. The common market is a remarkable achievement. But it has come about through the very forces which are simultaneously at work, and which are structuring the development of world trade. It is not surprising that the European common market does not naturally settle for some form of boundary, and the benefits which were put forward to dismantle protection inside Europe are also the objective set for the promotion of world trade. Commercial agreements and their incessant aftermath of quarrels and compromises have become the essential reality of European politics.

And, as all commentators agree, although social policy was not absent at the outset, it was delayed and held to be subordinate. To begin with, there were, in this matter, no real powers vested in the European institutions, and, as Sandra Fredman[1] expresses it neatly, both the Preamble and Articles 1, 17 and 1, 18 of the Treaty declared that the EC was committed to promoting better working conditions and improved standards of living for workers. But legislation to achieve this aim was not considered necessary. The social dimension was clearly a by-product of the promotion of economic objectives which were at the centre of the provisions on free movement for workers. In this context, only the principle of equal pay for equal work really did carry some impetus.

Now, it is true that the Protocol on social policy added on at Maastricht contains possibilities, in substance and in working procedures. The field of competence for Europe in these matters has been extended and more precisely defined; more scope has been given for qualified majority voting and much hope is invested in the original function of social dialogue. It is too soon to know how creative this method will be, but it has already shown its possibilities for parental and family leave and seems at least to have reinvigorated discussions on the dire consequences of unemployment, and on democracy at the work-place.

But, unlike the common market itself, social policy as a whole was not one of the achievements introduced by the period of economic growth and reconstruction which we in France describe as the '*trente glorieuses*', and it suffered both from this belated interest and from the unhappy provision that it was deemed acceptable to opt out of this part of the treaty.[2]

Building the common market could not entail for the Union, or the member states, responsibility for growth or an acceptable level of employment. It essentially meant dismantling obstacles to competition. And here we have been meticulously engaged in criticizing, discrediting and rendering obsolete much of what had been built by the will of preceding generations, as part of the collective responsibility of our respective governments.

Europe appears to be hopping along on one foot, the champion of non-interventionism in economic matters, but which intervenes incessantly in relations with our respective governments. They then have recourse to the European institutions for an explanation or an excuse; and our public opinion then discovers that we are committed to far more than a common market, a common creed and the belief that the invisible hand will procure not only wealth and harmony, but achievement of the union as well. The result should be painless, because all private interests will miraculously combine: history has not thus far proved the value of the theory. Indeed, on the contrary, this open Europe is on the defensive. The restructuring of global spheres of influence since the collapse of the Soviet Union and the reunification of Germany, as well as the effects of recession, have triggered off a defensive attitude in our countries. In a dangerous world, it is natural to fall back on familiar values.

This is also true of national identities. It should come as a warning that conflicts which appear so obviously detrimental to all parties fester very near us and seem unending when an issue of national identity is involved. And it is also ominous that the Europeans seem able to agree to keep other populations out, if not goods. The official stand taken in the name of Europe is to hold back immigration, discourage intermingling and renege on the right to asylum.

Europeans are sufficiently experienced to know that fortresses are more often than not traps and that strategy implies a capacity for moving beyond a preconceived plan. I am now convinced that we have made a mistake in putting ourselves in the hands of a particular power structure without reaching sufficient agreement about the type of society we want to live in. After all, history has rarely worked that way and, on the contrary, affords sufficient examples as, for example, in the case of the American Founding Fathers, or in the recent reunification of Germany, where a strong feeling for the political content of a far-reaching goal seems to be the only way to bring grand projects to fruition. So, we ought to be convinced, whatever our prejudices about Europe, of the necessity of discussing this political content, and of doing so openly.

This is where it becomes exciting to participate in a project which addresses the question by way of a debate on problems of culture and identity. We are in search of foundational principles to stow aboard our *Mayflower* and to transplant on the soil of what we would like to see as a new, young and attractive Europe. We would like to appeal to the democratic sensitivity of that generation which is on board the vessel, eager to build a new world, but which also fails to understand the issues behind a very intricate debate on the role and the limits of the Union.

One way to bypass that discussion and to go back to the people is precisely the one we are engaged in here. If we are to identify ourselves as citizens of a future Europe, we have to talk about identity and find some common language to describe what is important for each of us as an experience which is in effect shared, or can be put forward as a reality which others could be invited to share. If this refoundation process gets under way, the process of negotiation and the definition of who is responsible for what can find a new impetus.

3 REFOUNDATION, OR THE CULTURAL IDENTITY OF EUROPE

I am certainly convinced that we are now coming to the questions which should test our creativity. At this stage, I must be forgiven if I seem to participate in some new type of car-boot sale, by laying before the reader those problems or principles which are representative of my cultural baggage. Because, indeed, if I too am to board this *Mayflower*, I do have some expectations. That is, if we really mean to take the adventure seriously, as common citizens of a new world, we need to give a positive meaning to citizenship. We are not happy with being pushed around the chessboard by an invisible hand: we have the right to expect our commitments to be visible.

I shall suggest that, for citizens of Europe, the sense of political identity could be related to three themes: a definition of fundamental rights, the concept of solidarity and the recognition of differences.

We would expect Europe to be a society where the citizen exercises fundamental rights. Now this is where the lawyer is on familiar ground. We have firm reasons to think that identity is related to the affirmation of rights. Certain principles dealing with liberties and duties are in many constitutional systems, and certainly in all the countries involved in European construction these were regarded as fundamental, more fundamental than others because they tolerate no exception; and because mechanisms of guarantee are elaborated to protect them, and, finally, because the very meaning of the social contract is to ensure satisfaction of such rights.

We have reached a time when it is necessary to put these findings of constitutional law to a new test. On the one hand, their importance is more and more generally recognized in the field of anthropology: all human societies seem to refer to basic principles and, happily, many of those seem to be similar. On the other hand, in our 'old' Europe, our younger citizens are made to believe that this discussion is already behind them, when they in turn demand that they make their own appraisal of what they can recognize as fundamental.

I wish to suggest that the type of conference which underlies the present volume is a proper venue to make a take-over bid, as it were, for questions too fundamental to be left to traditional lawyers or politicians. They tend to believe everything has been said, especially in the different treaties, and so they focus on such technicalities as the application by the courts of the European convention in this or that country. They underestimate the fact that the definition of such rights in successive layers of national, European and international rules has become extremely intricate, the principle itself not necessarily being enhanced by such elaborate settings.

What we need is an active exercise of recognition, by our present day citizens, of what is so fundamental that it must be preserved in common. Let us ask them this precise question, which I myself would formulate in terms applicable in my own country, the purpose being, of course, not to impose this view, but to test the field of similarities and differences. Do we realize, do we believe that in our European society citizens are entitled to exercise a specific panoply of rights? These rights are related to the person, the very first of which is the affirmation of the dignity of the person, which goes with the eradication of torture, inhuman treatment and slavery; the right to life; the principle of equality and non-discrimination; the freedom of movement and the right to live in security; the right to privacy and to a normal family life; the right to possess property. These rights extend to intellectual activities, through freedom of thought, conscience and religion and the consequent liberty to express such ideas, to teach them and to expect a neutral approach from the authorities in such matters. Fundamental rights entail political and social action through free elections, freedom to associate, right of asylum and the separation of powers. They structure economic and social life through freedom of enterprise, the right to receive instruction, to work, to strike and to act collectively in the defence of a common and legitimate interest.

On the French scene, we may note that rights will be guaranteed by the right to an accessible and equitable system of justice and by the general principle of legality, which requires from any authority that it acts within the rule of law. And, for the sake of completeness, we must include the status of specific categories, which either enjoy fundamental rights as derived from the first category, or specially formulated rights: foreigners, prisoners, children, women, minorities, future generations.

Whoever harks back to the ambitions of the Founding Fathers cannot evade the recognition of the founding rights. Are we in agreement with this description and able to face together situations where it may be necessary to affirm that no derogation of such rights is acceptable, or else go through the process of interpretation that may be necessary in sufficient harmony?

We can go through the same exercise with solidarity. We would expect Europe to show understanding of this part of its heritage.

It is a difficulty for me – as a democrat and as a socialist – to accept that one of the 'pilgrims' can opt out of the social policy. This should not be interpreted as a criticism of a given country or even of the reasons which may at the time have made this compromise necessary. What worries me is the impact of this option on the common objective. It necessarily holds that social policy, the minimum wage or the expenditure for welfare is a handicap for development; and it is more than paradoxical that the circles that are so adamant about free competition should deem it possible to undercut all their partners on the basis of different social policies. This division of opinion inside an economic system which is governed by the same rules undermines what has made social policies possible in the history of all our old industrial countries. Now there are good reasons why this cannot be accepted as a principle for action. It would mean a definite breach in the feeling of solidarity that has held our societies together, and it would amount to a recognition that the European working class has acquired no rights from society from the long period of social progress which has led to the present day situation. People defend a territory; they also rally to defend history and we would be wise to realize that the essentials of social policy are not only a matter of costs, they are, in Europe, part of our history. Even if it is perfectly understandable that standards and objectives should be adjusted according to the needs of the present, it is a negation of our culture to hold social policy as subordinate.

And the proof of this lies with the right to work. Europe or no Europe, none of our democracies will survive if they tolerate a generalized risk of unemployment over a generation. It is work that knits our societies together and any substitute for its legitimacy can only cover temporary situations.

Another test of identity concerns the relationship between the people and government. I use the term in a general sense: to make things clear,

what are the functions of administration and government in modern, educated societies? Discussions about the future of the Union focus on the
responsibilities of the member states, with regard to what should or should
not be delegated to the Union. But it gets bogged down, or worse, leads to
compromise solutions which are unbelievably complex and do not, when
implemented, express the political will of the people. The nation, as a
nexus for solidarity, seems to thrive all the more, while its powers are
curbed in favour of institutions which do not seem to mobilize the same
political momentum. The reason for this is that our countries are not
answering the question: what is government? And we ignore the fact that,
for some of us, the role of the state and the devolution to public bodies
of an important fraction of our common interests is not only a matter of
political choice, dividing left- and right-wing opinion, which is already
important enough: it is, at least in France, and in countries which refer to
the same concept of public law, a matter precisely of cultural identity.
Underlying a system of public education which covers all children and
young people from kindergarten to university, for example, there is recognition of the service rendered by the teachers and the right of the public to
this service. In France, workers and consumers of these services, or the
utilities, will walk out to defend the fact that the service is *public*. This
does not mean that this characteristic should be regarded as eternal; very
similar results can be attained in other European societies by techniques of
regulation organized in the name of consumers' interests, and independently of the state authorities.

But if we are to understand each other, it must be clear that we do not
all see our well-being determined by privatization. And if this is to be the
case, one cannot seriously discuss the level of government without a precise view of the objectives of government. I suggest the following:

a. that a large sector of the population in our countries hold public bodies
   responsible for some aspects of their well-being, especially when it
   concerns equal rights;
b. that if this is the case, they should not be impeded in so doing by the
   provisions of the treaties;
c. that if this is not clear, the treaties should recognize as objectives for
   the Union the effective enjoyment of such fundamental rights, and provide that states and community organs are enabled to regulate, transfer
   resources or establish services if this is necessary to ensure the effectiveness of such rights. And this, to some minds, inevitably suggests
   that the European organs would be well served in having some spheres
   of influence where they provide service, with all the responsibilities

involved, and do not only appear to screen, supervise and eventually dismantle what has been attempted at national level, and through democratic decisions at national level.

We must in the future move towards the situation where Europeans would appear to have made positive provisions together.

This leads us to what I believe could be one of the most constructive themes for our discussions: it concerns precisely our differences. We would expect Europe to value differences.

We note, every day, that our populations are attached to what makes them culturally different: language, music, food, cafés and pubs, baguettes and sausages. If our proposed destiny means uniformization, it will never be popular. In this way, public opinion shows a remarkable sense of Europe's assets. Part of our countries' capacity for progress lies precisely in this wealth of differences. Is this not true for tourism, which is a large-scale resource based on different aspects of our European history, on the variety of our habits and ways of life, as well as on the fact that we seek to enjoy the company of our fellow-beings? What is true for tourism is also true for the everyday conditions of life. We are indeed deeply influenced by the cultural impact of the world economy, but we are all the more proud of the particularities which are built into our ancient and sophisticated experience. It seems to me that it could be very useful to recognize diversity as a part of our heritage and as a goal to be maintained. If we were to do so, we would eliminate the rivalry between European cultures as a cause of distrust and friction.

This of course addresses the question of the use of the English language; it is vital for Europeans and for English speakers that diversity in languages should be accepted. Of course, there is a waste in time and energy apparently involved in some activities, but it is the price we have to pay for more creativity in the long run, more ideas, more jobs, more works of art and more influence on the future.

Having for many years tried to communicate what was in my personal experience probably as a result of a mixed upbringing, I had the enlightening experience, a few weeks ago, to hear the same conviction expressed by Professor J. Weiler (in Craig and Harlow, 1998), who, as one of the most knowledgeable authorities on European affairs, has the privileged viewpoint of the independent observer. Europe is made of differences; its culture cannot afford to do away with differences; it must find some agreement on the way to deal with differences. To achieve diversity as a principle, it is very important to realize that our societies have, among their differences, a different way of dealing with differences.

Anyone who has been in a position to discuss the status of minorities will recognize a world of difference between what we see as the 'Anglo-Saxon' stand on minorities and *'égalité à la française'*. In the first case, the minority group is recognized as such, exercises rights and engages in dialogue with society as a whole on whatever it construes to be its relevant interests and through a leadership which has sprung from its ranks. This applies to religious groups, ethnic minorities, local communities, and so on. When in France we are faced with the same question, we have recourse to the principle of equal rights as set out in Article 2 of our Constitution. We are prepared to recognize equal rights to every man or woman, whatever group he or she may belong to, and whatever characteristic, sex, religion, ethnic origin, physical or intellectual originality might provoke discrimination. But we will not relate these rights to membership of a group. And this leads to the situation where the French Republic cannot ratify the international covenants on human rights without making reservations about the articles which define minorities.

Now, it seems that a reference to religious differences, which in our present times still provide fuel for uncertainty and insoluble conflicts, can be of use in the matter of developments in Europe. Here again, I am deeply indebted to Professor Weiler for his illuminating simplification of what came about in Europe after generations of failing to cope with differences. Yes, in France, you can say: I am French and I am Catholic (or Protestant or Jew or Moslem). This means that I have more than one normative identity. Now, how did we get there, how did we find the way out of the dramas which had affected generations, how did we in the end come to terms with what history would recognize as a basic contract for the expression of religious beliefs in a society which decided to cope with differences?

I do not seek to convert anyone to *'laïcité à la française'*; the word, anyway, defies translation. But there were two interesting ideas in the theory which helped the French out of the morass of religious strife. One was to find agreement, by an accepted consensus, on what is the public sphere, where the common rules take precedence, and what is the private sphere, where citizenship implies tolerance of different rules. The other idea was to strive for compatibility between the activities exercised in each different sphere. In the public sphere, anyone exercising authority will be required to be neutral; but a generous acceptance of freedom of opinion and expression allows the citizen to have several, compatible, identities.

Elaborating on this experience, I suggest that we are not necessarily looking for a dividing line between the traditional responsibilities of the old nation-states and the European entity, but for the capacity to combine two identities. We are not looking for uniformization or absorption, but for compatibility.

How can we set about this? We require an unconventional attitude to Europe. To begin with, we must be unabashed by lawyers, drafters and treaty-makers: they are only there to hold the pen. We are not in need of procedures, we are in need of substance. The type of material which was discussed in our very open-minded conference could be put to good use if it helps the ordinary citizen, simultaneously in all our countries, to set a goal for Europe. For this, we must be unintimidated by the accumulation of *savoir faire* invested so far in the European process. We must simultaneously address the national and the European level of politics.

This implies a change in perspective. The future goal for Europeans has been described so far as a common market, common currency, common policies, common institutions: to this we should add a common understanding of differences and this, of course, means that the objective is not uniformization. It could also mean we are not moving towards more power for the European institutions, but towards an original definition of what should be their sphere of competence.

An enterprise which could be more clearly founded on principle, on rights, solidarity and acceptance of differences as a value could be recognized by others and define its boundaries by way of explicit recognition. If we can clearly express why Europe, we are on the way to answering the other question: Which Europe?

One concluding remark: one of the advantages of this method is to cut across stereotypes. It should reassure conservatives, or conservationists, as it does not propose doing away with our inheritance. It should be of interest to progressives, as they like their politics with a dash of utopia. But someone might object: one of our European languages, the beautiful English language, has coined the word 'Euroscepticism'. May I venture to say that it expresses the one answer which is sterile? Sterile because you may not have recourse to scepticism to deny realities; and we are in a European reality. And sterile because we need to found a new world and you cannot do this without some degree of conviction.

NOTES

1.   I refer to opinions expressed by Sandra Fredman at a conference, the proceedings of which have been published in Craig and Harlow (1998).

2.   The recent provisions of the Amsterdam Treaty may hopefully initiate new developments.

REFERENCES

Craig, P. and Harlow, C., *Lawmaking in the European Union* (Amsterdam, Kluwer, 1998).

Lamaison, P. and Vidal-Naquet, P., *Généalogie de l'Europe* (Paris, Hachett 1994).

2 Why Europe?
Michael Tappin

INTRODUCTION

Eighteen months ago I was privileged to be in the European Parliament in Strasbourg when François Mitterand came to address the Parliament at the start of the French Presidency of the Council of Europe. He did not have much longer to live: always a small man, he was now showing all the signs of his illness, seeming frail, grey and withered.

The audience listened out of respect and interest to his presentation of Europe's position and future direction until it came to the point of 'why Europe was so essential', and suddenly, there was a pause, a change of stance, a change of mood. Mitterand put aside his notes and, leaning on the lectern, began to speak freely – from his heart.

He told the story of a young man raised in post-First World War France, then conscripted into military service to take up arms against a foreign aggressor in 1939. This was a young man who had seen his country raped, his friends die, his colleagues imprisoned, his whole world affected by the horror of war. Worse, for him, was the seeming inevitability of war, and he reminded us that three times during his family's memory – 1870, 1914 and 1940 – France had been invaded. Three times there had been deaths – loved ones lost to combat, famine and disease. He asked the questions, 'Why should this happen? What could stop this history being repeated? How could he, we, safeguard our children and grandchildren against the heritage of war?'

Mitterand's answer was co-operation. He held to that idea throughout his life. His delight at the Schumann Plan and the establishment of the European Coal and Steel Community was mirrored by his fears for Europe's future when de Gaulle vetoed Britain's application to the EEC. He wanted co-operation between the so-called great nations; the establishment of unifying ties which would make the taking up of arms impossible. In effect he was looking towards the principles which underlie the European Union.

WHOSE EUROPE? – SOVEREIGNTY

Very few people would disagree with the need for, or the value of, co-operation. Unfortunately, this is an issue which is rarely put to the public. What the public are confronted with is the question of sovereignty: co-operation is too often presented as capitulation.

In 1989 Edward Heath argued 'that we should beware of politicians who start to complain about the loss of sovereignty. What do they really mean?' he asked. All too often, by 'sovereignty' Heath felt politicians meant their own power. He added that sovereignty was an asset to be pooled for the benefit of all. In fact, the pooling of 'sovereignty' within the EU gives each nation the chance to influence the decisions of their partners which more than compensates for concessions they may have to make at home.

In reality, very few Western countries retain much in the way of sovereignty as most people would understand the term. Sovereign rights of defence are now largely dictated by our established alliances. Do we complain about our membership of NATO? Few people oppose inward investment or the flow of capital as a breach of our sovereignty. How many of our essential services (water, electricity, etc.) are owned by foreign companies? At one time the implications of this for national security would have been unacceptable. Even if we cut ourselves free of the ties of Europe, we would still find our agendas being set by the likes of the WTO, the UN and NATO, as well as the political and economic decisions of America, the CIS and the countries of the Pacific Basin. The tabloid debates hinge on smaller issues: the flavourings of crisps and straight bananas. Is this *really* how we want to define our sovereignty?

One thing that Mitterand certainly saw quite clearly was that co-operation may lead to harmonization, without creating conformity. For all he was a great European, he was still very much a Frenchman. Being both European and British or German is not impossible. He did not feel there was a contradiction in being both. Neither do I. I wish the media did not insist there was a distinction, but it is quite evident that the forces of racism, xenophobia and prejudice – the same forces Mitterand felt pushed us into wars – are still here. Why Europe? Because part of the work the EU is undertaking is to try on both micro- and macro-levels to eliminate those elements: to enlighten Europeans.

WHOSE EUROPE? – THE MICRO-LEVEL VIEW

It is accepted that one of the major causes of tension, nationalism (I use the word in its most negative sense) and exclusion stems from economic deprivation and social exclusion. The European Union currently has a range of programmes in operation which focus on job and wealth creation in less favoured areas. In the last five years Great Britain has benefited enormously from European regional development funding to regenerate economies which have suffered through industrial decline. In North Staffordshire, which forms part of my European Parliamentary constituency, we are now putting programmes together to counter the job losses in the coal and steel industries, so here we benefit from our membership of the European Union. At all times the commitments – written into our treaties – to promote equality of all citizens, ensure that special provision is made for women, immigrants, children, the long-term poor, and disabled people are honoured (albeit often in a limited way) to restrict social exclusion. It is a fact that almost all the rights and advantages that women have in the UK have come as a result of European legislation. As much as any law on straight bananas, legislation in this area is a product of the so-called breach of British sovereignty.

Education and training schemes are also available, and access to them is from the lowest possible level. It is possible for individual schools or small community groups to apply directly for European funding and develop partnerships with colleagues and institutions in other member states, which meet their particular requirements and interests. Subsidiarity – government at the lowest appropriate level – is built into all European programmes, ensuring local needs and circumstances are catered for. Sometimes subsidiarity is reinterpreted by member state governments to mean the renationalization of power, but that is another story.

There is also a commitment to maintaining the various cultures within the European Union. Money is given to support minority languages and cultures – particularly important in France where centralization has gone a long way to destroying indigenous minority cultures such as Breton. There is no aim or intention on the part of the Parliament or the Commission to turn the citizens of Europe into a bland mass of grey people. Harmonization and maintaining cultural identity are not mutually exclusive.

As far as the Council is concerned, national attitudes are fiercely maintained. For example, in the case of the Dutch, they are determined to have co-operation and tend to press hard for compromise. The British, on the other hand, are unashamedly determined that their role should be that of (and I quote from the White Paper of 12 March 1996 on the Intergovernmental Conference) '*An Association of Nations*'; 'a leading force in the EU for its own national interests'.[1] Since all EU legislation has to bear the stamp of the Council's accord – much of it with unanimous support – it is difficult to accept the argument that the UK is a victim of the Brussels dictatorship!

When, during the BSE crisis, the UK wielded its veto it managed to block about 120 decisions in just that month – showing that even on issues commonly supported by the rest of Europe, an individual country cannot be *coerced*. You don't get that message on the BBC or on the media in other countries.

WHOSE EUROPE? – THE MACRO-LEVEL VIEW

On a wider scale, the Union has taken up a support role with developing countries. As signatories of the Lomé Convention we are pledged to help with trade and aid. But as neighbours of Eastern Europe we have an extended role. Not only do we help with aid, training and trade association packages, we are also consciously helping to prepare countries for future accession to the European Union. The question 'why enlarge?' is answered with much the same type of reasoning as the question, 'why Europe?' The 'how' is rather more difficult. Political leaders in Europe all support enlargement. However, there is a problem and that problem is the matter of who is going to pay for enlargement. There is a political willingness, but no willingness on the part of the current 15 member states to fund such enlargement.

To fund accession will need at least one unpalatable scenario being acted out. Either we cut current Union expenditure – which would mean a huge reduction in the type of social and development programmes which benefit existing member states – or we increase Union income. The latter is problematical given that, politically, member state governments find it easier to blame Europe for all costs and less popular decisions, while taking credit for all benefits. Hence, as far as the public is concerned, it is the separate member states who are to fund enlargement, but the European Union which is insisting that the farmers fill out survey forms, or fishing communities limit fish-catch sizes. One may imagine how an additional Euro-tax would be presented. The idea of a European Union is not to unite the citizens in discontent!

Yet, upon the accession of just a handful of even the most prosperous Eastern European countries, to maintain existing standards of social support and agricultural policy, not only would all existing member states become net contributors – even the poorest areas of Greece may not qualify for subsidy – but the Union would become bankrupt. Under the terms of the Maastricht Treaty this is illegal. Much time is being dedicated within the Parliament, and especially within the Budget Committee of which I am a member, to find a solution. One thing seems likely: there will be no enlargement in the immediate future.

There is frustration, indeed, great frustration that the co-operation of which Mitterand spoke is still so limited. The Union has been unable to issue a communiqué on the US bombing of Iraq; we still do not have unity on the future of a Single Currency, or the UK's opt-out of the Social Chapter; the harmonization of tax structures; even the protection of children against exploitative employers. All these have failed to clear the hurdle of dissent at Council level. Yet, we cannot impose co-operation.

There are no dictators in the Union, and we don't want any. The Commission, which is most often presented as a dictator by the tabloids, is a small body – fewer in numbers than the Scottish Office, or most metropolitan councils – and has strictly controlled powers. When John Major summoned Jacques Delors to Downing Street, he came. As a civil servant, he had no choice.

On the other hand, democracy and accountability must be improved. The Parliament contains the only elected representatives of the people it serves. There is too much secrecy in the Commission and the Council of Ministers, by design and by chance. Most of the Parliament's meetings are open to the public and MEPs are accessible to their electorate. The Commission takes most of the blame for imposing laws on the helpless citizens of Europe, but, as civil servants, they are not allowed to explain, or defend themselves. Internally, there is often resentment that they take the blame publicly for other people's decisions. The Council has started making some meetings public, but it is clear that such meetings are carefully orchestrated. For transparency we need to be able to see behind those closed doors.

CONCLUSIONS

So, with all the limitations, with all the problems, warts and all, why Europe? Some arguments have been presented here, but I suspect there are as many others as there are citizens of Europe. There's a farmer in Kyrgyzstan who has called his new son Tacisbek in recognition of the support he received from the *Tacis* programme. There are people in my constituency who would not have jobs were it were not for EU schemes. There are networks of special interest groups (women, disabled, researchers, environmentalists) who have found more support by linking with similar groups in other member states than they had in their own areas. They all have specific reasons. The EU has given much to many and has a great deal more to give – and I am not just talking about finance.

But, most importantly, it has given all of us security – peace. My parents have not had to see their children killed by war as François Mitterand's did. There were few people at the 'Why Europe?' conference who had experience of war, and none that would want it. If we can make enlargement a reality, there will be even more of us in the Union of Peace. If for no other reason, that is 'why Europe', and that is why it is essential to continue the work against the forces of racism, exclusion and nationalistic prejudice that the Union is undertaking.

One final thought: is there an alternative? There is; the UK has the choice of staying in the Union as part of the world's largest trading bloc, helping to form one of the leading world powers (if not *the* leading power) by learning to co-operate with its partners, or it can pull out and stand in splendid isolation, as some politicians would seem to like. In my view, the result of this would be that the UK could wield all the international clout of a local council.

The big question for me is, 'why is "Why Europe?" such a difficult choice for some people to make?'

NOTE

1.   Quoted from 'White Paper on the 1996 Intergovernmental Conference', Vol. II, p. 159 (European Parliament, Directorate for Research, Political and Institutional Affairs Division, 1996) (my italics).

3 Towards a European Identity: Policy or Culture?

Hans-Joachim Veen

The former British Prime Minister, Harold Macmillan, was asked one day by a journalist, what had influenced him most in defining his policy and he answered: 'The circumstances, my dear, the circumstances.'

This seems to me a good approach for my topic too, because it is an empirical and a pragmatic one. So I would like to focus on three questions: first, what are the circumstances and challenges under which a specific political identity in Europe may grow? Second, of what kind, of what substance will a political identity have to be to make European integration acceptable for the people? Third, what was and actually is today the impact of cultural identity on European integration?

Beginning with the last question I offer a simple definition of what identity means in my view: I understand identity to be the collective knowledge of where one's historical roots lie, what one's foundations are and the direction in which one is heading.

It is thus immediately evident that historically Europe has always been based on different identities. Europe is the region of the world with the highest diversity of different languages, ethnic groups and nations, cultures and forms of life to be found in what is, comparatively speaking, an extremely restricted area. All these factors contribute and have always contributed to the shaping of European identity, sometimes in partnership, sometimes in conflict. Yet from ancient times until today, Europe has at the same time always perceived itself as a unit in more than merely geographical terms. As Ortega y Gasset so correctly and precisely observed in his major work of 1930, *The Revolt of the Masses*:

> Were we to take stock of our intellectual assets today, it would transpire that most of these assets stem, not from our respective fatherlands, but from our common European heritage. Within us all, the European by far surpasses the German, Spaniard or Frenchman. ... Four-fifths of our internal assets are common European resources.

Ortega y Gasset's (*Works*, III, p. 148) choice of nations is merely arbitrary: the Swede, Hungarian, Pole, Briton, Italian or Dutch could equally have stood beside his German, Spaniard and Frenchman.

41

Reducing complexity, with a certain degree of courage – an exercise for which the political sciences must always be prepared – the endless wealth of our common 'internal assets', i.e. what we have in common intellectually and culturally, can be subsumed under two complexes: the common Christian origins of European ethics and culture, and our common intellectual history (*Geistesgeschichte*), history of political ideas and constitutional history, in spite of temporal disparities and different forms of government.

The common Christian and intellectual heritage of Europe is an inescapable reality. It is present in our systems of higher and general education and continues to determine our ethics and everyday morals. Perhaps this is why it so often slips out of our minds: it is so obvious that we frequently take it for granted. But can one for a moment just try to imagine our streets and squares, our villages and towns without their churches and cathedrals, their chapels and Christian cemeteries?

The historical perspective, the common knowledge of where our roots lie, and what our foundations are, have certainly served to shape our identity, and, indeed, forms the basis of our European identity in intellectual and cultural terms right up to the present. Cultural identity once preceded the formation of the plethora of European nations with national identities and appears today as a necessary precondition within the current process of European political integration.

The same holds true for our common intellectual history (*Geistesgeschichte*) and our common history of political ideas, even leaving aside their Greek and Roman antecedents, as well as the Middle Ages. The major literary works of modern times, of the Enlightenment, Idealism, Realism and Romanticism, are to be found throughout Europe and belong to us all. Furthermore, the modern democratic state is a European product. It embarked upon its triumphant march via the USA throughout the entire world and has now become the universal model of a liberal democratic order. Basic rights and the separation of powers, the transition from classical natural law to modern human and civil rights, the state based on the rule of law and parliamentary democracy, checks and balances and state sovereignty – these are all achievements which stem from our common European heritage.

Thomas Hobbes and Montesquieu, John Locke and Immanuel Kant, John Stuart Mill and Rousseau and Thomas More have all equally contributed to this heritage. In an attempt more precisely to classify the contributions made by the various nations to the modern constitutional state, it could be said that England was the first to bring political freedom into the centre of the *raison d'état*; that the French Revolution later contributed to the concept of equality, so radically pushed through during the years of the revolution; and that Imperial Germany contributed the idea of the welfare state in the 1880s, which went back to the older, patrimonial conception of rule of the feudal lords and the absolutist princes in Germany (*Landesvatertum*). Europe was the historical testing ground for forms of state and government. The modern constitutional state therefore essentially co-determines the common European heritage, characterizing the political and cultural identity of Europe up to the present.

However, this heritage has long ceased to be specifically European; it has to a certain extent become universal property, just as the Christian cultural heritage of Europe has flourished far beyond its European roots and transcended the confines of the old continent. So, on the basis of all historical experience, the common identity of Europe, in terms of its *Geistesgeschichte*, its cultural and political ideas, evidently goes no further than the status quo of European diversity in its ethnic, economic and political dimension, comprising sovereign nation-states.

This demonstrates that the common Christian and cultural heritage of Europe and its unity of ideas, to which European politicians so gladly allude, are evidently insufficient to breathe life into the European Union in terms of economic and monetary union and political union with a common foreign and security policy. In other words, the virtual cultural identity of Europe does not lead to a political identity, nor to a unity of action which might promote the integration of Europe towards political union. And this is true despite the obvious Europeanization of everyday cultural trends, fashions, in sports, music and leisure-time activities. The lifestyles, clothes, consumer behaviour and the everyday standards of the French, the Swedes, the British, the Germans, the Italians and the Greeks are becoming increasingly indistinguishable and a common European everyday life culture is unmistakable. This is particularly evident among the younger generations for whom the dismantling of national borders throughout the EU no longer represents an achievement, but the natural starting position for their individual freedom of movement throughout Europe. One could call this a paradox: the virtual identity of Europe is not only rooted in history, but is also a living reality in our high-culture as well as in everyday culture, yet it does not give rise to a specifically political identity for Europe.

So how are we to achieve a political identity, which would then lead to common action? What can be its substance? These are questions which refer to 'the circumstances' Macmillan once addressed. What are 'the circumstances' in the post-1945 world and, more particularly, after the end of the East–West conflict in Europe? Since the Second World War it has been evident that the nation-state has had its day. Almost against their will, most peoples of Europe had entered into a community of fate, united by their common war experience, regardless of whether they were on the winning or the losing side. Poverty, hardship and economic ruin reduced the nations of Europe to the same level. Economic depression did not halt at borders, mutual dependencies had become inexorable. The European states had relinquished their role as great powers to the USA and Russia – even if France and Great Britain were loathe to recognize this. After the Second World War, it finally became clear that Europe needed new forms of co-operation since the coals of nationalism, aggression, racism, adversity and xenophobia simmered within the sovereign nation, requiring but a spark to burst into flames again and again. The danger of a regression into racist barbarianism and chauvinistic nationalism in Europe has by no means been warded off, as a glance at the tabloid press in the UK and elsewhere so painfully demonstrates. On the contrary: following the end of the East–West conflict, the trend towards 'renationalization' is evident, not only in the states of Central and Eastern Europe, but also in Western Europe. National or ethnic antipathies towards other peoples seem to be on the increase again, with a pioneer role perhaps being played by the United Kingdom in this respect. Another major challenge is the economic future of the old industrial states and the preservation of their welfare state character.

Against this background, my thesis is as follows: A political identity in Europe can only arise from the uncertainties of its future, the crisis in its present state and development, and the magnitude of the problems lying ahead of us which will integrate old nation-states into a Union capable of political action. The political identity of Europe accordingly means the common awareness that we are all in the same boat, confronted with the same challenges, and that we shall only be able to cope with the major tasks of our times by rowing the boat together. The political identity of Europe can neither be ordered from above nor conjured up. The political integration of Europe has thereby become a pragmatic task. And it is with pragmatism that we shall have to clarify more precisely what these major tasks are which can only be solved together.

Once again, with no pretension of being exhaustive, I should like to mention five European objectives in this context:

1   Securing a European Peace Order

The existing European peace order, whose core was established with the founding of the European Community and NATO in the 1950s, must be adapted to the requirements of changing times, expanded and secured anew.

With regard to Eastern Europe and Russia we have to realize that this peace order is on much thinner ice than many believe. We should keep in mind that a peace order is a prerequisite for prosperity, welfare and legal security all over Europe. This is especially relevant for a successful confirmation of the transformation process in Eastern Europe. Capital flees from insecure regions; therefore investment is only made in those places in which external and internal peace are secured. Peace in Europe presupposes a peace order in a complex sense in economic, social and legal policies. Its institutional enshrinement in the European Union and the link with the Atlantic Alliance are therefore the indispensable elements of such a stable peace order.

2   The Development of a Common Legal Order

A European peace order cannot only be effective 'externally', but must also constitute a common legal order 'internally'. This holds true for legal security and legal protection for the individual citizen, just as for protection against internationally organized crime. The latter has begun to undermine citizens' legal awareness and their belief in the ability of the state authorities to protect them, thus inducing a gradual delegitimization of state authorities with unforeseeable consequences for internal order, obedience to the law and the confidence of citizens in their state. Those who believe that internationally organized crime can be nipped in the bud at the level of a single nation are putting their own foundations at risk. Only a joint European approach can protect the state structures which guarantee the safety of the individual.

3   Europe's Capacity for Action in the International Arena

In the wake of the irreversible loss of their previous status as world powers, the individual European nation-states will only be able to assert themselves politically in the world of tomorrow if they pool their forces and interests. Europe will only be able to hold its own in the international power game and face the challenges of anti-Western forces of political ideology, totalitarianism and fundamentalism by means of joint, co-ordinated action. The old continent of Europe indeed does appear to be entering a new era of her history. Her great nations have lost their roles as colonial and world powers, even if the symbols are still cultivated. And her role as the focus of developments in world history, of culture, intellectual affairs and economic activity is at risk of fading into the annals of time. If the states of Europe wish to retain their status as global players and hold on to their prosperity, this can only be achieved in the context of a new supra-national formation. In this situation, it is probably easiest for Germany to redetermine its role and redefine itself in a supranational context. But it seems to me that France too has already realized this, while the United Kingdom has not yet offered a consistent response.

economic

4   International Competitiveness

The globalization of markets is also forcing Europe to make every effort to become internationally competitive and remain a base for the industries and service centres of the future. The creation of a single European market was an important step in this direction. The internal market must now be genuinely completed and rendered more efficient by the introduction of a single European currency. A regression to a mere free trade zone would fail to satisfy the requirements in this respect. Europe needs a common economic order which, in the long term, is inseparable from a common social order and corresponding legal harmonization, just as it is from a single currency.

5   Preserving Natural Resources

The increasingly pressing ecological problems can only be solved across frontiers. Preserving our natural resources for the generations to come is an urgent task affecting all Europeans in the same way. We cannot live today at the expense of the generations of tomorrow and permit the destruction of our vital resources. This sphere also requires the pooling of the entire forces of Europe.

This brief outline of European political objectives also shows, however, that there is a wide range of policy areas which do not need to be solved at supranational level and which, in fact, would be better not solved at that level. So we also need a discussion on what can better be solved on the national and the local level within a future Union. A European superstate would be contradictory to all of Europe's traditions and the diversity of its identities. For European identity has always been the dialectic of homo-geneity and diversity. And this concomitance of different cultural, national and religious identities must also be accepted in the future. The dialectic of unity and diversity which characterizes European identities have to remain the determining factor in the future. A political European identity therefore will always remain an identity in a restricted sense, confined to the common political objectives of European integration, alongside which other identities, just as national identities will always continue to exist.

European integration must not be taken too far. The idea of an all-embracing identification with a united Europe would not only be remote from everyday life, but, in my view, would be a highly problematic aspiration, one, indeed, from the realms of ideology. I openly admit that I have my misgivings about recent considerations of giving the united Europe 'a soul'; this is already dangerous at national level and would be even more compulsive in relation to Europe. Total identification with the European idea and the European superstate, which would take hold of all policy areas and seek to deal with them centrally, would be in contradiction to the vivid pluralism of European identities.

A political identity of Europe can thus only be achieved by a pragmatic approach, i.e. the growing common awareness of the common challenges nations and peoples are facing; in other words by means of a concrete political vision of a complex peace order and of Europe as a welfare union and a global player.

REFERENCE

Ortega y Gasset, J., *Gesammelte Werke III* (Stuttgart, Deutsche Verlagsamstalt, 1978).

4 Identity, Citizenship and Democracy in Europe
Wolfgang Ullmann

1 EUROPEAN IDENTITY

There is more than one reason to start a statement on citizenship and democracy in Europe with an explanation of the concept of identity and what it could mean on the European level. One of these reasons I will try to explain by referring to a discussion, which took place in the Institutional Affairs Committee of the European Parliament some months before September 1996, when I presented the paper which forms the basis of this chapter.

The members of this committee were discussing the concept of European citizenship and what this might entail, in connection with the Parliament's position in the negotiations of the Intergovernmental Conference, which was dealing with amendments and additions to the Maastricht Treaty. In the midst of this discussion one of our British colleagues made the point that citizenship in the European Union, seen from the perspective of legal clarity and effectiveness, seems a rather vague and idealistic concept, whereas national citizenship gives legal security and is thus much more meaningful to citizens than the more or less indefinite title of citizenship of the Union.

What I would like to emphasize over against this one-sided affirmation of national citizenship and identity is to underline the fact that there is a special European identity; a European identity not only in terms of culture and history, as might be commonly accepted, but also in terms of politics and social structures, and even in terms of psychology and consciousness. And precisely this kind of European identity is the reality and occurs as the impact of the nation and the nation-state. It is, moreover, fundamental: fundamental not for some Europeans and not for others, but fundamental for *all* Europeans, a unique historical and cultural feature. And this is why a 'Europe of the nations' is not a goal which lies only in the future. Europe consists of nations, and in some respect this is actually the historical definition of what it means to be European.

German textbooks usually say: Europeans have in common their origin in Antiquity, Christianity and Germanic pre-Christian traditions.

This answer, while not totally wrong, is in more than one respect incomplete, because it does not explain this unique and complex structure of a special group of nations; nations which are, on the one hand, clearly distinguished from each other by languages, institutions and traditions and at the same time connected or even unified by a common history, a special kind of interrelatedness and connectedness.

Where does the latter come from? The origin of European nations lies in the Middle Ages, more precisely in the medieval university. In this institution a new type of socialization was created by scholarly activity, a new kind of co-operation and communication between teachers and disciples (*'universitas docentium et discentium'*). This co-operation and communication connected young people from all parts of Europe. At the same time it gave the opportunity to bring together groups which were unified by language and common origins (*nationes*).

This was a really extraordinary type of socialization – co-ordination and assimilation, integration without merger and absorption, which means without loss of identity. This unique institutional and social environment became possible thanks to the co-ordination and synchronization of different and even contradictory traditions: the Bible with its Hebrew, Greek and Latin versions; Greek philosophy, Roman and canon law. This last may in particular be seen as the classical paradigm of what we mean by the synchronization of contradictory traditions. *Gratians 'Decretum'* as a *'Concordantia discordantium canonum'* gave the watchword for a whole epoch of scholarly work, aimed at gathering together and harmonizing different traditions. And we can see this secular endeavour of harmonization as preparing a new kind of democracy and democratization, creating relationships between different and competing traditions within one newly created framework on a new level of equal communication, which can be clearly distinguished from Greek democracy and Roman governance by the rule of law and military power, based only on one tradition and one body politic.

So, the enormous impact of this new paradigm explains very well why it came to be the leading concept in the struggle to overcome the deep crisis of medieval Christianity in the fourteenth and fifteenth centuries. When the councils for universal reform (Constance, 1414–18; Basle, 1431–45) were looking for a model of universal representation, they eventually took over the organization of nations from the university (see the famous decree, *Haec sancta synodus*, 30.3.1415 in the *Conciliorum Oecumenicorum decreta*). This decision should not be seen as astonishing, because representation would never have been universal if it had been based on secular or ecclesiastical institutions, which at this time, the beginning of the fifteenth century, were a reason merely for fissure and fragmentation. On the other hand, the nations of the universities, which were parts neither of secular nor ecclesiastical powers, were nevertheless a clearly defined social entity, and could be used as a means of combining independent and parallel social structures. Secular power, the Church and the university – all three were dominating institutions, independent from each other, which, in their horizontal parallelism excluded any hierarchical structure as well as all the tensions and conflicts raised by hierarchical claims.

This brief outline of the common heritage of all European nations, of their common historical identity, reveals the panorama of their common pedigree. This was a sequence of revolutions, commencing with the struggle of the Pope and the Roman church for its independence from the medieval emperors and their influence over the church, which took place at the end of the eleventh and the beginning of the twelfth centuries. This revolutionary struggle was completed and settled in 1122 by the so-called *Edict of Worms*, which distinguished between Italy and Germany as areas in which different relations pertained between secular and canon law.

This was the first step, continued by similar steps of emancipations and independence, which may be tabulated as follows:

1517–55   The German Reformation which entailed a distinction between Latin and German Scandinavian Europe, the latter being beyond the remit of any kind of jurisdictional influence of the Pope or his representatives.

1641–88   The British Revolution ('Restoration of Freedom'), which led to a distinction between absolute and constitutional monarchy.

1789–1815 The French Revolution, which brought the separation of monarchy and democracy, and unitarian national and multi-ethnic states.

Since 1914 this distinction has been called into question by the breakdown of these last, particularly in Eastern Europe, but this breakdown has also endangered cultural and legal equality in Central and Western Europe.

This rather short overview nevertheless leads to an ineluctable conclusion: European democracy will be more and more destabilized and the identity of Western nations will decline yet further if the concepts of nation and nationality, and of democracy forget and exclude their roots in the pre-1789 European traditions. This means that European identity includes participation in the following:

a. conciliarity – the ability to co-ordinate different and non-contemporary traditions;

b. reformation – the freedom to change constitutions without restraining or removing fundamental rights;

c. enlightenment – free access to all kinds and levels of culture.

So, the strength and cultural vitality of national identity depends on participation in all these aspects of European identity. The opinion that there is a contradiction or at least a conflict between national and European identity has to be rejected as deeply mistaken. If the latter identity is weakened, the result will be the decline and fall of the former identity. Germany is the most obvious and minatory example of this connection.

2   NATIONAL AND EUROPEAN CITIZENSHIP

What are the consequences for the concept of citizenship in the EU and for Europe as a whole?

Let us first consider the present state of affairs. Since the Maastricht Treaty we have had a special EU citizenship, based on national citizenship in one of the member states. In any evaluation of its impact and practicability one should have in mind the competences accruing to this citizenship, which are:

a. freedom of movement and residence on the territory of the member states;

b. the right to vote and stand in municipal and European Parliament elections, purely by virtue of the residence criterion;

c. the right of petition and the right to apply to the European Ombudsman;

d. the entitlement of non-nationals to diplomatic protection afforded by any member state.

Of course, everyone knows the limitations for freedom of movement under the conditions of Schengen and Dublin or the deeply unsatisfactory situation of third country nationals. We have, therefore, an ongoing debate in the European Parliament which is considering the deletion of those limitations, and giving third country nationals rights on the same footing as EU citizens after five years' residence in the EU. Nobody knows how far the IGC will go in debating or accepting those suggestions.

Independently of these possibilities the European Parliament is discussing the fact that the EU Treaty entails only a very poor number of limited political rights. These discussions have so far had one major result: an application to the European Court for a decision on the possibility that the EU join the European Human Rights Convention. Meanwhile the negative result of the European Court's decision has meant the failure of the above-mentioned initiative.

Under such circumstances another position has gained in strength: the idea of including a kind of Magna Carta of fundamental rights within the EU Treaty, based on the text of 1989, as adapted by Parliament and completed by additional amendments against discrimination, for the protection and guarantee of rights, for an ecologically sound environment, self-determination (for example, in bio-ethics) and data protection.

3   EUROPEAN DEMOCRACY

The Maastricht Treaty declared, as the major and final goal of the EU, that the Union would become 'a union of peoples' – astonishingly not a 'union of nations'! But at present it is still merely a market union in combination with agreements on co-operation in the fields of security and external politics (the so-called 'second pillar'), and in justice and home affairs (the 'third pillar'). All this leaves us a considerable distance from being a 'union of peoples'!

And this is why a Magna Carta of fundamental rights could become the gravitational centre for the post-Maastricht programme for a real union of peoples, based on an identity which would be defined and structured by this charter of fundamental rights. Of course this would call for the formulation of rights to freedoms which go far beyond the present regulations in Articles 8a ff. of the EU Treaty. In this respect, I see the following priorities: self-determination on the basis of free access to all levels of European culture; the guarantee of this freedom by a peace structure based on the elimination of all forces and possibilities of aggression; and a charter of fundamental rights as stated above.

There is still one major task to be accomplished: the claim of the OSCE (Organization for Security and Co-operation in Europe) Charter of Paris to overcome the gap between Western and Eastern Europe. Only after this gap has been closed can we be sure that we have succeeded in transforming national democracy into European democracy; a European democracy which has not absorbed, but which includes and protects, national cultures and traditions.

Part II
Political Commentary

5 European Identity

Christopher Brewin

The title of this volume, and the conference which gave rise to it, make the point that European identity is more problematical than national identity. After 1989 the German sense of identity enabled Chancellor Kohl to integrate the Eastern Länder into the Federal Republic despite the resentment of Ossler and Wessler. There was no comparable sense of European identity sufficient for an *immediate* raising of loans and eventually taxes to integrate Eastern and Central Europe into the new European Union.

However, the question remains whether, despite the variety of peoples and cultures, there is sufficient political identity to enable Central and Eastern Europe to be integrated into the military and economic structures of Western Europe. This question of whether Europe is capable of organizing itself on a larger scale involves two further challenges. The first is whether Europeans as a body will be capable of acting together to stabilize their neighbours in the Mediterranean and the successor states of the USSR. The alternative national concept is that it will be in Germany's national interest to stabilize the East while France will take a special interest in the Mediterranean. In other words, are Europeans prepared to do more out of a sense of identity with this Continent than they will do for New Zealanders, Africans, Latin Americans and Asians with whom individual states have historically strong cultural links, but with whom there is no identification as fellow-Europeans?

The second question is whether a European order can contain the irredentist and secessionist ambitions of groups with strong ethnic and cultural identities. Germany itself has dormant claims to Silesia and its 1938 frontier; Greek pan-Hellenism has claims to Macedonia and northern Epirus as well as to union with Cyprus. The Basques and Catalans, Scots and Ulstermen, the Russians in Estonia, the Abkhazians, the Hungarians of Romania, the Albanians in Kosovo provide examples where there is a potential European interest distinct from the national interests of individual European states.

In trying to describe what distinguishes contemporary Europeans from non-Europeans I shall consider only two attributes, geography and culture. I shall argue that, unlike German identity, physical geography is now the most important criterion and that human geography has lost much of its former importance. Culture will also be divided into the two categories of

Kultur and *Bildung*. I shall argue that, again unlike German identity, *Kultur* – those more permanent elements like language, music, religion and cuisine which are difficult for political authorities to alter – is less important than *Bildung*, the deliberate promotion of identity by national and European bureaucracies.

In the final section I shall tentatively suggest that European identity is formed more by dialectic than attributes. The analogy of a football team will illustrate my thesis. A team requires players chosen for their footballing *attributes* – pace, skills of dribbling and passing. But its character changes by playing other teams, and by internal interactions between the players, and between the players and the management. In preparing for this argument, I begin with some remarks about identity.

1   IDENTITY AND A PHILOSOPHY OF HISTORY?

In its modern unphilosophical usage, 'identity' is a new word, in marked contrast to the word 'European' which has a long but discontinuous usage over three millennia since the eighth century BC (Duroselle, 1990). It is a term of social psychology, in which institutions create meaning for those in them – as in families, schools, European and national bureaucracies. Identity can be expressed by external signs like clothes and hairstyles. It can express internal attitudes, ranging from the ferocious remembered histories of threatened groups in the Balkans to the taught ethics of tolerance of minorities and defence of their rights.

Identity is often conceived of as an individual matter, with elements both of calculation and emotion ascribed to the choice of identity. I cite the definition of group identity given by the European Henri Tajfel (1978, p. 402) as typical:

> the individual's knowledge that he or she belongs to certain social groups together with some *emotional* or *value* significance to him or her of the group membership. (emphasis added)

However, national identity has been more collectivist and top–down than this individualist account suggests. Since about 1900 states have issued identity cards to civilians and identity discs to soldiers. For this, two elements have been required. The first has been an issuing authority. The second element has been objective criteria whereby officials can decide who is entitled to receive the card or disc. In the Maastricht Treaty, the states members piggy-backed on this notion of a top–down conferral of identity by ascribing European citizenship to all nationals of member states.

It is also important that this term has been particularly popular in America, where older terms like allegiance, and ties to birthplace and religion were politically incorrect. The elements of the Constitution of the United States, the English language, love of country and myths about the Founding Fathers are deliberately taught to all American schoolchildren and all recruits to the federal army. As befits its democratic origins, identity emphasizes a shared *similarity* rather than, say, the hierarchy of allegiance linking the estates of the medieval period. The American concept is self-consciously *secular*, not tied to ethnic origins or birthplace or religious faith. Moreover, it is oriented *to the future* as well as past. For example, a German–*American* has a hyphenated identity where German refers to origins and American to present and future commitments.

Although political identity can be taught, the content has to be appropriate to the circumstances of the time. No teacher however brilliant and no authority however absolute could recreate what were in medieval times allegiances to town or guild or nobles expressed in the heraldry of banners and coats of arms. There is an implicit philosophy of history in every account of identity. Thus national identities inconceivable in the Middle Ages could be created in Western Europe from the seventeenth century, in Italy and Germany in the nineteenth century, and in Eastern Europe after the collapse of three empires at the beginning of the twentieth century. The doctrine of untrammelled sovereign statehood enabled politicians to commercialize agriculture, industrialize, create networks of post, railways and air routes centred on national capitals, and institute mass education and mass armies. Although national identities were justified by their foundation on culture communities, in most cases the size of the state was also based on élite calculations of how to deal with external pressures, both military and commercial. For example, according to von Treitschke, a real state had to be of sufficient size to win battles on its own:

A defenceless state may still be termed a kingdom for conventional or courtly reasons, but science, whose first duty is accuracy, must boldly declare that in point of fact such a country no longer ranks as a State.[1]

Now that nationally-based commercial policies are either futile or dangerous to their own peoples, and few states can rely for their security on their own military forces, some philosophies of history claim that there are objective determinants requiring the development of a European identity. By describing the 1914 and 1939 wars as civil wars, American historians make the assumption that Europe has been an entity throughout this century.

Hitler's aggressive nationalism had the aim of substituting a European self-sufficiency area for what he claimed was a dangerous reliance on Wall Street and colonial suppliers.

After 1945, European federalists expected a popular revolution on the model of 1789 to sweep away the historic provinces and institute a European polity on the level of Continental war-making, production and marketing. Even the British Secretary of State for India argued in 'A Note on Post-War Reconstruction', dated 29 October 1940,[2] that peace in Europe required the development of a European identity:

> The most effective way of limiting the danger from aggressive national patriotism is to subsume it in a wider, but still concrete and definite patriotism. The best hope of European peace lies not in any political machinery but in awakening a positive European consciousness and a patriotism for Europe as an entity with a character and interest of its own.

What is revealing about this quotation is not just the British hostility to institutions, what Amery went on to call the distraction of 'fancy European or world reconstruction'. It was that the British did not include themselves as Europeans, but responded to Hitler's racism with a comparable racial identification with the Anglo-Saxons of the USA and the white Commonwealth, sometimes expressed as the cultural unity of the English-speaking peoples. Amery went on to argue that:

> to preserve and yet further develop the informal co-operation between the British Empire and the United States which has grown up in this war is by far the greatest practical contribution that we can make to world peace in the future. This should be the first objective of our post-war policy.

Fifty years ago, there were competing philosophies of history. Some saw Europe as a context for imperialist rivalries, some as a common European home in which reconstructed states would emulate the national plans of the USSR, some as a region in an internationalist environment characterized by the 'Open Door' to American investment and protection. From our present perspective it would seem that two kinds of authority have been influential in determining from above the nature of post-war European identity – the nation-states that were reconstructed on both sides of the Iron Curtain, and the pan-European organizations for military and economic co-operation. Before examining the content of European identity, it is worth looking at the authorities which have been concerned for differing reasons to promote a sense of European identity.

2 THE AUTHORITIES: NATIONAL AND EUROPEAN BUREAUCRACIES

After 1989 all national bureaucracies in both Eastern and Western Europe, and all regional authorities, have asserted their European credentials. Sometimes, as shown by referenda in Norway and Switzerland, they have been more European than their peoples. Sometimes, as in the UK and the USSR, they have imagined themselves as more than just another European power. Sometimes, as in the case of Germany and some of the states of Central and Eastern Europe, they have promoted a European ideology as an instrument of recovering sovereignty with the agreement of their neighbours. Milward's 1992 thesis that national bureaucracies join institutions for their own national purposes has a point even if it does underplay the sense of duty and European idealism of many statesmen and intellectuals. All states have come to appreciate the need for reliable institutions of joint rule.

However, in contrast to the enthusiasm of Robespierre and Napoleon for their post-1789 French identities, they have generally been constrained in promoting any new European identity by the desire to go on governing in their national jurisdictions. In contrast to the USA, the states have retained full control over national education systems and the major say in the recruitment and use of all military and police forces.

The 'internationals', the new class of European bureaucrats, show considerable variation in their enthusiasm for European identity. NATO officials are often seconded from national bureaucracies and see their organization as instrumental to national purposes. Council of Europe officials see Europe in Amery's cultural terms as an antidote to chauvinism. Jacques Delors found that while the corporate directors of major European-owned electronics companies accepted that they could no longer be viable as national champions, they saw their future not as European champions but in technological alliances with leading firms in Japan and the USA, and in using cheap labour outside Europe (Ross, 1995, pp. 120–4).

The strongest promoters of European identity are the career civil servants of the European Union, but they show considerable circumspection with regard to the nation-states who constitute the twin decision-making bodies of the European Union, the Council and European Council of heads of state and government. I have before me an information pack for schools 'to mark the Fourth UK Presidency of the European Community'. Its authors write: 'It is not our task to promote any particular way forward, but you may like to discuss some of the following questions ...' This is far from the language of the American Declaration of 1776. As well as maintaining a posture of neutrality, the European civil servants are living embodiments of Raymond Aron's jibe that Europe appeals more to the intellect than the emotions. Beethoven's 'Ode to Joy' was chosen as the European anthem. Europe is promoted through youth orchestras and yachting festivals. There is a European University Institute in Florence. The focus of the Directorate-General for information is on élite opinion-formers. Similarly, the claims of the European Parliament to represent the peoples of Europe are never accompanied by any threat to resign when they are sidelined by successive intergovernmental conferences. The success of the Court of Justice in Luxembourg in establishing the doctrine of its own supremacy in matters of European law has been established in discreet remoteness. There is the potential challenge to its supremacy implicit in the 'states' rights' doctrine of the Brunner Judgement handed down by the German Constitutional Court (11 January 1994). Its reluctance to offend member states is shown in its judgement against the Commission in the case of the unilateral Greek embargo on the Former Yugoslav Republic of Macedonia.

This low-key approach to promoting identity is most evident in the actions of the most powerful of the EU institutions, the Council of (national) Ministers. It was in 1969 that the heads of state and government at the Hague Conference (final communiqué) first referred to developing a European identity, based on the past but looking to the future, 'consonant with its traditions and its mission'. In 1983 the 'Solemn Declaration on European Identity'[3] was proclaimed to cover the failure of the Genscher-Colombo Plan to establish a common foreign policy. In 1985 the member states established the Adonnino Committee to develop a greater mass appeal for the European Community, but few of its suggestions were included in the Single European Act. When in 1986 the Council adopted the 12 stars of the Council of Europe flag as the emblem of the EC, it did so without fanfare in a low-profile Minute. In 1988 it resolved:

> to strengthen in *young people* a sense of European identity and make clear to them the value of European civilisation and of the foundations on which the European peoples *intend to base their development* today, that is in particular the safeguarding of the principles of democracy, social justice and respect for human rights.[4] (emphasis added)

This resolution encapsulates the states' reliance on what in the USA would be called the teaching of civics, in which the only specifically European content consists of teaching the history of the European communities, and the advantages and challenges it offers.

This short survey of the national and EU authorities' promotion of a sense of pan-European identity shows that while both have an interest in the subject, each has been constrained in promoting a sense of identity based on values and appealing to popular emotions. In comparison with the banners of medieval corporations, or the flags and anthems of the age of nationalism, the 12 stars of the European Union have more in common with the appeal of modern corporate logos. The aim is silent recognition rather than noisy enthusiasm.

Let us turn from bureaucratic authorities to discuss the *rational basis*, the attributes and dialectic of contemporary European identity.

3   EUROPEAN IDENTITY: ATTRIBUTES

3.1   Geography: Physical and Human

Physical geography presently takes primacy over race and culture as the best starting point in determining Europeanness. While most Americans and Australians are racially and culturally of European extraction, they would be insulted to be identified as Europeans. They have given themselves new identities, politically constituting themselves Americans and Australians. This argument is even stronger where the racial identity is absent. Africans may speak French or English, Latin Americans may speak Portuguese or Spanish, Asians may speak Dutch or Portuguese or English; but none of them would thereby claim to identify themselves as Europeans. More controversially, I would argue that where colonists with a European allegiance have not given themselves new identities in territories geographically distant from Europe, as is the case with the Falkland islanders, their claim to be Europeans and not Latin Americans is now anachronistic even though they rely on the principle of self-determination set out above. I would also argue that all those individuals legally resident within the geographical boundaries of Europe are entitled on human rights grounds to participate, if they so wish, in the making of the rules under which they live. This option might well be rejected by those with a non-European identity; thus American and Japanese and Arab citizens living in Europe would prefer their existing status as resident aliens. However, Russians in Estonia and Turks in Germany, even though the Turkish Republic has itself opposed such assimilation, might well want to apply for citizenship of their host states.

The status of Russians, Estonians and Turks raises the question of where the eastern boundary of Europe lies within a Eurasian landmass which is continuous. Physical geographers can offer no satisfactory answer to this question. Jean Gottman and other French geographers have offered a solution based on mountains, rivers and seas:

> The Eastern limit follows traditionally the 'line of the Urals', that is the crest of the Ural mountain range from the Arctic shores southward, then the course of the Ural river which empties into the Caspian sea; the limit crosses the Caspian southward and swings to the Black Sea westward along the crest of the Caucasus range.
>
> (Gottmann, 1950, p. 8)

Although the Russians have co-operated by erecting a signpost pointing east to Asia and west to Europe, the Urals are a low rolling range like the Chilterns. One problem is that they have never constituted a political, religious, linguistic, racial or administrative border, ever. A second problem is one of human geography. For example, the Estonians and Russians who have been exiled to, or employed in, Siberia have never thought of themselves as Asians. Also most Georgians and Armenians would claim that they are as entitled to consider themselves European as Abkhazians or Ossetians.

Physical geographers who divide Europe from Asia at the Bosphorus face a similar problem of human geography. Although the Turks themselves distinguish between the European and the Anatolian/Asian sides of Istanbul, the Turks, Lazars, Circassians and Kurds who cross the Bosphorus every day are the same on both sides. Moreover, even if it is the case that the Turks are like the Japanese in having Europeanized themselves over two centuries, the difference is that geographical proximity now entitles the Turks to consider themselves not only in but of Europe. On the island of Cyprus there is no difference in the European credentials of the Greeks and Turks.

Israel does pose a difficulty for my thesis. Should the Jews of European origin and culture be counted as non-European because they have chosen to emigrate to Israel where they are outnumbered by the Arabs and Sephardic Jews? Or should they be counted as European because of their geographical proximity? The European Union's answer has been to refuse to contemplate accession, but to grant Israel trade concessions comparable to those of Scandinavian non-members.

Like the Turks, the British can choose whether to consider themselves European. In terms of physical geography they are linked to the Continental landmass but their weather pattern can be considered Atlantic rather than Continental. In terms of human geography they can consider themselves as having been peopled and civilized by contact with the

Continent, or give priority on the Churchillian lines offered above by Amery to their links to other English-speaking peoples and the independent states of the British Commonwealth.

The question of whether there is a European race or Indo-European family of peoples has been answered in the negative in the aftermath of Hitler's attempt to base a European order on a racial hierarchy. No serious author would claim that Jews cannot be Europeans because they are Semites or that gypsies are excluded by race from citizenship. It is true that, from an external perspective, genetic descent from natives of Europe has continued to be an attribute of European identity. Asians, Africans and Latin Americans know what they mean when they refer to Europeans both within and outside Europe.

The racial category of Caucasian invented by Johann Friedrich Blumenthal (d. 1840) is still favoured by policemen and other state authorities in Australia and America despite the lack of any evidence for an Indo-European family of 'white' races descended from Noah after his ark beached on Mount Ararat. In popular parlance, Caucasian includes European types differentiated by skin colour and skull shape. The several classifications include fair-skinned and dark-skinned Celts; Teutons; Mediterraneans, including Greeks and Turks; Slavs (which Estonians, following Metternich, still claim are Asians). Merely to list these types should be enough to show that there is no single racial component in the make-up of geographical Europe's population which is at the same time exclusive to Europe. To the successive invasions from the east can now be added all those who have immigrated to Europe as a consequence both of global communications and of far-flung European empires.

The discovery of DNA in 1953 has changed for ever the scientific understanding of how genetic material is transmitted and the relative insignificance of skins and skulls. Hitler's assertion of the racial superiority of a pure Aryan race, and consequent inferiority of the Semite, Romany and Slav has become as unconvincing as the counter-claim of the liberal historian of Europe, H. A. L. Fisher, that European superiority was due to their being 'energetic mongrels' (Fisher, 1936, p. 12).

However, in laws on nationality and citizenship, and in some party political platforms, race remains important in contemporary self-definitions. The 1981 British Nationality Act added *jus sanguinis*, the polite Latin phrase for descent by blood-line, to the right of nationality by birth on British geographical territory, *jus solo*. This novelty has the unifying pragmatic consequence of harmonizing the bases of entitlement throughout Europe and lessening the long-standing division between '*Gemeinschaft*' and '*Gesellschaft*' conceptions of statehood. The Federal Republic of

Germany for its part has also acknowledged that guest workers born *and* educated in Germany may apply for citizenship. Germany remains unique in having, like modern Israel, a law of return allowing all those descended from German parents the right to demand citizenship as of right. Perhaps even more surprising is that race can still be affirmed as the basis of political movements. The pan-Hellenic party in Greece, PASOK, was not set up to unite all cultural philhellenes, but to foster the racial values of those of Greek race, including the right to rule Greater Greece. The national front organizations to be found in many European countries from Northern Ireland to Russia proclaim racial as well as cultural agendas.

However, while it is true that the notion is widespread that Europeans belong racially to an Indo-European family of 'European peoples', or that European is a synonym for white skin, it is now indefensible as a criterion of European identity. This is so for two reasons. The first is a guilty recognition that Hitler's attack on Jews and Romanies has had its counterpart at some point in history in every major European country. Few would dare to assert that Jews cannot be citizens and cannot be Europeans, although the European doctrine of individual human rights has the markedly anti-collective basis first articulated in 1791: 'The Jews must be refused everything as a separate nation, and be granted everything as individuals' (Davies, 1996, p. 843). The second reason is that European cities have become cosmopolitan. Immigrant Jamaicans, Chinese, Bangladeshis, Algerians, Moroccans, Lebanese and Turks can no more be denied the status of citizenship in European states, and hence of being Europeans if they so choose, than can similar communities in North America. The cultural reception of human rights doctrine carries with it the implication that humans legally resident should be able to participate in the society where they live and work. Education by the political authorities against the racism and xenophobia that is widespread in Europe brings us to the next attribute of European identity, that of culture.

3.2   Culture: *Kultur* and *Bildung*

Like geography, the attribute of culture can also be divided into two parts. The first is *Kultur* – what is difficult for political authorities to change – cuisine, language, religion, music, sport, common experience of war, the recent commitment to democracy and the rule of law. The second is *Bildung* – what political authorities teach through schoolbooks, or by (dis)incentives – such as knowledge of foreign languages, a view of history, participation in the political or cultural process, toleration, rights to health-care and education.

The nub of the cultural argument is that communities united by a shared language or history ought to rule themselves as political entities. Culture can be used to promote either unification or secession. Thus the unification of Germany was justified in terms of *Kultur*, of its single language and literature, music and art. On the other hand, the differences between Catholic and Protestant, '*hochdeutsch*' and Southern speech, Saxon and Rhinelander, Prussian and Bavarian have been used to justify the weakening of Germany by the victorious Allies' imposition of a federal system. In a third variant, advocates of a federal European order invoke both theses to weaken the monopolistic tendency of territorial national identity. They claim that Europe has sufficient cultural unity to justify a federal government with one economic and monetary order. Simultaneously, they invoke the principle of subsidiarity to suggest that Walloons and Scots, Basques and Bretons, Slovaks and Northern Leaguers can govern themselves by seceding from larger states which are no longer needed for the defence of culturally defined communities from larger neighbours. Here it is the claim that European unity must be based on a common *Kultur* with which I want to take issue.

In the first place the cultural arguments based on a common family of languages, or on identifying Europe with Christianity or industrialization, have become unteachable over the last hundred years. To base European culture on a common family of Indo-European languages would lead to the absurd conclusion that Hungarians, Basques (Euskadi), Finns and Turks were not European. There is, however, some mileage left in the weaker version of this thesis which points to the syllabus of languages taught to children. Even in the age of imperialism, children learned Latin, perhaps Greek and a neighbouring language like French or German, but not Urdu or Swahili. Also there is a cultural as well as a scientific vocation in the teaching of English, German and French by Russians and Turks, although this was not reciprocated by the teaching of Russian and Turkish in Western Europe.

Similarly, it is no longer possible to identify Europe with Christianity now that there are more Christians outside Europe and some 13 million Muslims in the EU alone. Although the Christian Democrat prime ministers have tried to suggest that Christianity is essential to European identity, this seems as anachronistic as to suggest that the Holy Roman Empire has been reborn. For the secular successor states of Western and Eastern Christendom to attempt to exclude the successor states of Islam from the Council of Europe, or of Western European Union, would be monstrously inconsistent.

However, it has to be admitted that, as with past racism, the millennium during which there was no positive contact between Western Christendom, Greek Orthodoxy and Islam points to a cultural dissonance which *Bildung* needs to counter. The diatribes of Erasmus and Gladstone (1876) against the Turk, identification with the victory over the Saracens at Poitiers (732) or the defeat by the Ottomans at Mohacs (1526) are dangerous materials for defining current identity.[5] They are as anachronistic as taking pride in the consistency with which imperialists of all national origins promoted missionary Christianity.

Third, the most impressive, and misleading, account of the cultural content of European civilization is that it is a unique *mixture* derived from Athens, Rome and Jerusalem.[6] Athens is depicted as the Hellenistic source of myths celebrating Nature rediscovered in the Renaissance, and the model for democracy. Rome is depicted as the model for a pan-European system of law and order, and as providing the Latin elements of Western European languages and a common élite culture. Jerusalem is depicted as the source of Judaeo-Christian morality, making all European peoples into people of the Book.

The intellectual problem with this picture is historical as well as contemporary. For a thousand years Athens was not part of Europe. Jerusalem, at least since the end of the Roman Empire, has been occupied by the Crusaders and the British Empire, but has never been European. The political problem has been that Romanticism and liberal history have misunderstood the links and antipathies between Greeks and Turks, regarding Athens as essential to Europe but the Ottoman and Seljuk Turks as uncivilized barbarians, in but not of Europe. If Balkan history is to be regarded as European, then it is difficult to understand why the successors of its Ottoman rulers, especially after Turkey's reformation on European models, should be regarded as non-European. Somewhat tentatively, I argue that it is a matter of calculation by the authorities of the EU and its member states whether the contested sense of identity in Western Europe will be strengthened or weakened by treating Turkey as fully European. If the decision is to include Europe's second country in terms of population, it would be easy to emphasize the cultural importance in classical and religious and civilizational terms of the area between Ephesus and Antioch. At present the decision has been postponed on the grounds that identity will be weakened by Wessler-type resentment at yet more immigrants from Anatolia and more taxation to benefit those temporarily much poorer in the east. It is a matter of *Bildung*, not *Kultur*.

Fourth, industrialization is no longer a distinctive part of European society as was the case in the last century when Europe was differentiated by its technology of iron and steel, and steam.[7] However, the nature of European identity in developing pluralist capitalism is again a matter of unresolved calculation.

Now that national subsidies are no longer adequate on the scale of global competition, some firms look to maintain market share by moving production to Asia and by technological alliances with Japanese or American firms. Others argue for European protectionism to safeguard ownership and jobs as has been done in agriculture. The decision has been postponed by agreement on a Single Market enlarged to Central and Eastern Europe, which has found greater support among the large industrialists than did the Treaty of Rome.

Fifth, a European high culture is sometimes affirmed in Matthew Arnold's sense of a distinctive tradition in seeking after perfection in literature, music, painting and architecture, and philosophy. As in the case of language, the dominant category is national, but most artists have been profoundly influenced by their European neighbours. At one end of the literary spectrum Umberto Eco is more European than national, perhaps because of his focus on medieval Europe. At the other end of the spectrum Rushdie and V. S. Naipaul are more international than European or national. In music and painting, the case for a distinctive tradition is even stronger. Most musicians are recognizably national within a European tradition that sounds different from Arab or Asian or African music. Sephardic Jews in Israel, on the whole, do not go to listen to the same music as Ashkenazi Jews. However, popular music is Americanized or internationalized; and Japanese and American artists and audiences seem happy with the music of Beethoven. With painting and architecture, national and European traditions can still be discerned in picture galleries and domestic architecture (Kultermann, 1994). However, commercial city centres and communications like bridges and airports are no longer recognizably national or even European, but rather international. Moreover, in philosophy, de Rougemont's claim (1965) that Western philosophy has a progressive spiral quality which differentiates it from the circular philosophies of Confucius, the Buddha and Hinduism has become unteachable. Moreover, it is increasingly difficult to associate nations with philosophical schools as in English utilitarians, French Cartesians, German Hegelians. As with architecture, economics and philosophy have become more international than European or national.

The same pattern can be discerned in sport and cuisine. When Real Madrid failed to reach the European finals in football and basketball, a newspaper headline screamed, 'Out of Europe'. However, football and chess are the only games played throughout Europe, and neither are distinctively

European. Similarly, the existence of three great cuisines in Europe – Northern smorgasbords, French cuisine and Turkish meses – does not make those of us who eat Chinese, Indian and Indonesian food, or hamburgers, less European.

In short, the common values and emotional attachment of European identity are bound to be weaker in terms of their component cultural attributes and deliberate *Bildung* than has been the case for communities and societies built on linguistic or national or ideological similarities. Within the geographical area of Europe, the basis of this weaker sense of identity lies on the one hand in differences, and on the other hand, in the individual inadequacy of historically formed political units to act on their own on the scale required by modern production methods and military technologies. One possible way of safeguarding their unequal identities as communities and societies is for the historically and culturally various territorial entities in this peninsula of Asia to unite rather as persons of different gender like to unite, because they are *different* not identical. Instead of subordinating themselves to Washington or Tokyo, they have the option of agreeing rules. Instead of putting up with the aggressive nationalism exhibited by Croats and Serbs they have the option of combining forces on a European basis, or alternatively under American leadership. They have the option of updating the Enlightenment project of linking republics in a league as an alternative to empires and Hitler's racially ordered self-sufficiency so that human rights and toleration of minorities are taught, rather as in American civics courses civil rights and republicanism are taught. Whether this is to be by co-operation among separate entities, or by greater integration, will be a function of calculation in the face of an internal dialectic and an external dialectic, the subjects of the next section.

4.1   External Dialectic

There is no statue erected in Stalin's honour in Brussels. Nevertheless, the fear inspired in Western Europe by the Red Army's remodelling of the social systems and states of Eastern Europe was important in inducing institutionalized co-operation of different kinds in Western and Eastern Europe. The USA was persuaded to set up NATO and to put Marshall Plan dollars into Europe rather than, say, India. This was not the first time that Europe owed its sense of itself as a unit to an external federator. The chronicler of the battle of Poitiers in 732 records that 'leaving their houses in the morning the Europeans espied the well-aligned tents of the Saracens' (Wilson and van Durren, 1995, p. 26); and in Eastern Europe the Habsburg dynasty developed its role as protector of Christendom against Islam after the defeat by the Ottomans of the last Jagiellon king at the battle of Mohacs. The collapse of the USSR in 1991 has ended this motive for the political unification of Europe. However, the collapse of the Soviet empire has offered motives for political identity which so far have kept pace with the resurgence of nationalism. Essentially, German leaders have wanted to reassure their neighbours that a reunified Germany is not about to recreate an expansionist *Ostpolitik* in Eastern Europe, and their neighbours' leaders have recognized the advantages of joint action, offers of future access to markets and military and economic organization, in stabilizing Eastern Europe, North Africa and Turkey. The inability of the separate sovereign states to prevent ethnic cleansing in Cyprus and Bosnia, where individual national interest is not directly threatened, has reinforced the need to protect minorities and human rights on a collective basis.

Some see a future role for Islamic fundamentalism in provoking another clash of civilizations, but this seems unlikely as fundamentalists lack the most elementary political unity. A more likely cause of European togetherness under threat is the development of global economic *Machtpolitik* between the dollar, the yen and the euro. However, many large firms in Europe prefer internationalism as an alternative to the development of a European industrial protectionism comparable to that of agriculture. They see links with global partners for technology, and production in Asia or Latin America for cheapness.

4.2 Internal Dialectic

There have been many lines of division in Europe, and not all of them have produced dialogue between contending sides. In the Cold War period we got used to the categories of Western and Eastern Europe where supposedly sovereign societies aligned their social, economic and educational systems according to the model acceptable to their respective superpower. Conceptions of *societas*, social market and liberal capitalism could be set against *Gemeinschaft*, five-year national plans and Communist fraternity. There is a much older and deeper division between North and South, Germanic and Latin, Protestant and Catholic, beer and wine which runs conveniently along the 50th Parallel. There are cross-cutting divisions of ideology, so that the narrowest geographical conception of Europe – from Poland to Portugal – is shared by the peace movements of the Left and the nationalist right who are equally opposed to American and Russian participation and are united by prejudice against Turkey as the heir to the Ottoman empire.

However, in this section I want to focus on the present internal dialectic as radically unequal powers try to come to terms with the reunification of Germany and potential enlargement of the European Union. When Bismarck in 1866 called Europe a 'geographical expression' he was denying that there was an internal order which depended on the continued division of Germany (Wilson and van Durren, 1995, p. 76). I want, on the contrary, to suggest that there is an internal order formed by the relative power and differing conceptions of its units, rather as Switzerland is a way of meeting external pressures by compromises between differing cultures and cantons (Wæver, 1992).

5   CONCEPTIONS OF EUROPE

5.1   The French Conception of Europe

The French of all political colours conceive of Europe as being an entity like France. As in France, what de Gaulle called the '*éléments de dispersion*' need to be kept in check by a strong cultural mission, a defence identity, institutions, a clearly defined border, and above all a will capable of making and enforcing decisions with a clear sense of what is internal and what is external. A strong European identity is the foundation for this state-like entity with its core in Western Europe but contributing to stabilizing an Eastern Europe characterized by a weaker sense of European identity. Western Europe is conceived as the magnet to which other entities will adhere like separate iron filings. In economic terms, Europe could develop as a fortress protecting workers and owners in industry as the CAP (Common Agricultural Policy) has protected farmers. However, there is a nationalist sub-theme which sees Europe as no more than a mosaic of cultures, of more interest to élites than ordinary people.

5.2   The German Conception of Europe

Post-war Germany has been more inclined to see the state as a problem, an aspect of a pluralist process, a system to be kept neither too weak nor too strong. A low-profile state system enables networks of culture and economy to work without provoking anti-German alliances. Europe is not about defining borders but changing what borders mean. Geographically the core of this Europe is a *Mitteleuropa* which is mostly German-speaking but also includes Poland, the Czech and Slovak Republics, Croatia and Slovenia. Eastern Europe means the lands like the Ukraine beyond historic Prussia. Germans seem to want a Europe that is anarchic, in which individual states can ask for loans in return for meeting the conditions set by the Bundesbank. Jan Knoll from Polish Silesia can say, 'I want to live in a Europe without borders'.

5.3 The Russian Conception of Europe

The USSR was, until recently, a superpower on the global stage where Brezhnev's idea of a common European home consisted of triumphant Communist parties under Russian leadership. The Russian Federation still seems anxious not to be thought of as just another European power, and Gorbachev's common home seemed to stress variety rather than unity.

5.4 The British Conception of Europe

The British too fear integration, stressing their overseas links and the separation from the Continent of an island subject to Atlantic rather than Continental weather patterns. The British idea can be summed up as one of addition rather than integration, contributing their troops and their markets to enable the UK to be on the level of events while retaining a separate, pro-Atlantic and economically internationalist identity.

5.5 The Swiss Conception of Europe

Like the Norwegians, the German cantons of Switzerland rejected the federal government's attempt to institutionalize their role at the centre of Europe. Relying on their historic isolation, and an internal federation of culturally various cantons combined with external neutrality, the Swiss provide a strong counter-example to the argument of this article. They are secure in their cultural identity as Europeans but reluctant to replace an ideology of neutrality and self-reliance.

6 CONCLUSION

An anonymous Eurocrat is quoted in *Agence Europe* of 29 June 1992 as saying:

The term 'European' has no official definition and combines geographical, historical and cultural elements which together contribute in forging
the European identity, and whose content is likely to be subject to
review by each succeeding generation ... It is not a sum of parts but a
dialectic over time and space.

In the same spirit I have argued that criteria of physical geography have for our generation replaced those of racial origin. My thesis is that European identity will be taught less as a matter of past common *Kultur* but, as in the USA, as *Bildung* based on future needs to act together. The states need a European identity to make common rules, develop Continental-scale assurance of boundaries of states unequal in size, of human rights within those states which are mutually assured against revolution, of production and market and currency that is world competitive, of common action to stabilize neighbours which it is not in the national interest of any particular state to perform. Such an identity would have more emotional appeal than the alternative of a commercially driven internationalism. It would be more agreeable than the nationalist alternative in which Germany takes the hegemonial role on the model of the USA in the free world.

As Václav Havel pleaded on 8 March 1994 to the European Parliament in asking for entry even if Czechs will need help, 'We may all be different, but we are all in the same boat.'

NOTES

1. H. von Treitschke, *Politics* Vol. 1, transl. Dugdale, B. and De Bille, T. (London, Constable, 1916), pp. 29–30.
2. Leopold Amery, *Cabinet Papers*, WA(40)7, 29 October 1940 (Public Records Office).
3. Bulletin EC-6-1983, point 1.6.1.
4. EEC Council Resolution – C/177/02/88, 24 May 1988.
5. Neumann, I. and Welsh, J., 'The Other in European Self-definition: Addendum to the Literature on International Society', *Review of International Studies*, Vol. 17, No. 4 (1991), pp. 327–49.
6. See de Rougemont, D., *The Meaning of Europe* (London, Sidgwick and Jackson, 1965).
7. Hartmut Kaeble in Lützeler, 1994, pp. 89–113.

REFERENCES

Davies, N., *Europe: a History* (Oxford, Oxford University Press, 1996).
Duroselle, J.-B., *Europe: a History of its Peoples* (London, Viking, 1990).
Fisher, H. A. L., *A History of Europe* (London, Edward Arnold, 1936).
Gladstone, W. E., 'The Bulgarian Atrocities and the Question of the East' (1876 Pamphlet).

Gottmann, J., *A Geography of Europe* (New York, Holt, Reinhart and Wilson, 1950).

Harle, V. (ed.), *European Values in International Relations* (London, Pinter, 1990).

Kultermann, U., 'The Context of Tradition and Cultural Identity', in Lützeler, P. M. (ed.), *Europe after Maastricht: American and European Perspectives* (Providence, RI, Berghahn Books, 1994), pp. 285–95.

Lützeler, P. M. (ed.), *Europe after Maastricht: American and European Perspectives* (Providence, RI, Berghahn Books, 1994).

Milward, A., *The European Rescue of the Nation-State* (London, Routledge, 1992).

Ross, G., *Jacques Delors and European Integration* (Oxford, Blackwell, 1995).

de Rougemont, D., *The Meaning of Europe* (London, Sidgwick and Jackson, 1965).

Smith, M., 'The European Union and a Changing European Order', *Journal of Common Market Studies*, Vol. 34, No. 1, March 1996, pp. 5–29.

Tajfel, H., *Introducing Social Psychology* (Harmondsworth, Penguin, 1978).

Toynbee, A., *The Western Question in Greece and Turkey* (London, Constable, 1922).

Wæver, O., 'Three Competing Europes: German, French, Russian', *International Affairs*, Vol. 68, No. 1, 1992, pp. 77–103.

Wilson, K. and van Durren, J., *The History of the Idea of Europe* (London, Routledge, 1995 revised edition).

6 Who are 'We'? Populists, Democrats and the People
Margaret Canovan

The last Olympic Games were accompanied by a stream of complaints in the British press about the poor performance of our athletes. This reached such a pitch that it was even suggested, half seriously, that the only thing to be done (if we were to be able to look forward to the next Games without shame) was to promote the formation of a European Olympic team. The EU as a whole ought to field a single team, for that would mean (so it was argued) that the reserves of talent available to it might well be enough to win more gold medals than the USA. We would at last be able to relax in front of our television sets and take pride in the performance of 'our' boys and girls.

It may be that as a popular symbol of European Union, such a team would be a great deal more potent than the European Parliament or the adoption of the euro (Billig, 1995, p. 121). But my reason for mentioning it is that it focuses attention on an important and neglected aspect of citizenship and community in the European Union, the question of collective identity: who are 'We'?

I shall argue in this chapter that projects for community and citizenship cannot avoid the first person plural: citizens are 'us', and (by implication) not 'them'. Insofar as Europhiles seek greater integration and more democracy in the EU, they project a first person plural on a European scale: we, the people of the European Union. But this projected democratic European people is shadowed by other 'peoples', often invoked in populist discourses that make much of more deeply-rooted contrasts between 'us' and 'them'. In the latter part of the chapter I shall consider how this populism is related to democracy, and whether plans to integrate the EU by bringing it closer to the people would simply play into the populists' hands.

1 COMMUNITY, CITIZENSHIP AND 'US'

'Community' and 'citizenship' are warm words, generally taken to signal inclusion. Neither, however, can avoid the first person plural. 'We' form the community, and citizens are 'us'. It will help us to understand the political grammar of European identity if we reflect a little upon this, focusing on citizenship because it will itself lead us to community.

In the theoretical literature on citizenship there are (to oversimplify an exceedingly complex matter) two different ways of approaching the subject, one often termed 'liberal', which is focused upon individual rights, the other called 'republican', concerned with political participation. The liberal approach, which is dominant both in political theory and in ordinary speech, understands citizenship in terms of the rights and entitlements of individuals. For example, have I got a passport, and if so, from which state? Do I have the right to reside in Britain and the EU? Am I entitled to social security benefits? Can I vote? The answers to these questions are matters of enormous significance for individuals, so it is not surprising that liberals, who inherit traditions of humanitarian cosmopolitanism, should sometimes have been tempted to think of citizenship as a universal human right. Short of the existence of a world state, however, citizenship can only mean membership of a particular polity, and even the supranational citizenship of the EU must be limited. Inherent in the concept of citizenship, therefore, is boundedness, and the issue of where the boundaries of citizenship are drawn.

Rules on the granting of citizenship vary enormously between different states. Even within the European Union, some are markedly more generous than others (Brubaker, 1992). What is invariable, however, is the existence of a core of citizens whose citizenship is simply inherited, who are by chance of birth members of 'us', a bounded community. Furthermore, it is the representatives of that given community – 'our' representatives – who make or amend the rules that loosen or tighten the boundaries of citizenship. In other words, although (on its liberal interpretation) citizenship may seem to be all about individual rights, it actually presupposes the existence of a defined community with the capacity for collective action – a 'we'.

This is one version of a point frequently made by communitarian critics of individualistic liberalism (Mulhall and Swift, 1992). Another version criticizes the liberal emphasis on the rights of individual citizens, on the grounds that the core of citizenship should not be a matter of individual entitlements but of shared political responsibility. Citizenship, seen from this republican viewpoint, means being an active member of the polity (Oldfield, 1990). Political theorists who think of themselves as 'republican' rather than liberal like to recall the classical tradition of active citizenship coming down from the ancient city-state. In the Athenian democracy or the Roman Republic (according to this tradition) being a citizen meant being co-responsible for the fate of the republic, filled with a public spirit that could indeed make it an enviable fate *pro patria mori*. Citizens were an élite group, exclusively male and distinguished from the majority of the population. But their privileged status entailed weighty duties. Since these ancient cities were continually involved in warfare, their citizens could expect to be called on to demonstrate their patriotism on the battlefield (Rahe, 1992, pp. 46–57). Modern political thinkers who seek to revive the spirit of republican citizenship rarely think in such military terms, and take for granted that women and other long-term residents should be included. But they do seek to foster public spirit, active involvement in politics and a sense of shared responsibility for the polity.

In being more demanding than the liberal approach to citizenship, republicanism depends even more obviously on a conception of political community, a distinct 'us'. For that patriotic involvement with and concern for the polity has to be commitment to a *particular* polity – '*our*' polity, in fact. Republican citizenship cannot be a matter simply of enjoying the rights available to one as an individual and treating the polity as a 'service station' (Taylor, 1993, p. 121) from which one can move on when it becomes convenient to do so. Instead, it implies and presupposes a strong sense of belonging: though its theorists lay stress upon the virtuous circle through which the practice of citizenship *itself* binds citizens together into a political community, thereby reinforcing its own foundations and allowing the incorporation of newcomers (Barber, 1984, pp. 133, 189).

2   A EUROPEAN PEOPLE?

The point of these brief remarks about citizenship and community is to focus attention on a neglected aspect of the European project, and to remind us of the magnitude of the undertaking. In some ways, of course, we already have European citizenship (Meehan, 1993). But it exists as something added on to citizenship of nation-states that form the substance of the EU. For the promise of this wider citizenship to be fully realized, something else is needed. Whether we understand citizenship in liberal terms as a matter of individual rights, or in republican terms as a matter of joint responsibility, it is clear that citizenship requires and presupposes political community, in the sense of a political body that exists in the first person plural: a *we*. If we are to have a Europe that is genuinely a community of citizens, we need a Europe whose members are aware of being part of a first person plural that stretches from Ireland to Greece, from Portugal to Finland, not to mention from Essex to Bavaria. At present no such 'we' exists (Hayward, 1995). How might it be created?

As political leaders have always known, by far the simplest way to foster a sense of 'us' is to focus hostile attention on 'them'. All the strongest national identities in Europe were formed or reinforced in the course of wars against historic enemies, and military mobilization can on occasion merge older local loyalties into a wider sense of nationality, as happened in eighteenth-century Britain in the course of its long struggle against France (Colley, 1992). That sense of a British 'us', which had been weakened by the half-century of peace after 1945, has recently been reinforced in many quarters (particularly but not exclusively in England) by disputes with 'our European partners', who can readily be represented as wicked foreigners across the Channel who insist on stealing 'our' fish, slaughtering 'our' cattle and so on.

The time-honoured tactic that might suggest itself to a Europhile wishing to foster a sense of European identity would therefore be to mobilize negative solidarity against those outside, notably against the Muslim countries that are the source of mass immigration. The rhetoric of fortress Europe, defending Christendom against the Saracens, is of course ready to hand, and has considerable appeal in some quarters (Smith, 1992, pp. 75–6). Needless to say, Europhiles in general fear that kind of militant Europeanism, and feel that a sense of community bought at such a price would not be worth having. Instead they are more inclined to stress a quite different path to integration, one that runs through democratic citizenship. This is a line of thought influenced by republican notions of citizenship. The argument is that Englishmen, Frenchmen, Italians and the rest will not feel European unless they are actively involved in the European polity. But increased political participation that fostered a sense of common responsibility would produce a common European public spirit, a common patriotism and genuine European citizenship. A Europe able to do this would of course need to be much more democratic, with an enhanced role for the European Parliament and public debate within a well-informed public that would be European in scope (Tassin, 1992, pp. 187–90).

This conception of active European citizenship may appear to offer a democratic route to true European community, a means of generating positive integration into a new EU-wide 'Us'. Instead of a reactive, defensive 'Us', united only by hostility to those outside, the EU can (according to this theory) develop a confident, democratic union of European citizens that would be comparable to the better aspects of American democracy. Famously, 'We, the people of the United States' appears at the start of the American Constitution, and many Europhiles would argue that if EU citizens had a more well-grounded sense that the Union was democratic and belonged to them, then 'We, the people of the European Union' would have as strong a sense of common citizenship as Americans.

This notion of a European Union united by democracy has obvious appeal; furthermore, the American parallel seems to show that a sense of belonging to 'us' can exist on a surprisingly large scale, and among people of enormously diverse origins. To say this is not to ignore the sometimes bitter disputes about difference and identity in the USA, nor the salience of regional conflicts of interest and anti-federal sentiment. What is striking, however, is that so much of the backwoods opposition to Washington is itself framed in the form of an appeal to American traditions and values. The frequent American upsurges of populism, in other words, do not actually challenge the sense of an American 'us', but tend if anything to reinforce it. It may be that (in the very long run) a comparable sense of belonging to a democratic 'us', 'We, the people of the European Union' will come into existence.

However, there are some very large obstacles along the way, and in the remainder of this chapter I shall focus on one of them that arises, ironically, from the ambiguities of democracy itself: the problem of populism. This problem (to put it in a nutshell) is that any attempt to democratize the EU in the interests of integration, in the hope thereby of generating a sense of common identity, is bound to offer a golden opportunity for political mobilization *against* integration by Europhobe populists: and in such a contest, the populists have the advantage of appealing to versions of 'us' that have a good deal more resonance than does the European identity that is yet to be created.

There is a serious dilemma here, both forks of which look ominous. Where the project of democratization is concerned, it seems that Europhiles are damned if they do and damned if they don't. The founding fathers of the Union promoted European integration at the level of the élite without making much attempt to mobilize the people behind the project, no doubt suspecting that in the short run this would not be possible. They are sometimes criticized for this; but the rift between a transnational élite and a locally-minded populace at the grassroots is not simply a European phenomenon that might have been avoided by more sensitive policy-making. It is a feature of the modern world much more generally, part of a dialectic whereby the same forces that in some ways produce cosmopolitanism simultaneously set off populist reactions against it.

In a striking analysis of a widespread tension between what he calls '*Macworld*' and '*Jihad*', Benjamin Barber (1992) has pointed to this dialectic. This era of global communications and global markets is on the one hand the post-national era of 'Macworld', a world in which national differences have become irrelevant as people from China to Peru surf the Internet, watch satellite television and buy and sell the same consumer goods. This new integration of the human race is symbolized by the world-wide spread of Big Macs and Coke (which, mysteriously, people of all countries and

cultures seem to want). But this in itself sparks off the other side to the
dialectic, what Barber sums up under the heading of 'Jihad': the backlash
against cosmopolitanism, the recovery of particular roots, the mobilization
of nationalism, tribalism, religious fundamentalism.

Barber paints with a broad brush, but echoes of his dialectic can certainly be observed in Europe, where the process of integration, symbolized
by the Maastricht Treaty, has itself set off counter-movements in many
countries that have exposed the gap between a Europhile political élite and
Eurosceptic grassroots (Hayward, 1995). Many Europhiles, of course
(pursuing the line of argument explored above), would say that the answer
is straightforward: the way to close the gap between élite and grassroots is
to democratize the European project. But this response is too facile. For a
neat illustration of the pitfalls of integration through democracy one need
only turn to the case of Switzerland. Members of the Europhile Swiss élite
have for some time wanted Switzerland to join the EU, and if they had as
much power as political élites do in other European countries, they would
no doubt have managed to bring this about. But Switzerland is the most
democratic country in Europe, devolving decision-making to ordinary citizens to an unusual extent. To the frustration of many of its members, the
élite cannot move faster than the grassroots, with the result that they have
not even managed to get their country into the EU's waiting room, the
European Economic Area, rejected in a popular referendum in 1992
(Kobach, 1994, p. 132).

It is no accident that referendums are so popular with Eurosceptics from
England to Austria, for while Europhiles may talk of integrating Europe by
empowering the people and thereby building a pan-European sense of 'us',
their opponents can make democracy work for exactly opposite purposes.
Indeed, the opponents of further integration pride themselves on being the
true democrats, those who are willing to trust the people and allow them to
take decisions (Haider, 1995, pp. 88, 104; Marcus, 1995, pp. 54, 100, 115).
Meanwhile they find it easy to play on *anti*-European senses of 'us' versus
'them'. Even the minimal institutions for European democracy that already
exist can be grist to the Eurosceptic mill. The European Parliament may or
may not work as means of integrating the citizens of the European Union,
but it certainly provides a splendid platform for anti-integrationists such as
the members of the French *Front National*. The paradoxes of this situation
are nicely revealed in Jean-Marie Le Pen's provocative slogan, 'Nationalists
of all countries, unite!' (Marcus, 1995, p. 164).

The point is that plans for generating a single European People by
means of democratic participation run up against the fact that a lot of
alternative 'peoples' already exist inside the EU, much easier to mobilize

since their sense of 'us' is so much more deeply rooted. Not all these 'peoples' correspond to nation-states, and EU institutions have provided opportunities for the instrumental use of federalism by sub-nationalisms in Catalonia, Scotland and elsewhere. But the fact remains that on the road to integration through democracy stand the intimidating roadblocks of populism.

3   POPULISM, DEMOCRACY AND 'THE PEOPLE'

Despite obsessive interest by political thinkers and scientists in the theory and practice of democracy, little attention has been paid to populism, and still less to its ambiguous relation to democracy. 'Populism' has many different senses within different discourses (Canovan, 1981; Ionescu and Gellner, 1969), but it is used in the present context to refer to attempts within liberal democracies to appeal from the élite to 'the people' against the established power structure (including the parties) and against the dominant public values (which are now liberal values). Within American traditions populism of this sort is comparatively respectable, boasting an ancestry that goes back not only to the People's Party of the 1890s but beyond that to Jacksonian and even Jeffersonian democracy (Kazin, 1995; Goodwyn, 1976). In Britain and continental Europe, by contrast, for a politician to be called a 'populist' is almost invariably an insult, and populists are widely seen as posing a danger to democracy by stirring up popular prejudices on emotive subjects such as immigration, law and order – and Europe (Betz, 1994). But those accused of populism retort that *they* are the true democrats, representing the views of ordinary people in the face of élites who have stolen democracy from the grassroots. In their view, in other words, democracy is not functioning properly, and party politicians who are supposed to be the people's representatives are actually out of touch (Haider, 1995, p. 88).

In one sense, the populists' claim to be the true representatives of the people is self-defeating, in that they rarely command a majority in elections, and often get only a ridiculously small share of the vote. If they did win more elections, they would themselves rapidly turn into part of the élite and lose their claimed link with the grassroots. Nevertheless, they inspire alarm because their opponents fear that they do indeed represent the people, at any rate in articulating views and grievances that may be prominent in opinion polls but are not shared by the élite.

This is not the place to explore the complexities of the relation between populism and democracy, which owe a good deal to ambiguities within democracy itself, and particularly to the tension between the pragmatic side of democracy as a working system of government, and what one might call democracy's 'redemptive' side, its promise of power to the people to make a better world. What matters in the present context is that the democratic rhetoric of popular sovereignty cannot but hand advantages to Eurosceptic populists, and give democratically minded Europhiles an uphill task. The problem lies in the wonderfully ambiguous concept that lies at the heart of democracy – 'the people'. This term has a great many different but intertwined senses, and all the most emotive and resonant of those senses favour Eurosceptic populism (Canovan, 1984).

'The people' can, of course, have a relatively neutral political meaning, referring simply to the population legally resident within a given territory (such as the EU) and implying no definite claims about their nature or unity. Perhaps this neutral sense of the term could be said to correspond to the liberal understanding of the citizen that we looked at earlier, as a citizen with rights. In the rhetoric of democracy, however, the term 'people' is usually employed in ways that carry more contentious political implications. For example, it is often used to mean the *sovereign* democratic people, which implies 'we, the people' as a collectivity able to act. This sense corresponds to the republican understanding of citizenship as membership in a collective people who are joined in responsibility for the polity they share. In principle, this sense is one that European integrationists could use to refer to the pan-European 'people' of their aspiration. But the difficulty is that that sovereign European people is a collectivity that has still to be formed and is therefore not available for mobilization, whereas the French people or the British people are ready to hand.

In other words, attempts to appeal to the people in this republican sense tend to merge with evocations of a more explicitly limited people: *our* people, understood in terms that are national or ethnic. 'Our people' are defined by contrast with outsiders, as when Le Pen promises to give France back to the French people. Furthermore, in the debate over European integration, republican and national senses overlap with another politically potent meaning, for 'the people' can also refer to what used to be called 'the common people' as distinct from the élite. While populists regularly mobilize 'the people' against the élite in their own countries, such appeals gain an extra edge when they are directed not just against the powers that be in Paris or London, but against a remote élite in Brussels. And since the European project is associated not only with foreigners, professional politicians and the educated upper classes but also with big business, plenty of class resentments are available for mobilization in the name of that democratic divinity, the People.

Populists can appeal to all these different senses of the term (and hardly anyone will notice when they switch in mid-speech from one to another). What makes things so easy for them is that these senses all refer to images of the people as they already are, with their existing identities, loyalties, interests and grievances. By contrast, those Europhiles who hope to integrate Europe through the practice of democracy must also appeal to the people, but in their case this means an appeal to the people as they *will* someday be, with a new identity, new loyalties, new interests (Wallace and Smith, 1995, p. 144). The case for democratic integration relies (explicitly or implicitly) on the *transformative* power of democracy, the faith that democratic practice will itself educate and enlighten citizens and inculcate in them a wider identity.

In terms of democratic theory, there is nothing remarkable about this. Transformative views of democracy have actually formed a strong strand in democratic traditions, motivating many campaigning reformers. Since at least the time of John Stuart Mill, articulate democrats have often shared the belief that one of the main purposes of democracy is to change people for the better (Mill, 1910, pp. 193–5, 277–9). On this view, the masses were not given the vote just to record their existing wishes and sentiments: on the contrary, it was part of a process of education, intended to turn the ignorant into democratic citizens.

There is a strand within this transformative view of democracy of the old republican tradition that active citizenship fosters patriotism and public spirit; but mixed with it is a strong dose of the more modern belief in enlightenment and progress through reason. On this view, democracy is a matter of public debate led by those in the vanguard of knowledge and opinion. If ordinary citizens can be induced to participate in these debates, then enlightenment will filter down, people will become better informed, more liberal, and less narrow in their attachments (Barber, 1984, pp. 152–4; Pateman, 1960, pp. 42–4; Fishkin, 1991, p. 81).

The idea of transformative democracy may or may not be persuasive in theory, but within the practical context of the EU it presents a number of problems. One of these is to do with scale. The trend of democratic theory is to stress the importance of face-to-face discussion if democracy is to be real, and therefore to aspire to move decision-making downwards from the nation-state. In that sense, the notion of democracy at the European level runs counter to the logic of democratic transformation. Integrationists might answer that in these days of electronic communication, size no longer presents such problems of communication. There is no reason why public debates carried on at the level of the Union should not be widely accessible. But this merely highlights another problem, the problem of language. If the citizens of the Union are to have an enlightening public discourse they need to be able to communicate and to understand one another. Indeed, much of the theory of transformative democracy relies heavily on Habermasian ideas about undistorted communication. But how can there be an enlightening public discourse at the European level without a shared language? Insofar as serious attempts were made to foster such a discourse, the rift would widen between the multi-lingual Europhiles and people at the grassroots, who would not be able to follow the discussion and whose suspicion of the élite would be even more readily mobilized by populists.

Is there any way, then, in which Europhiles *could* go about building a European 'us', and generating real European community and citizenship? Probably not: new political collectivities are normally a result of historical contingencies that are unpredictable and beyond control, while deliberate attempts to manufacture new identities often backfire. Nevertheless, a Europhile determined to give history a push in the right direction might do worse than to take a leaf out of the populists' book, and go straight to the grassroots. Perhaps the only kind of move to integrate the EU that will cut any ice with the man in front of the TV set is to build a new European 'Us' by making use of the power of modern sporting loyalties. There is already an élite of football players who are trans-European stars, and perhaps what the Commission ought to be doing is building world-beating European teams in all sports, including the next Olympics. Success in this endeavour would generate its own television coverage of 'our' victories. If someday the European flag adorns the shirts of football hooligans from Copenhagen to Calabria, it will at last be clear that 'we' are really on the way to European community and citizenship.

REFERENCES

Billig, M., *Banal Nationalism* (London, Sage, 1995).
Barber, B., *Strong Democracy: Participatory Politics for a New Age* (Berkeley, CA, University of California Press, 1984).
Barber, B., 'Jihad vs McWorld', *The Atlantic Monthly*, Vol. 269, No. 3, 1992, pp. 53–63.
Betz, H.-G., *Radical Right-Wing Populism in Western Europe* (London, Macmillan, 1994).
Brubaker, R., *Citizenship and Nationhood in France and Germany* (Cambridge, MA, Harvard University Press, 1992).

Canovan, M., *Populism* (New York, Harcourt Brace Jovanovich, 1981).

Canovan, M., ' "People", Politicians and Populism', *Government and Opposition*, Vol. 19, No. 3, 1984, pp. 312–27.

Colley, L., *Britons: Forging the Nation 1707–1837* (New Haven, Yale University Press, 1992).

Fishkin, J. S., *Democracy and Deliberation: New Directions for Democratic Reform* (New Haven, Yale University Press, 1991).

Goodwyn, L., *Democratic Promise: the Populist Moment in America* (New York, Oxford University Press, 1976).

Haider, J., *The Freedom I Mean* (Pine Plains, Swan Books, 1995).

Hayward, J. (ed.), *The Crisis of Representation in Europe* (London, Frank Cass, 1995).

Ionescu, G. and Gellner, E., *Populism: Its Meanings and National Characteristics* (London, Weidenfeld and Nicolson, 1969).

Kazin, M., *The Populist Persuasion: an American History* (New York, Basic Books, 1995).

Kobach, K. W., 'Switzerland', in Butler, D. and Ranney, A. (eds), *Referendums around the World: the Growing Use of Direct Democracy* (London, Macmillan, 1994), pp. 98–153.

Marcus, J., *The National Front and French Politics: the Resistible Rise of Jean-Marie Le Pen* (London, Macmillan, 1995).

Meehan, E., *Citizenship and the European Community* (London, Sage, 1993).

Mill, J. S., *Utilitarianism, Liberty, Representative Government* (London, J. M. Dent and Sons, 1910).

Mulhall, S. and Swift, A., *Liberals and Communitarians* (Oxford, Blackwell, 1992).

Oldfield, A., *Citizenship and Community: Civic Republicanism and the Modern World* (London, Routledge, 1990).

Pateman, C., *Participation and Democratic Theory* (Cambridge, Cambridge University Press, 1960).

Rahe, P. A., *Republics Ancient and Modern: Classical Republicanism and the American Revolution* (Chapel Hill, NC, University of North Carolina Press, 1992).

Smith, A. D., 'National Identity and the Idea of European Unity', *International Affairs*, Vol. 68, No. 1, 1992, pp. 55–76.

Tassin, E., 'Europe: a Political Community?', in Mouffe, C. (ed.), *Dimensions of Radical Democracy: Pluralism, Citizenship, Community* (London, Verso, 1992), pp. 169–92.

Taylor, C., 'Institutions in National Life', in Laforest, G. (ed.), *Reconciling the Solitudes: Essays on Canadian Federalism and Nationalism* (Montreal, McGill-Queens University Press, 1993), pp. 120–34.

Wallace, W. and Smith, J., 'Democracy or Technocracy? European Integration and the Problem of Popular Consent', in Hayward, J. (ed.), *The Crisis of Representation in Europe* (London, Frank Cass, 1995), pp. 137–57.

7 Being and Doing in Europe since 1945: Contrasting Dichotomies of Identity and Efficiency

Jolyon Howorth

The definition of 'European identity' is a major headache. As Edgar Morin (1990, p. 37) has stressed, there was never any internal founding principle. The Greek and Roman bases came from the periphery, Judeo-Christianity from Asia Minor. Successive waves of migrations and invasions produced a hopelessly confused ethnic cocktail. European values have always existed as contradictory dichotomies: right and might, democracy and tyranny, socialism and liberalism, spirituality and materialism, communism and fascism. At the turn of this century, Paul Valéry's imaginary Chinese scholar had already noted the 'insane disorder of Europe':

> I cannot even understand the continuance, however short, of such confusion. On your continent power is powerless. Your politics is one of changes of heart. It leads to general revolutions, followed by regrets over revolutions, which are also revolutions.
>
> (Valéry, 1951, p. 115)

By 1939, Europe's three oldest democracies, France, Britain and Holland, were ruthless colonial empires, while almost all her other leading nations, Russia, Germany, Italy, Spain and Portugal had stumbled into insanity. If Europe had ever had a collective identity, it had certainly lost it by the outbreak of the Second World War.

After 1945, however, Europe's definition (and to a very large extent its identity) were superimposed from the outside. Although there was an endogenous process – European integration – which arose quite naturally from the inner dialectics of Western European history, this process was subsumed under an exogenous systemic constraint: superpower global confrontation. The old continent was strait-jacketed into what Edward Thompson called the 'permafrost' of Cold War confrontation. In the West, identity meant alignment with Washington and the adoption of the absolute values of 'liberalism', the 'open society' and 'democracy'. In countries like

Germany and Italy, a new national party, based on Christian Democracy, temporarily smothered the genuine diversity of regional distinctiveness – chickens which were to come home to roost after 1989. In the East, enforced obeissance to Russian autocracy produced an official culture underpinned by another set of absolutes informed by words like 'peace', 'socialism' and (there too) 'democracy'. Although the two forms of hegemony defy detailed comparison, both constituted a somewhat artificial diversion from the natural flow of European history and identity. They also generated equally artificial forms of dissent, which took their cue from the external model rather than from internal realities. In both blocs, the scarecrow of the other was massively used to create a forced bonding, an internal ideological conformism, a false and fragile identity. Almost six hundred years ago, the dying Henry IV had recommended to his son Henry V this age-old trick of statecraft, designed to forge internal cohesion: 'Therefore my Harry/Be it thy course to busy giddy minds/With foreign quarrels'. Asking, in 1982, the question, 'What is the Cold War now about?', Thompson (1982, p. 17) concluded:

> It is about itself. ... The Cold War may be seen as a show which was put, by two rival entrepreneurs, upon the road in 1946 or 1947. The show has grown bigger and bigger; the entrepreneurs have lost control of it, as it has thrown up its own managers, administrators, producers and a huge supporting cast; these have a direct interest in its continuance, in its enlargement. Whatever happens, the show must go on.

That 'show' is responsible for having skewed the natural progression of European integration in ways which it is almost impossible to apprehend, but which it is worth examining. In particular, it retarded or actually diverted the natural process of harmonization between identity and function – between 'being' and 'doing' – which is the hallmark of normal historical development, the essence of political culture.

BEING, DOING AND IDENTITY[1]

At the risk of oversimplification, it is useful to consider that human beings come together for two main purposes: to be together and to do together. Being involves identity, doing does not – or, at any rate, not necessarily. An association or a committee is for doing together; society is for being together. Being has to do with the deeper communicative dimensions of a collectivity: language, psychology, empathy, values, memory. It speaks to a sense of continuity and collective destiny. Doing involves the more organizational dimensions of collective action: institutions, hierarchies, structures.

It has no necessary association with the past, but looks resolutely to the future. The rule of being is consensus; that of doing is the majority. In short, being is essentially about what we call culture, while doing is about what we call politics. When the two are in harmony, that is what we mean by the expression 'political culture' (see Figure 7.1). In Western Europe, this harmonization between being and doing has, over the last two centuries, tended to exist in the form of the nation-state. But there is no reason to assume that history has now come to a full stop. Units of being and doing have evolved and shifted considerably over the centuries.

If we take the example of France, for instance (see Figure 7.2), the feudal system, by the late Middle Ages, had gradually given rise to an ideal unit for both being and doing: the commune.

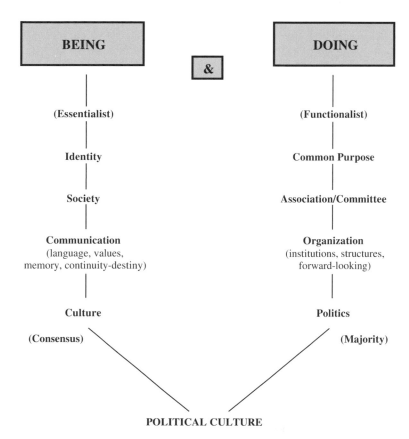

Figure 7.1   Being and Doing

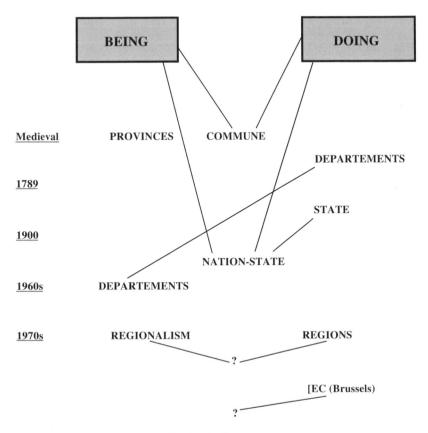

Figure 7.2   Units of Being and Doing in France

Here, the enfranchized bourgeoisie worked and lived together, adminis-
tering their affairs harmoniously in their own interests. By contrast, the
provinces had primarily become places of being, characterized by little
more than distinctive patois, customs, festivals and traditions. Prior to
1789, the nation, for the vast majority of people, was little more than an
absolutist abstraction. After the Revolution, the departments were created,
above all as instruments of national administration, and therefore of doing.
The department, however, never succeeded in gelling as a locus both of
doing and of being. There has never been such a thing as a departmental
political culture. This was in large part as a result of the parallel rise of the
nation-state – which soon became the primary locus of both being and
doing, the crucible of political culture. Indeed, gradually, the department

lost its original function and became essentially a place of being (they live in the Dordogne, we come from the Var). The nation-state reigns supreme as the crossroads of being and doing.

Recently, two new forces have arisen as apparent challengers to this political-cultural supremacy of the nation-state. First, regions, which have re-emerged both as units of being and as units of doing. The advent of regional political cultures is not impossible – and they could easily cut across national borders – witness Lotharingia, or Catalonia. The second apparent challenge has come from supranationalism. But the EEC/EC/EU has only really ever been a place of doing. The key question is: could Europe ever become a place of being, a place of identity? One of the major problems in the emergence of such an identity is the impact of the Cold War on the recent identities of the major European nations. If we examine the picture since 1945, we see that only in one instance (that of France) have being and doing been in harmony within the European context.

Germany was for forty years overwhelmingly concerned with doing: with existing, with creating a functioning system, with reviving her economy and especially with contributing to the functioning of international organisms such as the EC and NATO. Her being was sublimated, subsumed for the most part within her new European and international credentials. In part this was an understandable act of amnesia; in part a consequence of Cold War realities. Since 1989, Germany has been in desperate search of her being, of her true identity. Harmonization between being and doing offers her two models: the historical one of a German Europe and the futuristic one of a European Germany. It is partly out of fear of the former that the entire political class has identified the way forward as being via the latter.[2]

Italy also was primarily concerned with doing. Equally keen to prove her European credentials as a way of atoning for her recent waywardness, she cobbled together an artificial form of constitutional unity around a party machine forged in the furnaces of the Cold War – Christian Democracy – which helped perpetuate an equally artificial sparring partner, the Communist Party. These two *frères ennemis* helped keep each other alive (and seemingly popular) – along with the myth of national unity – just so long as the Cold War continued to exist. Italy identified more closely than any other country with the European project, in large part because her real identity actually existed (and is now re-emerging) at the sub-cultural level of the family, the local community or the region. When the Christian Democratic coalition inevitably fell apart in early 1992, the *Financial Times* saw this as 'the Berlin Wall claiming its last victim' (8 April 1992, p. 18). When Italy eventually brings her being into harmony with her doing, it is not unlikely that this will involve a new regionalism within a broader Europe.[3]

Spain also failed to harmonize being and doing. For thirty years, the Franco regime purported to incarnate the eternal being of the nation. But it was an atavistic and false form of being which effectively marginalized Spain from the mainstream of Europe and prevented her from doing anything very constructive. In the early 1980s, Felipe Gonzalez gambled on doing, on practical involvement with the EC, as a means of leading Spain, almost unquestioningly, towards a new – European – form of being. The experiment is still in process. But as the Europe of Maastricht's convergence criteria began to hurt, Spain too began to question the desirability of the European identity Gonzalez had held out. The election victory of the conservatives in 1995, and the subsequent attempts by prime minister Aznar to revert to a tense combination of doing in Europe and being in Spain, shows just how crucial this dichotomy has become in the Iberian peninsula.[4]

Britain, by contrast, has totally subordinated her doing to her perceived sense of being. Convinced for a decade or so after 1945 that she was still a world power, she urged 'Europe' on the 'continentals' and sought to hang on to an Empire nobody else wanted. Neither her being nor her doing was European. From 1956 (Suez) to 1973 (EC membership), she gradually, and very painfully, began to realize that her best chance of doing what it is she does best – trade – was in Europe. But because she steadfastly continued to identify her being somewhere else (mid-Atlantic? Sceptred Isle? Bolsover?) she has continued to do her European thing with neither enthusiasm nor success. The Euro-aberration of Thatcherism only made matters worse by consecrating the rift between being and doing. Europe as a continental Stop and Shop, yes; Europe as a serious political project, no. In 1997, Britain remains stuck, all dressed up in national atavism and nowhere at all to go. New Labour failed even to address this issue in opposition and, at the time of writing (June 1997), there are no signs of the Blair government coming to terms with it in office. If the Single Currency were to come into being and were to prove a success, the moment of truth for the UK in Europe would finally have arrived.[5]

France has been the one country in the post-war world which has succeeded in harmonizing her being and her doing – within a European context. Having realized very soon after the war that she would not be granted the status of 'most favoured nation' that she sought from Washington, she began, very early under Jean Monnet, to seek primary national fulfilment through carving out a major role in Europe. That project was continued not only by de Gaulle but also by every subsequent president. As a result, France has, basically, got the Europe that she wanted. The one danger for

France in playing the European card so vigorously lay in German unification. That is why the end of the Cold War has actually produced a new identity crisis in France, resulting from her need to come to terms with the fact that the leadership role which used to be that of Paris has now passed to Bonn (or Berlin). But it did not take François Mitterrand long to realize that Europe is still the only show in town. Disharmony between being and doing is to be avoided at all cost. Jacques Chirac soon learned the same lesson on entering the Elysée. For a brief moment, British politicians and journalists seemed to believe that Chirac would prove a worthy Eurosceptical ally. They were rapidly disappointed. A similar phenomenon occurred on the surprise election of prime minister Lionel Jospin in June 1997. Anglo-Saxon journalists commented sagely on the inevitability of a new European crisis as the conflicting recipes of market economism (Kohl and Blair) and social solidarity (Jospin) proved to be irreconcilable. But if the journalists keep looking, they will see why France sees Europe as the best way of backing France.[6]

Now the crucial question raised earlier has to do with the possible emergence of a European form of identity. Will doing lead to being? There are several ways of looking at this. It could be argued that, since the EU is essentially about doing, there is no real need to identify with it in order for it simply to function effectively. People do not identify with Marks and Spencers or with British Telecom or with their Ford Sierra in order for these services to fulfil their needs. At the same time, it could be said that true identity – meaningful being – will only ever exist at the most immediate level: the family, the village, the peer group or local community. On the other hand, it is also perfectly possible to enjoy multiple identities, no single one of which is exclusive of or contradictory to the others.[7] In this author's case, Bath, the South West, England, the UK, France, Western Europe, continental Europe, the Atlantic area, Judeo-Christianity, the Human Race. But they all have different intensities and different meanings. And only rarely do being and doing connect in serious ways.

But if we accept my earlier definition of political culture as the harmonious combination of being and doing, of culture and politics, then there are signs that a growing European identity is not altogether improbable. The key here is that much abused term 'sovereignty'. Despite all the nonsense that is talked about 'national sovereignty', the fact is that sovereignty is often no longer identifiable or applicable in the vertical mode of the nineteenth century. Many decisions – increasingly crucial decisions which directly affect our lives – are simply beyond the scope or competence of national governments. Interdependence has created a horizontal – almost layer cake – structuring of sovereignty, which has, in its turn, generated the concept of subsidiarity. Decisions on upgrading B roads or on the opening date for the fly-fishing season or on planning permission for a lean-to in the neighbour's garden are the prerogative of local authorities and, to the extent to which individuals in a community are affected by those decisions, they will both involve themselves in the decision-making process (doing) and they will identify with the outcome (being). At a much higher level, despite all the huffing and puffing of the Eurosceptics, certain very crucial decisions can and should only be taken by the European Union (or by an even broader instance of the international community). In the era of Chernobyl, of acid rain and of wholesale maritime pollution, the environment in which we live cannot be managed at local or even at national level. In the era of the Single Market, internationally agreed standards are indispensable. Most Europeans accept the need for European watchdogs to blow the whistle on BSE, raw sewage on Blackpool beach, the unregulated liquidation of international fish stocks. In the age of the jet engine and the TGV, transport policy must be European or international. In the era of global capital flows, many workers in Swindon and South Wales and the North East, know perfectly well that their jobs and livelihood depend crucially on Britain's membership of the EU. And a growing number of people recognize that a Common Foreign and Security policy is the only meaningful successor to the increasingly meaningless notion of 'national defence'. All these are functions. They are things that 'Europe' can, should and does do. But they have an increasingly direct effect on people's lives. As the peoples of Europe gradually realize that the purity of the air they breathe, the security of the jobs they hold, the quality of the goods they purchase, the definition of the rights they enjoy, and even – one day – the origins of the soldiers safeguarding their security are European rather than national, then the notion of 'being European' will not be far behind. Few would reject the broad definition of 'nation' offered by Anthony Smith in 1992 (p. 60):

> A named human population sharing a historical territory, common memories and myths of origin, a mass, standardised public culture, a common economy and territorial mobility and common legal rights and duties.

Is there any reason to suppose that that definition could not, eventually, be applied to a collective identity in Europe?

As regional (and indeed global) interdependence continues to impinge on our daily lives, it will surely become more and more natural and more and more acceptable to look to the EU as the locus of coherent, co-ordinated transcontinental policy initiatives and decisions. Of course, there is still massive room for improvement, beginning with democratic control.

'Brussels', like any other form of government or administration, will often get things wrong – even terribly wrong. There is an enormous amount that needs improving. But these are still early days. What is involved here is a historical process. Even in the late twentieth century, there are many local worthies in France who resent intensely the fact that decisions on, say, the building of a viaduct across the Tarn valley have to be referred primarily to Paris. But the strength of local feeling did not prevent the nation-state (which was a logical historical development) from generating a viable political culture. In exactly the same way, nationalistic bleatings from MPs uncomfortable with their own relative insignificance or from Australian or Canadian newspaper proprietors interested only in cashing in on tribalism, will not get in the way of historical progress.

The point I am making is this, and it is quite simple. The medieval village as a place of being and doing was eventually superseded by larger and larger units, leading eventually to the nation-state, precisely because the interdependences created by doing gradually gave rise to broader, vaster forms of identity. Units of human collectiveness which begin life naturally as units of doing, normally evolve into units of being, and hence of identity. The articulation between being and doing is in a state of constant flux. There is, of course, a major difference between the processes which forged the nation-state and those which may help bring into existence a sense of identification with Europe. Whereas the functionalist consequences of standards uniformization (money, weights, measures) and the communications revolution (roads, rail, canals) gave impetus to the nation-building project throughout the nineteenth century, it was at the same time enormously boosted by the centralist power of the state. In today's world, that is a feature which is almost totally absent in the forging of Europe, and attempts by the European Commission to kick-start a sense of European identity have had minimal impact.[8] Would the nation-state have developed as a result of purely functionalist impulses?

The problem today is precisely the function and durability of the nation-state. The nation-state is being radically transformed. It is not clear which decisions will, in fifty years time, logically or legitimately be taken at national level. Analysts interpret this rapid transformation in radically divergent ways. Robert Reich (1991) considers that the role and function of the nation-state in the era of 'global webs' is changing almost beyond recognition. Alan Milward (1992), on the contrary, has reinterpreted the EU as revitalizing the nation-state through the growing importance of intergovernmentalism. Clearly, the Union will remain a complex mix of integration and intergovernmentalism. Yet Milward's thesis about the positive symbiosis involved in EU/nation-state relations seems unduly static.

The nation-state was a staging post in the dynamic forward march of history. Its role is increasingly being undermined from every direction: subnational regionalism, supranational Europeanism and transnational globalism. Where identities will eventually be located is still anybody's guess. In the post-war world, interdependence has proved at least as powerful a glue as nationalism. In both the Western and Eastern parts of Europe, localisms, regionalisms and nationalisms are learning to coexist with federations and confederations. Being and doing are restructuring themselves in a host of new and interlocking forms, the whole in a state of constant evolution. The emphasis is on diversity-in-unity. That is the truth and distinctiveness of Europe. Perhaps the ultimate lesson Europeans will have learned from the catastrophic experience of their own totalitarian folly will be that pluralism also can be a viable and enriching form of identity.

In any case, Europe is not a fixed quantity. And it is quite possible, indeed probable, that the EU itself – as a historically generated regional regime – is little more than a staging post on the road to globalization. That process may happen much more swiftly than we can anticipate, with the result that a European identity could well be superseded even before it actually takes shape.

NOTES

1. I am grateful to Edgard Pisani for first suggesting this approach in his 'Foreword' to Maclean and Howorth (1992), pp. xii–xiii.
2. For discussions of this, see Zimmerman (1997); Gabriel (1994); Knischewski (1996).
3. See Bull (1997); Gundle and Parker (1996); and the special issue of *Modern Italy* (Journal of the Association for the Study of Modern Italy) on 'The Italian Crisis 1989–1994', Vol. 1, No. 1, Autumn 1995.
4. See Lopez-Aranguren (1991); Maliniak (1990); Perez-Díaz (1993).
5. See George (1994); see also George (1992) and Lunn (1996).
6. See Allègre and Jeambar (1996); Jenkins and Copsey (1996); Howorth (1995); Rioux (1996).
7. See Marks *et al.* (1996).
8. See Shore (1993).

REFERENCES

Allègre, C. and Jeambar, D., *Questions de France* (Paris, Fayard, 1996).

Bull, A., 'Italy and the Legacy of the Cold War', Inaugural Lecture (Chair of Italian Studies), University of Bath, May 1997. University of Bath European Research Institute Occasional Paper No. 8, 1997, 20 pp.

Gabriel, O. W., 'Politische Kulture aus der Sicht der empirischen Sozialforschung', in Niedermayer, O. and von Beyme, K. (eds), *Politische Kultur in Ost- und Westdeutschland* (Berlin, Akademie Verlag, 1994), pp. 22–42.

George, S., *Britain and the European Community: the Politics of Semi-Detachment* (Oxford, Clarendon, 1992).

George, S., *An Awkward Partner: Britain in the European Community* (Oxford, Oxford University Press, second edition, 1994).

Gundle, S. and Parker, S. (eds), *The New Italian Republic. From the Fall of the Berlin Wall to Berlusconi* (London, Routledge, 1996).

Howorth, J., 'France and European Security 1944–1994: Re-reading the Gaullist "Consensus" ', in Jenkins, B. and Chafer, T. (eds), *France from the Cold War to the New World Order* (London, Macmillan, 1995), pp. 17–38.

Jenkins, B. and Copsey, N., 'Nation, Nationalism and National Identity in France', in Jenkins, B. and Sofos, S. A., *Nation and Identity in Contemporary Europe* (London, Routledge, 1996), pp. 101–24.

Knischewski, G., 'Post-War National Identity in Germany', in Jenkins, B. and Sofos, S. A. (eds), *Nation and Identity in Contemporary Europe* (London, Routledge, 1996), pp. 125–51.

Lopez-Aranguren, E., 'Naciolanismo y regionalismo en la Espana de las autonomias', in Vidal Beneyto, J. (ed.), *Espana a debate. Vol. 2 – La Sociedad* (Madrid, Tecnos, 1991), pp. 48–73.

Lunn, K., 'Reconsidering "Britishness": the Construction and Significance of National Identity in Twentieth-century Britain', in Jenkins, B. and Sofos, S. A. (eds), *Nation and Identity in Contemporary Europe* (London, Routledge, 1996), pp. 83–100.

Maliniak, T., *Les Espagnols: de la Movida à l'Europe* (Paris, Centurion, 1990).

Marks, G., Hooghe, L. and Blank, K., 'European Integration from the 1980s: State-Centric v. Multi-level Governance', *Journal of Common Market Studies*, Vol. 34, No. 3, September 1996, pp. 342–78.

Milward, A. S., *The European Rescue of the Nation State* (London, Routledge, 1992).

Modern Italy (Journal of the Association for the Study of Modern Italy): Special issue on 'The Italian Crisis 1989–1994', Vol. 1, No. 1, Autumn 1995.

Morin, E., *Penser l'Europe* (Paris, Gallimard, 1990).

Perez-Díaz, V., *The Return of Civil Society: the Emergence of Democratic Spain* (Cambridge, MA, Harvard University Press, 1993).

Pisani, E., 'Foreword' to Maclean, M. and Howorth, J. (eds), *Europeans on Europe: Transnational Visions of a New Continent* (London, Macmillan, 1992), pp. xii–xiii.

Reich, R., *The Work of Nations* (London, Simon and Schuster, 1991).

Rioux, J-P., 'Maastricht et après', *L'Histoire*, 201, July–August 1996, pp. 108–9.

Shore, C., 'Inventing the People's Europe: Critical Reflections on EC "Cultural Policy"', *MAN: Journal of the Royal Anthropological Institute*, Vol. 28, No. 4, 1993, pp. 779–800.

Smith, A. D., 'National Identity and the Idea of European Unity', *International Affairs*, Vol. 68, No. 1, January 1992, p. 60.

Thompson, E. P., *Beyond the Cold War* (London, Merlin/END, 1982).
Valéry, P., 'The Yellow River', in *Reflections on the World Today* (trans. by Francis Scarfe) (London, Thames and Hudson, 1951), p. 115.
Zimmermann, E., 'Germany', in Eatwell, R. (ed.), *European Political Cultures: Conflict or Convergence?* (London, Routledge, 1997), pp. 88–106.

8 From Nation-Building to the Construction of Europe: the Lessons and Limitations of the French Example

Brian Jenkins

One of the problems associated with attempts to promote a popular sense of *European* identity is that there are no obvious historical models to serve as a guide. The most inviting analogy is with the process of nation-building in Europe itself in the nineteenth and early twentieth centuries, but this raises a number of problems. Given what one author has called 'the novelty of our historical circumstances' (Gray, 1996, p. 19), the drawing of parallels between such different periods is clearly a hazardous undertaking. Furthermore, the very success of the national idea has itself raised obstacles to the development of supranational identities.

At another level, however, the objections are less persuasive. It is often assumed that the processes of nation-building have little in common with those involved in the construction of Europe; that Europe is not, and can never become, that 'community of culture' which nations are deemed to embody. However, this view offers a one-sided perspective on the mechanisms of nation-formation, and raises issues that lie at the very heart of the debate on nationalism and the national question.

If we believe that nations are shaped primarily by some pre-existing sense of collective identity – a common language and history, shared belief systems and 'psychological make-up', all contained within well-defined territorial boundaries,[1] then the prospects for emulating these conditions at European level will indeed appear slim. If, on the other hand, we give what I would regard as proper recognition to the *politics* of nation-building, and acknowledge that nations are socially and ideologically *constructed*, then there are grounds for greater optimism about the European project. This is not to deny that the cultural raw material of nationhood (what Hobsbawm has called 'popular proto-nationalism' [Hobsbawm, 1990, pp. 46–79]) may sometimes have played a significant role in nation-state formation, though far less than *nationalists* themselves routinely pretend. However, to borrow the terms used by Jolyon Howorth elsewhere in this volume, '*doing*' has often been the most powerful agency for the development of a sense of '*being*', and this metaphor seems particularly appropriate in this context.

The first point is that there were many different paths to nationhood, and that the 'raw material' mentioned above was rarely present in the 'necessary' or 'desirable' combination. Examples abound where nation-states were constructed despite considerable linguistic or religious diversity, where historical traditions were 'invented' rather than 'discovered' (Hobsbawm and Ranger, 1983) and where national boundaries had little rationale beyond the *realpolitik* of conquest or diplomacy.

To say this is to recognize that nations are political *artefacts*, and that as often as not they are the *creations* of states rather than the *creators* of states.[2] Even in those cases where a sense of nationhood had to be promoted as a *precondition* of the struggle for statehood, this was always within the firmly *political* context of opposition to existing state structures.

If nation-states first emerged in the context of the decay of the prenational dynastic structures of *Ancien Régime* Europe (a process itself associated with the broader phenomenon of 'modernity'), it may be argued that today we are witnessing a period of equally significant social and cultural change. Whether or not the overarching concept of 'post-modernity' is appropriate or helpful in this respect, terms like post-industrialism and post-colonialism (not to mention post-materialism and post-socialism) are suggestive of a number of related transitional phenomena. Against this wider background, the nation-state is experiencing the full effects of economic globalization, and the attendant problems of reduced autonomy arguably presage a generalized crisis of political legitimacy. In this context it is relevant to ask the question whether, just as in the last century prenational state structures crumbled in the face of nationalism, so in the late twentieth century the nation-state model is itself being superseded.

In the contemporary context of economic and cultural globalization, it is easy to regard all nations and nationalisms as essentially parochial and exclusive, and the recent resurgence of ethnic nationalism in the post-communist successor states has reinforced this image. It is important, therefore, to remind ourselves that in the nineteenth and early twentieth centuries the nation-building process frequently involved a dramatic widening of the cultural, political and spatial horizons of ordinary people, expanding social consciousness beyond the ties of kinship, trade and locality (*Gemeinschaft*) to invoke an 'imagined community' (Anderson, 1983) based on the more abstract notion of *Gesellschaft*. To borrow Tom Nairn's image of nationalism as the 'Modern Janus' (Nairn, 1977, pp. 329–63), if one face of the phenomenon looks back to the past, revealing the features of ethnic particularism and fear of the 'other', the reverse face looks to the future in a more generous and optimistic spirit of universalism – nations as constituent parts of an emerging world community.

Of course, this simple polarity fails to convey the full complexity of the national question. Nationalism may be mobilized by established states, or by movements that challenge existing state structures. It has, at different times, been harnessed to ideologies of every shade across the political spectrum, to projects of social emancipation and to those of social integration, to the cause of imperialist expansion and to that of liberation, to authoritarian populism and to liberal democracy. Nationhood has been defined by the determinist principles of descendance (*droit du sang*) and by the voluntarist principles of residence (*droit du sol*), has been inspired by both *ethnic* and *civic* solidarities, has been achieved by state-led assimilation or by a more tolerant incorporation of subsidiary identities in civil society. The sheer diversity of this experience warns against attempts to generalize about the processes of nation-formation or the ideological characterisitics of nationalism(s), and indeed case studies of individual countries would reveal an infinitely more nuanced picture than can be conveyed by the set of contrasts outlined above.

THE CASE OF FRANCE

In examining the case of nation-formation in France, some necessary distinctions suggest themselves. In an age where virtually every state in the world claims to be a *nation-state*, and where 'nation-speak' permeates political discourse everywhere, we are faced with a terminological and conceptual morass. *Nation, nationality, nationhood, nationalism* (and *patriotism*), *nationalist* (and *nationalistic*), *national identity, national consciousness, national sentiment* – such terms are used with little precision in everyday parlance, and specialist scholarship has scarcely helped to clarify matters. Problems of definition are endemic to the ideological and methodological debate on the national question, and there is no more consensus on terminology than there is on the explanation and interpretation of the phenomenon. The precise terms used below are therefore less significant than the underlying intent, which is to distinguish conceptually between different features of the nation-building process.

National Consciousness

I will use the term '*national consciousness*' to denote the process whereby the 'nation' becomes a significant collective reference point in the lives of

ordinary people. Clearly, variables of geography and ethnicity will affect
the feasibility of this process, but in more general terms it will be facilitated by socio-economic transformations – industrialization and urbaniza-
tion, improved communications, expanding labour and commodity
markets, rising levels of literacy, etc. This will hasten the gradual transcen-
dence of local and regional identities which become subsumed in the
wider national 'whole'. However, the key framework for such developments is the emergence of the nation-state and of the notion of 'citizenship', whereby the masses acquire a sense of 'having a stake' in the
national community. As the focus of decision-making, conflict mediation
and interest representation, the nation-state will endeavour to 'integrate'
diverse social categories (whether defined by class, gender or ethnicity)
and to promote allegiance to the 'nation'.

The role of the state in this process was particularly prominent in the
case of France. The absolutist monarchy of the seventeenth and eighteenth
centuries may indeed be seen as a necessary compensation for the country's linguistic, cultural and geographical diversity, and for the perceived
fragility of its long land frontiers. The intense political divisions created by
the Revolution provided a further pretext for the preservation of this centralized state apparatus, and successive regimes mistrusted regional identities, not only as potentially disintegrative but also as a possible power base
for political opposition. Under the Third Republic, the attempt to create a
homogeneous national culture was intensified through the agencies of
mass schooling and mass conscription, through the deployment of national
symbols and the 'invention' of national traditions, and through the identification of an external enemy in the shape of the newly unified Germany.

National consciousness under absolutism had largely been limited to
social élites, and to the regions that were least remote from the capital.
The Revolution, by invoking the concept of citizenship and politically
mobilizing millions of ordinary peasants and town-dwellers, therefore
marked a decisive stage in the construction of nationhood (Jenkins, 1990,
pp. 13–26). This was an ideologically precocious development given the
economic backwardness of large areas of the country, and the degree of
mass politicization it accomplished should not be exaggerated. However,
there is no doubt that the 'slow re-run' of the Revolution (1815–70) pro-
gressivly widened the political community and raised levels of popular
political consciousness. The social compromise of the Third Republic,
based on the property-owning middle classes and peasantry, was consolidated by rural modernization, representative democracy and the state-led
inculcation of national values, turning 'peasants into Frenchmen' in Eugen
Weber's famous phrase (Weber, 1976).

The emergence and extension of national consciousness in France may thus be seen as a gradual process of social and political 'integration'. However alienated many industrial workers felt under the *bourgeois* Third Republic before 1914, the nation-state was an unavoidable reference point for political and trade-union activity, though arguably it was not until the 'new deal' of the Liberation reforms (1944–6) that the industrial working class acquired a more concrete sense of 'membership' of the nation. The formal recognition of women as full members of the political community came only with the granting of suffrage in 1945, and in terms of the wider notion of equal citizenship the process of integration is far from complete. The same might equally be said of those immigrants who, despite acquiring citizen rights under the relatively liberal nationality code of 1945, nonetheless continue to experience discrimination in civil society.

National consciousness may thus be defined as a politically neutral sense of membership of the national community, based primarily on the recognition that the nation-state is the main institutional framework for the satisfaction of individual and collective aspirations. At a more affective level this may be combined with a sense of 'belonging', an attachment to a familiar spatial environment or 'way of life', and it is at this level that terms like '*national sentiment*' or indeed '*patriotism*' come into play. However, a distinctive feature of the French experience is the significant role of the centralized state in inculcating this sense of nationhood, and the integrationist (some would say 'assimilationist') logic that has consistently underpinned this project, irrespective of the ideological colour of successive regimes.

This has had two negative effects. The first is that, in as far as French nationhood has been shaped more by the state than by spontaneous forces in 'civil society', the present decline in the capacity of that state to fulfil national aspirations risks has caused something of an 'identity crisis'. The second is that the integrationist attempt to create a homogeneous national culture is no longer feasible in the context of an increasingly multi-ethnic and pluralist society. These are themes to which we shall return.

Nationalism and National Identity

These last observations raise a different dimension of the 'national question'. What exactly *is* French 'national identity', what *is* the homogeneous national culture that successive regimes have allegedly sought to construct? Here we are in the force field of *nationalism* proper, where attempts are made to appropriate the past in the name of political and social values deemed to be characteristically 'French'. And the essential point to be made is that 'national identity' in France has never been subject to any comfortable consensus; it has been a highly contested area. In 200 years punctuated by war, invasion and revolution, issues of national sovereignty and state legitimacy have repeatedly emerged to colour the discourse and imagery of political conflict. Diverse movements and ideologies have, in such circumstances, presented themselves as the authentic expression of national values, as the true 'patriots', as the legitimate defenders of the 'national interest' (Jenkins, 1990).

In this short chapter it will not be possible to explore the full ideological and political diversity of French nationalism(s), which was already apparent in the very different (though related) phenomena of revolutionary *Jacobin* republicanism and Bonapartism. These two traditions made equal use of the 'dangerous' concept of the popular nation in their opposition to the social and political élites of the restored monarchy (1815–48) and to the European settlement imposed by the 1815 Congress of Vienna. Nationalism in this period was thus mobilized in opposition to the established regime, setting the 'nation' (the *pays réel* of the 'people') against the 'state' (the unrepresentative *pays légal* seen as subservient to international interests). During the 1848 Revolution, and even more so during the Paris Commune of 1871, the convergence of the themes of social and political emancipation with those of national self-determination (and in the latter case national liberation) gave nationalism a decidedly left-wing coloration.

By the turn of the century, however, popular anti-state nationalism had undergone a complex ideological transformation in the context of opposition to the liberal *bourgeois* Third Republic, and eventually became identified with an extreme Right that many have seen as 'proto-fascist' in character.[3] Though some have seen this process as a metamorphosis of the previous left-wing Jacobin tradition, in the context of the times it represented something new – an inter-class coalition of the discontented and marginalized, extending from conservative Catholic to *petit-bourgeois* and plebeian milieux, attracting monarchists together with populists of diverse political persuasions, and initially even some socialists who saw the Boulangist movement of the 1880s as a vehicle for undermining *bourgeois* democracy. This new nationalism was *externally* aggressive and chauvinist in its call for revenge against Germany, while *internally* it sought to redefine nationality on deterministic and exclusivist ethnic lines. Racism, especially in the form of anti-semitism, was a key theme, but ethnicity was conceived as much in cultural as in strictly biological terms, allowing a whole range of *outsiders* to be identified as hostile to core national values – Protestants and Freemasons, liberal intellectuals and 'corrupt' bourgeois politicians, international socialists. So-called 'integral' nationalism promoted (a particular vision of) the 'nation' as an overriding and unconditional loyalty, as an instrument of collective unity, therefore invoking an authoritarian state which would transcend the divisiveness of both representative democracy and social class struggle.

'Nation' has thus been deployed by movements of both Left and Right as a mobilizing theme for popular opposition to the prevailing regime. Arguably, these forms of 'anti-state nationalism' have never truly 'captured' the state and translated their value systems fully into practice, even in the exceptional conditions created by the defeat of 1940 and the period of Nazi occupation. While the collaborationist Vichy regime gave considerable scope to the ideologues of right-wing integral nationalism, it was also shaped by more traditional conservative forces and indeed by external pressures. Similarly, although the Resistance movement revived the left-wing discourse of national liberation and social emancipation last heard at the time of the Paris Commune, its reform programme was compromised by the political divisions and the economic and international realities of the post-war era.

It was through the agency of the *state*, therefore, that efforts were made to construct a more consensual form of national identity which would transcend these polarities of left and right. In this respect it is important to recognize that, though the Third Republic adopted the once revolutionary iconography of *Marseillaise*, tricolour and Bastille day as symbols of nationhood, it did so on the ruins of the Paris Commune and in a spirit of reconciliation which claimed that the Revolution was now complete. Furthermore, while conservative enemies of the regime denounced the secular education system as a vehicle of republican indoctrination, in reality Lavisse's history textbooks emphasized the continuity of *La France éternelle*, invoking the achievements of Charlemagne and Richelieu and treating the Revolution as an episode in the unfolding tale of French *grandeur* and *rayonnement* (Citron, 1987, p. 68).

Thus, in seeking to build consensus, the Republic was inevitably open to other more conservative influences, especially those generated by traditionalist Catholic milieux which were barely reconciled to the advent of democracy and the age of mass politics, resented the regime's anti-clericalism, shared the anti-semitism of the extreme-Right nationalists, and saw the Army and the Church rather than the Republic as the true incarnation of national values and national continuity. The representatives of such attitudes were entrenched in the administrative and political institutions of the Republican state, and while they resigned themselves to republican *forms*, they had little sympathy for republican *ideals*. Their ambivalence was amply illustrated by Vichy, and indeed by the collapse of the Fourth Republic when the Army again emerged as a potential counter-pole for the definition of national interests in opposition to the civilian authorities.

These tensions and contradictions within the republican state itself also allowed a certain dilution of the republican concept of nationhood, and this reflected the inherent dangers of the 'assimilationist' logic of '*La République une et indivisible*'. The ideal may have been the promotion of equal citizenship in an open and tolerant civic order, but at the same time the insistence on a homogeneous national culture as a necessary basis for that order raises the possibility that some categories may be judged 'non-assimilable' or 'unwilling' to assimilate, and therefore designated as outsiders or 'internal aliens' (Silverman, 1992, p. 111). As we have seen, this exclusion may be on political or religious as much as on 'ethnic' grounds, but in the contemporary context it has a particular resonance in the case of immigrants and their descendants. The central point, however, is that the boundaries between the 'civic' and the 'ethnic' models of nationhood are permeable, and that symbiosis between the two has been a persistent feature in the *practice*, if not in the official *discourse*, of the Republic.

These ambiguities were particularly evident in the widespread reluctance to come to terms with decolonization, most strikingly in the case of Algeria. Whatever the diversity of political motives from left to right, there was a lowest common denominator in the concept of France's 'civilizing mission', the belief that Algerian independence was an illogical choice when set against the prospect of participation in a superior metropolitan culture. Whether this mission was conceived in secular or religious terms, as geared to emancipation or domination, to eventual 'equality' or subservience, it betrayed a fundamental condescension towards colonial peoples which was at least a 'sub-text' even in left-wing articulations of national identity.

National Sentiments in an Age of National Decline

The opposition of two rival models of French national identity as represented by Vichy's *Révolution nationale* and the anti-fascist Resistance and Liberation movement has never since been duplicated in such stark terms. After 1945 the ideological divide between competing nationalisms (Gaullist, Communist, Poujadist) became increasingly blurred as France struggled to come to terms with lost status in the world of the superpower blocs. In the 1960s Gaullism indeed appeared to have achieved a new nationalist synthesis which reconciled old antagonisms behind presidentialism, economic modernization, and the slogan of an 'independent' foreign and defence policy.

Ironically, the state-led modernization of the 1960s decisively opened the French economy to the international forces which would progressively reduce the autonomy of national government in the sphere of economic and other related policy fields. The failure of the Socialists' interventionist programme in 1981–2 ('Keynesianism in one country') was taken as confirmation that in the age of 'market globalism' governments no longer had sufficient leverage over the domestic economy to implement a nationalist industrial regeneration strategy. The end of the Cold War and the demise of the bloc system has similarly undermined the bases of France's discourse of national independence in foreign and defence policy (Chafer and Jenkins, 1996, pp. 1–14). The current 'crisis of political representation' in France reflects widespread disillusionment with the incapacity of governments to 'deliver the goods', itself a symptom of the crisis of the nation-state as the primary agency of decision-making in an increasingly supranational world.

In this context, it is not surprising that nationalism has lost its credibility as a political ideology and programme, and has been largely jettisoned by mainstream French political parties. However, other factors have also contributed to this process. Politicized versions of national identity were based on other collective solidarities, value systems and institutions which have since been eroded by social and cultural change: on the Left working-class communities, trade unionism, social egalitarianism, the *école républicaine*; on the Right religious belief, Church and Army (Mendras and Cole, 1991). The advent of a more individualistic, socially and culturally pluralistic, multi-ethnic society has weakened the appeal of the historic myths which bound *nation* and *state* together.

This growing *separation* was already visible culturally in the events of May 1968, which may be seen as a revolt of *civil society* against prevailing state structures. It was significant that the main political targets of the movement were Gaullism and Communism, which in their different ways incarnated the bureaucratic, centralizing, homogenizing logic of French national identity formation. It is significant too that the social movements of the 1970s, for which May 1968 acted as a catalyst, reflected a challenge to the assimilationist model of French nationhood – regionalism, feminism, anti-racism, Third Worldism.

The rise of the *Front national* may be seen as a symptom of the difficulties of transition and adaptation to a post-industrial, post-colonial, post-national society. Le Pen's movement feeds on the insecurities engendered by this process, appealing to those who feel most threatened by market globalism, and exploiting in a racist direction the ideological space opened up by the mainstream parties' abandonment of nationalist discourse.

Significantly, the FN's nationalism is not geared to the development of a coherent and credible political programme, but to the populist exploitation of identity crisis at both local community and national level (Jenkins and Copsey, 1996, pp. 116–21). It feeds on fear for the future and nostalgia for the past, and may be seen as a form of resistance to what Hobsbawm has called the 'supranational restructuring of the globe' (Hobsbawm, 1990, p. 182).

Before turning finally to the relationship between France's self-image as a nation, and the idea of 'Europe', let us summarize the implications of the preceding observations.

1. *National consciousness* in France is well established, but the central reference point in the historical process of nation-formation, namely the *nation-state*, no longer provides a convincing focus for political aspirations. There is an increasing separation between the long-cultivated sense of 'belonging' to a national community, and the logic of self-government on which that community was originally based.[4]

2. As a result, *nationalism* as a political programme has lost credibility and *national identity* has become less tangible. While Gaullism appeared to have attenuated the sharp ideological polarizations of the past, and to have laid the foundations for a more comfortable and less conflictual sense of nationhood, those who subsequently hailed a new era of 'consensus' and 'la fin de l'exception française' now appear too complacent in their predictions (Mendras and Cole, 1991; Furet, 1978).

3. What exactly *are* the 'national sentiments' of ordinary French people, assiduously cultivated over 200 years by rival regimes and movements, but now deprived of any realistic and coherent political expression? At this point, it is worth reminding ourselves that public opinion at large is rarely as sensitive to ideological nuances as the politicized milieux of '*minorités agissantes*'. It was only at critical moments – when national territory was threatened, or when the legitimacy of the state was seriously called into question – that rival conceptions of national identity achieved a wider popular currency. And, indeed, when such circumstances encouraged national consensus (e.g. the *Union sacrée* of 1914) the imagery was depoliticized. Socialists and conservatives may have rationalized the need for war in very different terms, but this had limited popular resonance because these different motives led to the same conclusion. On the other hand, in the period before and during the Second World War rival nationalisms became sharply polarized, invoking not only different histories and value systems, but different forms of state, different external enemies, different policies. In this context,

the stark political choices involved inevitably impinged more heavily on popular consciousness.

4. However, in periods of greater stability it is safe to assume that, for the majority who were not politically active or engaged, *national sentiments* were more amorphous – an attachment to a familiar spatial environment, to its traditions and way of life, mediated perhaps through regional, religious or class loyalties, but only vaguely 'political' (that sense of having a stake in the national community which Hobsbawm has called 'state patriotism' [Hobsbawm, 1990, pp. 80–100]). In the case of France, however, there is perhaps another more widely shared sentiment, equally difficult to *demarcate* politically but 'political' nonetheless, namely that sense of France's exemplary universal mission and its past status as a 'great power' (both continental and colonial). Part of the success of Gaullism was that it found ways of nurturing that illusion even in the changed world system of the superpowers, and it is that illusion which is increasingly exposed in the era of accelerating globalization.

FRANCE AND EUROPE

In the post-war period the construction of Europe as a transnational institutional entity has become a crucial reference point for defining French political movements as more or less 'nationalist'. Under the Fourth Republic in the 1950s, the debate over the proposed creation of a European Defence Community appeared to polarize opinion between the nationalist 'extremes' (Communists, left Socialists and Gaullists) on the one hand, and, on the other, a centre ground stretching from moderate Socialists to conservative 'free-marketeers' whose pro-Europeanism has been identified as implicitly 'non-nationalist'.

This is a simplistic dichotomy for several reasons. First of all, in the context of the emerging post-war structures of the Cold War and bloc politics, it would be facile simply to *equate* Communist and Gaullist 'nationalisms', each of which had its own distinctive ideological rationale, both domestic and international. Admittedly the themes of their opposition to the European enterprise sometimes overlapped, and reinforced one another at the level of public opinion – the resistance legacy, fear of a renascent Germany, a shared though far from identical anti-Americanism. But the differences in their social constituencies and domestic political aspirations, and above all their different *locations* in the Cold War divide, can hardly be presented as minor nuances, as marginal differences of emphasis in the rhetoric of national sovereignty and independence.

Similarly, it would be misleading to separate the pro-European project from this wider international context. While (most) Socialists, Christian Democrats and the *droite modérée* shared a fundamental anti-communism, they did not have an identical vision of the kind of Europe they wished to create, or of how this emerging entity should position itself in world affairs. At one level there were (and arguably still are) tensions between a Europe shaped largely by economic liberalism and one based on the model of social democracy. At another level, not all pro-Europeans saw the future community as part of the bloc architecture of the 'free world' and the Western Alliance. At least in the early 1950s there remained a significant Left-neutralist element which aspired to a non-aligned Europe as a third force in the world system, equidistant between American capitalism and Soviet Communism, a kind of socialist prefiguration of the Gaullist discourse of the 1960s (Cornick, 1996, p. 49).

This mention of de Gaulle brings us to a further point of contention. Orthodox historiography implies a 'break' between the foreign policy of the Fourth Republic (ineffective, compliant, undermined by internal divisions) and that of the Fifth (decisive, independent, and based on an emerging Gaullist consensus). As Jolyon Howorth has suggested in a recent essay (Howorth, 1996), this perspective underestimates the degree of continuity in the French state's quest for international influence and status in the post-war era, and the persistent importance of 'Europe' in these calculations. For successive French governments, the formal transfers of sovereignty involved in the creation of transnational structures were compensated by the prospect of increased leverage on world affairs if France could shape the emerging community in line with its own institutional and ideological preferences.

De Gaulle's endorsement of the Treaty of Rome when he came to power in 1958, his subsequent advocacy of an *Europe des patries*, his vision of an enlarged European space independent of the power blocs, confirmed his own particular (and in the event highly seductive) conception of how French and European interests might coincide. But, by the same token, those who advocated different institutional models and international roles for Europe were not necessarily any less preoccupied with the furtherance of *French interests*, they simply perceived these through a different ideological prism. In other words, the contrast between *nationalist* and *non-nationalist* responses to the project of European integration is not the most helpful analytical framework.

The notion that something called 'Europe' exists, and that France should have a leading role in determining its shape and direction, is widely shared across the political spectrum. The obsessive use of the barometer of 'nationalism' tends to obscure the fact that different kinds of 'Europe' are on the agenda – one defined by the liberal market economy or by more social-democratic principles, a community integrated 'vertically' through national governments or more 'horizontally' through transnational institutions, a community open to the world or an economic and cultural 'fortress'. In other words, Europe remains a 'potentiality', and needs to become a genuine political 'space' in which these different conceptions can freely compete rather than being dressed up and disguised as the rival 'interests' of *nations* (that is, states).

EUROPE AS A POLITICAL 'SPACE'

To return to our central theme, the French model of nation-building is instructive for the creation of Europe precisely because it embraced rival conceptions of national identity. *National consciousness* did not imply consensus, a single hegemonic image of essential 'Frenchness'. Rather it reflected growing recognition of the nation-state as a framework within which different visions of the 'nation' could be articulated. In this respect, 'doing' helped to create a sense of 'being', and to the extent that the European Union achieves popular recognition as a significant decision-making agency, it too could become a framework for the development of a growing European consciousness. But this 'consciousness' should not be equated with 'identity', which in the *European* context would necessarily be highly pluralistic both regionally and ideologically.

However, for this process to take full effect the institutions of the EU need greater political legitimacy. A sense of being directly affected by, and implicated in, the decision-making process is a necessary precondition for the emergence of a genuine popular European consciousness, and this can only be achieved if institutions are transparent, accountable and representative. The construction of European 'citizenship' is therefore of central importance, and this raises crucial questions about the patterns of integration in the European Community.

The present model is essentially one of *vertical* integration through member nation-states. The key source of collective decisions is intergovernmental, and the approval of the legislative and administrative outcomes is entrusted to national parliaments. This process has negative implications for the development of European consciousness for a number of reasons:

1. Decisions are taken at an élite level at several removes from the arena of public scrutiny and debate. Their implementation emanates from

what is often perceived as an unaccountable bureaucracy, and national parliaments absorb the details into their routine business. As a result, the affairs of the European Union have only limited 'visibility', and thus even the basic prerequisite of democratic accountability is unfulfilled.

2. Since the representative principle is deemed to be assured by the democratic legitimacy of national governments and parliaments, the affairs of the European Union are forced into a framework which emphasizes the plurality (and rivalry) of *national* interests. This imagery inevitably promotes popular perceptions of 'Europe' as an *external* agency constraining the freedom of manoeuvre of national governments, and identified with the hegemonic aspirations of other nation-states.

3. What is 'lost' in this imagery is the recognition that in these vertical structures 'nations' are represented by 'states', and that these states reflect the ascendancy of particular sets of vested interests within their respective communities. In reality, within each nation-state there is a diversity of views about the future shape and role of 'Europe', but this diversity is stifled by an institutional straitjacket which reifies the member states (rather than the European 'citizenry' itself) as the legitimate democratic 'actors' in the European Union.

In other words, the spread of popular European 'consciousness' requires the promotion of *horizontal* integration, permitting the cultivation of collective aspirations which transcend the purely *national* divisions favoured by the present institutional arrangements. It would be naive to pretend, of course, that two hundred years of nation-building have left no mark; that linguistic and cultural differences, historical animosities, uneven economic development, dissimilar political and social structures, count for nothing. But it is equally the case that economic globalism, mass migration and mass communication have narrowed such differences, that the efficacy of national decision-making is increasingly called into question, and that the political issues that mobilize public opinion increasingly transcend national boundaries, invoking transnational solidarities and inviting transnational solutions.[5] In short, it is only when (if) the European Union reflects the *ideological* diversity of its political community (rather than just its vertical *national* components) that it will become the kind of political 'space' which will promote a sense of 'citizenship'.

EUROPE: 'STATE' AND 'CIVIL SOCIETY'

There is another respect, however, in which the French nation-building process may serve more as a 'caution' than as an example for the European community. Whatever their ideological differences, the movements that competed for control of the French state were always tempted to use the centralized apparatus to create a homogenized national culture, ironing out linguistic differences, discouraging local and regional identities, and seeking to assimilate immigrant communities. If this state-led integrationist model now appears to have foundered on the realities of an increasingly pluralistic and multi-ethnic France, then all the more reason for rejecting it in the wider context of Europe where cultural differences are even more complex and even less amenable to 'top–down' strategies of this sort. *Doing* will not create a sense of *being* if it is foisted on reluctant peoples from above by institutions that enjoy little democratic legitimacy.

This is not to say that institutional change is irrelevant. Indeed, there is an urgent need to remedy the so-called 'democratic deficit' in Europe, by widening the opportunities for citizen participation and representation, and making the executive agencies of the EU more accountable to transnational representative bodies. However, it will (persuasively) be argued that institutions like the European Parliament lack the democratic credibility to be entrusted with greater power, and lack the power to achieve greater credibility. Such arguments are usually underpinned by the increasingly unconvincing rhetoric of *national* sovereignty, but they are also deployed by 'free-market' pro-Europeans who see no reason to encumber the process of economic integration with democratic controls.

That said, there is a 'chicken and egg' problem about the creation of a more democratic Europe. The democratization of transnational institutions has to be accompanied by the development of a representative infrastructure in 'civil society'. Political parties, interest and pressure groups, social movements and non-governmental organizations of every kind have to learn to co-operate across frontiers and to develop a distinctly European agenda. The incentive to do so is, of course, reduced by the relative weakness of organizations like the European Parliament, but in turn the case for strengthening the latter's role is undermined by the absence of a developed European 'civil society'. The only way of resolving this problem is by making the democratic reform of EU institutions a central campaigning theme around which 'civil society' activists could begin to coalesce.

Further progress with EU integration through the present vertical intergovernmental processes would tend to reinforce fears of an élite-led project leading to a super-state, one which would govern 'subjects' rather than 'citizens', and which would be enslaved to the principles of market globalism. Indeed, these fears have already found sufficient political expression to jeopardize the whole enterprise. European consciousness cannot be forged from above by unrepresentative and unaccountable institutions.

It will emerge only though the effective practice of citizenship within a democratized institutional framework, and the pressure for such reforms can only come from below through the agency of 'civil society'.

CONCLUSION

The construction of a democratic European 'space' through horizontal integration would also help to resolve the tensions between different levels of allegiance – regional, ethnic, national, European. The cultural diversity of Europe should be perceived as a rich resource rather than as an obstacle to be 'ironed out' by bureaucratic homogenization. European consciousness will need to coexist with a plurality of other social identities. However, 'difference' does not lead remorselessly to antagonism and conflict, unless cultivated in that direction by political actors. But that is precisely the effect of the current 'vertical' integration through member states, which constantly emphasizes the alleged *contradiction* between 'national' and 'European' interests.

'Horizontal' integration would on the other hand emphasize aspirations that are *shared* across the frontiers, and would facilitate collective action on policy issues that clearly require European mediation. This would be quite compatible with recognition that other areas of policy are more appropriately dealt with by nation-states, regions or municipalities. Indeed, the notion of 'subsidiarity' implies a functional distribution of policy-making competences, and the emergence of a multi-layered civic community from local to European level. The former British Conservative government's deliberate distortion of the term to justify a centralized and unitary 'nation-state' reveals all the dangers of the 'vertical' model of integration.

As Eric Hobsbawm has pointed out, each individual has a multiplicity of 'identities' (Hobsbawm, 1990, p. 123). These are not exclusive of one another, not interchangeable 'like shoes'. They coexist, even though circumstances may make one form of identity more salient at a given time. There is always the possibility that these identities will enter into conflict with one another, but this does not indicate that they are *fundamentally* antagonistic and irreconcilable. Genuinely *painful* choices are normally imposed by problematic historical situations, and indeed by the willingness of politicians to exploit and magnify the particular 'identity' which suits their purposes. Attempts to forge a European consciousness will therefore need to acknowledge and respect cultural pluralism. Failure to do this is grist to the mill of those who feed politically on Europe's ethnic and national divisions, or who envisage a 'Fortress Europe' closed to the outside world.

In this respect, it is the inclusive 'civic', rather than exclusive 'ethnic', model of nation-building which should serve as an example. Social identities are secured and stabilized by political empowerment, and this applies as much to the *creation* of a sense of being 'European' as it does to the *protection* of older national, regional or local loyalties. Indeed, the current wave of 'Euroscepticism' reflects popular frustration at the inability of national governments to 'deliver' what has traditionally been expected of them. It has been easy to lay this 'loss of sovereignty' at the door of Europe, and to present the integration process as a *vehicle* of market globalism rather than as an attempt to regain a degree of sovereignty at a higher level.

These 'conflicts of identity' can only be resolved within decentralized structures of democratic accountability, through the various territorial levels from European Union to locality. But these structures must be based on a realistic assessment of the policy constraints at each level and on a clear demarcation of policy-making functions. Only on this basis will it become possible to narrow the gap between expectations and outcomes, to restore credibility to political processes, and to build a European citizenry based on 'multiple' but mutually compatible identities.

NOTES

1.   Stalin's famous definition runs, 'A nation is a historically constituted, stable community of people, formed on the basis of a common language, territory, economic life and psychological make-up manifested in a common culture' (Stalin, 1973, p. 61).
2.   Thus, for example, Immanuel Wallerstein writes, 'in almost every case statehood preceded nationhood, and not the other way round, despite a widespread myth to the contrary' (Balibar and Wallerstein, 1991, p. 81).
3.   See for example Sternhell (1978) and Smith (1979).
4.   In the words of Stanley Hoffmann, 'Thus today, for domestic and external reasons, the French state no longer defines or crystallizes French nationalism, and nationalism in French society no longer serves as a forceful inspiration for the state' (Hoffmann, 1974, p. 483).
5.   David Goldblatt and David Held wrote recently that 'we live in a world of overlapping communities of fate in which transboundary problems require common, democratic, transboundary solutions. At the level of the EU this requires the active promotion of policies to overcome the democratic deficit

and the deployment of transnational referenda on major Europe-wide questions' (Goldblatt and Held, 1997, p. 26).

REFERENCES

Anderson, B., *Imagined Communities: Reflections on the Origin and Spread of Nationalism* (London, Verso, 1983).

Balibar, E. and Wallerstein, I., *Race, Nation, Class: Ambiguous Identities* (London, Verso, 1991).

Chafer, A. and Jenkins, B. (eds), *France: From the Cold War to the New World Order* (London, Macmillan, 1996).

Citron, S., *Le mythe national: L'histoire de France en question* (Paris, Editions Ouvrières, 1987).

Cornick, M., 'French Intellectuals, Neutralism and the Search for Peace in the Cold War', in Chafer, A. and Jenkins, B. (eds), *France: From the Cold War to the New World Order* (London, Macmillan, 1996), pp. 39–52.

Furet, F., *Penser la Revolution française* (Paris, Gallimard, 1978).

Goldblatt, E. and Held, D., 'Bring Back Democracy', *New Stateman*, 10 January 1997, pp. 24–6.

Gray, John, 'What Liberalism Cannot Do', *New Statesman*, 20 September 1996, pp. 18–20.

Hobsbawm, E., *Nations and Nationalism since 1780* (Cambridge, Cambridge University Press, 1990).

Hobsbawm, E. and Ranger, T. (eds), *The Invention of Tradition* (Cambridge, Cambridge University Press, 1983).

Hoffmann, S., *Essais sur la France: Déclin ou Renouveau?* (Paris, Seuil, 1974).

Howorth, J., 'France and European Security 1944–94: Re-reading the Gaullist "Consensus"', in Chafer, A. and Jenkins, B. (eds), *France: From the Cold War to the New World Order* (London, Macmillan, 1996), pp. 17–38.

Jenkins, B., *Nationalism in France: Class and Nation since 1789* (London, Routledge, 1990).

Jenkins, B. and Copsey, N., 'Nation, Nationalism and National Identity in France', in Jenkins, B. and Sofos, S. (eds), *Nation and Identity in Contemporary Europe* (London, Routledge, 1996), pp. 101–24.

Mendras, H. and Cole, A., *Social Change in Modern France: Towards a Cultural Anthropology of the Fifth Republic* (Cambridge, Cambridge University Press, 1991).

Nairn, T., *The Break-up of Britain* (London, New Left Books, 1977).

Silverman, M., *Deconstructing the Nation: Immigration, Racism and Citizenship in Modern France* (London, Routledge, 1992).

Smith, A. D., *Nationalism in the Twentieth Century* (London, Martin Robertson, 1979).

Stalin, J., 'The Nation', in Franklin, B. (ed.), *The Essential Stalin: Major Theoretical Writings 1905–52* (London, Croom Helm, 1973), pp. 57–61.

Sternhell, Z., *La droite révolutionaire 1885–1914: Les origines françaises du facisme* (Paris, Seuil, 1978).

Weber, E., *Peasants into Frenchmen: the Modernisation of Rural France 1870–1914* (Stanford, Stanford University Press, 1976).

9 Constructing a European Identity: Problems of Supranationalism

Aleksandar Pavković

Who counts as a European? Where are the outer frontiers of Europe? Are Russians Europeans? Are they Europeans even if very few of them very seldom think of themselves as Europeans?[1] Are Turks Europeans? And if so, what about the Turkic nations, Turkmens and Azerbaijanis? And their non-Turkic neighbours, Georgians and Armenians? The uncertainties surrounding these 'hard' or 'frontier' cases do not present any insurmountable obstacles to the constructing of a European supranational identity. For an identity in the process of construction, the controversies over its outer boundaries are not only natural but also welcome: such a controversy appears to assume that there is a core European identity which allows us to debate the exact location of its outer boundaries. In this debate about who counts as a European, the French, the British and the Germans, indeed the original six or the present 15 European Union members are assumed to be, without any doubt, Europeans. It is only the membership of other border nations that is possibly in doubt.

Yet a controversy such as this reveals not only that this identity is in the process of being constructed but that it is constructed as an identity inclusive of other, well-established – some would say primordial – national identities. Including the established identities, it attempts at most to transcend but not to replace them. This indeed differentiates supranational identities from those of an ordinary national variety: the latter exclude, often aggressively so, any other national identity and attempt to replace or subordinate any other collective – religious, regional, ethnic, tribal or even professional – identities. One can indeed raise the question as to whether a Breton is a Frenchman or a Protestant Ulsterman a Briton. However many Bretons may disagree, non-Breton French (and, indeed, many other fellow Europeans) are going to regard them as French; and however British many Ulstermen may feel, they still may end up as Irish, whether they like it or not. These well-established nations inhabit nation-states; and these states tend to settle the questions of national belonging without leaving much room for doubt. Supranations mostly inhabit imaginary spaces created by enthusiastic intellectuals or bureaucrats who often lack both the power and the need to settle decisively the questions of supranational belonging. This is one reason why the question of whether Russians are Europeans appears at present so open-ended while similar questions about Bretons and Ulstermen do not.

Why is there no doubt as to whom the finger from a military mobilization poster is pointing? Its target, I would think, is firmly defined by its presumed national identity. When the drums roll and the call '*Allons, enfants de la Patrie ...*' or its equivalent echoes through the streets or media, those who are not sure of whether they are being called up are called traitors and dealt with accordingly. Among the many roles which national identities are called upon to play, that of a recruitment master is perhaps the simplest and most effective one. Not so with supranational identities. There are no mobilization posters (perhaps not as yet) with the finger pointing to the Europeans, and Schiller's 'Ode to Joy' is not a call to Europeans to fall in and march. The now defunct supranation of Yugoslavs was never mentioned in any of the myriad proclamations, posters and marching songs of the Communist Party of Yugoslavia during or after the Second World War. The Yugoslav Communists, perhaps better than any other supranationalists, knew that pointing the finger of mobilization at Yugoslavs would be pointing it at no one in particular. Perhaps this makes it clearer why one can debate at length who belongs to the honorary club of Europeans: when the chips are down and the drums roll, who belongs to this club would matter very little; or so it seems at this stage of the development of a common European identity.

SUPRANATIONALISM: OVERCOMING A VIOLENT PAST AND REACHING FOR A RADIANT FUTURE

This is no accident: the post-1945 project of construction of a European supranationality adopted an explicit anti-war stance, the stance which clearly dominates the most engaging outline of the project, Edgar Morin's *Penser l'Europe* (1990). Morin's book celebrates the peace in Europe, the peace which dawned on Europe after two suicidal European wars this century; according to him, the sense of common European (supranational) identity originates in the realization that these and previous European wars were suicidal and potentially destructive of common Europeanness. The spread and permanent establishment – let us call it rootedness – of a common European identity would no doubt prevent any future suicidal wars.

The idea of the war-preventive qualities of common Europeanness had found its most forceful expression in several proclamations of Second World War resistance movements. Thus, Declaration I of the Geneva conference of Resistance Movements of 20 May 1944 identifies the sources of a new European solidarity:

> The heroic struggle being waged against the common enemy on all fronts of the internal resistance is not only a signal proof of patriotism and faith in the resurrection of their countries, but that the sacrifices and suffering accepted for the same cause have created ties of brotherhood among them and have given birth to a new awareness of solidarity among the free peoples, the maintenance of which will be one of the essential guarantees of peace.
>
> (Lipgengs, 1985, pp. 678–9)

The chief cause of the world conflicts in the past generation, Declaration I states, was 'the existence of thirty sovereign States in Europe'. To remove this cause, the signatories of Declaration I proposed a Federal Union of Europe, directly responsible to the peoples of Europe, with a European army as the sole military force in Europe and an independent Supreme Court. Only this type of restriction of the sovereignty of nation-states, they argued, could bring permanent peace to Europe. Noting the rising sense of solidarity among the peoples of Europe, the Italian Movement for the European Federation, in its open letter of August 1944 to the French Committee for the European Federation, for the first time referred to the peoples of Europe by their common name 'Europeans' and proceeded to urge the oppressed Europeans to create a free community of all nations of the continent (Lipgengs, 1985, p. 693).

Originating in the European resistance vision of the common struggle against the extremes of European nationalism, the European identity propagated by Morin, Rougement, Duroselle and Brugmans, to name the few prominent Euro supranationalists, is naturally anti-nationalist as well: the intolerant and thus war-oriented nationalism is not only incompatible with an inclusive European identity but is also destructive of peace and the well-being of all peoples of Europe. Of course, European supranationalists – like their predecessors in the European resistance movements – are ready to distinguish the good from the bad variety of nationalism. The first is tolerant of diversity while the second is not only intolerant but leads to violence and war. However, the anti-war and anti-(bad)nationalism aspects of this supranational concept of common European identity not only make it useless as a potential instrument of military mobilization but also rule out the strategies which appeal to a nation's military glory and to its superiority over the Other.

As Anthony D. Smith (1992, p. 73) points out, (supranational) European identity is not constructed on a memory of glorious military feats – both those of victory and of defeat – the memory which lies at the core of every European national identity. There are no war memorials, remembrance days and wreath-laying ceremonies which glorify the Europeans. However, it would not be difficult, if it ever proves necessary, to construct a memory of European military glory: the defeat of Atilla, the victory at Lepanto, the lifting of the siege(s) of Vienna – and with a little ingenuity – the Normandy landings; surely all these and many more could be packaged to reveal the unbroken European struggle for European values on European soil. Once this is done, there would be no obstacle to building a series of more or less monumental war memorials extolling the struggle and the fallen for the European cause.

The Euro supranationalist project is incompatible with any such monumental 'struggle for freedom' model, not only because of its explicit anti-war stance. The glorification of the alleged European feats of arms, in their view, would clash with the very values which stand at the core of the supranational conception of Europe and European identity. The victory of European values of liberal democracy, equality, individual autonomy which, according to Morin and other Euro supranationalists, makes the core of European values, was not a feat of arms; and, in any case, these values could not be imposed by the sheer force of arms. In rejecting the glorification of war in the name of European anti-war values, Euro supranationalists also reject one of the successful strategies of constructing national or supranational identities. This strategy, as we shall see at the end of the present chapter, still provides an alternative (albeit at present not too plausible) model for the construction of European identity.

The anti-nationalist stance, on the other hand, prevents Euro supranationalists from defining their European identity by way of contrast with the intolerable or simply inferior Other. Thus, the Europeans, according to Morin, not only are not superior to Asians, Africans, Americans or any Others, but their Europeanness is not defined by any – negative or positive – contrast to non-Europeans and their traditions and values. This makes the Euro identity project quite abstract and restricts the construction of effective European supranational or national markers. For the Euro supranationalists do not tell us how to distinguish at a glance a European from a non-European. Racial features are, of course, ruled out from the start; so are the manners and the style of dress. We are left only with the European values and traditions, none of which form a part of the outside apparel of Europeans and can serve as visible markers.

This, of course, does not mean that the concept of common Europeanness is all-inclusive and that it tolerates all cultural or social innovations taking place in Europe. Morin, for one, vehemently rejects:

the homogenization of customs and the cultural standardization which is irresistibly spreading throughout Europe: jeans, shirts, westerns, serials, shows, hamburgers, Coke, Pepsi, papers, self-services and supermarkets.

(Morin, 1990, p. 172)

These processes of Americanization, Morin argues, are the results of capitalist commodification and standardization as well as techno-bureaucratic anonimization, all of which are 'native' to Europe. While the phenomena of the process – from jeans to supermarkets – originate in the US, the underlying processes are firmly rooted in Europe. It is these processes of the homogenization of customs and standardization of cultures that threaten to destroy the diversity and nonconformity of European cultures – their unique and defining mark – and thus degrade the very concept of European culture. They are to be resisted not because of their foreignness, not because they originate in the intolerable (in this case, American) Other, but because they threaten the uniqueness of European cultures. This uniqueness needs to be defended not from a foreign Other, but from its indigenous degradation.

With no memory of military glories and no enemy Other, Euro supranationalists are left with few other tools of traditional national identity construction. The traditional national identity requires a common past usually in the form of a tale of a united and goal-oriented collective endeavour of an emergent nation. Some Euro supranationalists, notably the historians Duroselle and Brugmans, are ready at least to attempt to tell a similar tale; Duroselle (1990, pp. 20–1) lists nine 'phases of shared experience' of western, northern, central and southern Europe (from the megalith to the recent Imperial phase) and discerns 'a general if halting growth in compassion, humanity and equality' in European history. These are possibly only some of the 'solid historic reasons' which led Duroselle to regard 'Europe not only as a mosaic of cultures but as an organic whole' (Davies, 1996, p. 40). While not quite a tale of 'a united endeavour' of Europeans which inevitably leads to a Europe united, Duroselle's story aims to demonstrate the persistence of a European 'core' ('unity') throughout its history, independent of the apparent disunity and conflict among its nation-states (Duroselle, 1990, p. 411).

In contrast to Duroselle, Morin admits that the European past offers no tale of this kind. Yet not all is lost: instead of united endeavour, there is, according to Morin (1990, p. 56), a European whirlpool resulting in 'a permanent euro-organizing anarchy'. This anarchy, Morin argues, was producing a Europe of permanent metamorphosis, of a creative diversity and of an ongoing dialogue. Ignoring this cascade of metaphors, one sees Morin here valiantly facing the absence of any kind of unity in European history and turning an abundance of conflict into a unique and possibly unifying and defining feature of the European past. This strategy, however unconvincing it may seem at first, at least avoids blatant falsifications to which many historians of a 'united endeavour' are prone. Moreover, it allows each of the European nations to continue to have its own separate and glorious past of 'united endeavour' and 'struggle for freedom'. Admitting to the abundance of conflict as well as of dialogue, Morin appropriates the latter for the supranational European identity, thus leaving to each separate nation its own tale of unifying purpose and military glory. In his view, the Europe of wars and violence is intrinsically related not to its common identity but to the bad and destructive nationalisms. Yet in this mythical division of responsibility, Morin (unlike Duroselle in his *L'Idée de l'Europe dans l'histoire*) ignores Hitler's idea of a Europe united and purified by the Nazis and perhaps less a barbaric but no less violent vision of Europe united by Napoleon's Grande Armée. His strategy thus seems rather simple: the wars and the conflict are, in his recounting of the past, conveniently left to the egocentric nation-states and their destructive nationalisms.

Morin constructs a non-violent and tolerant European past of traditions and cultures in dialogue. In addition to this somewhat purified past, he also recruits the future for the cause of Europe and its common identity. The European 'community of destiny', the *Schicksalgemeinschaft*, which, according to Otto Bauer, characterizes every true nation, can emerge, Morin (1990, p. 197) avers, only from the future:

> Our European historical memories have nothing in common but the division and war. They have no common heritage except for their mutual hatreds. Our community of destiny could not emerge from our past which only contradicts it. *It would hardly emerge from our present because it is our future which will impose it upon us.* (emphasis in original)

Europe's destiny lies, Morin is convinced, in this 'accelerated future'.

AN IDENTITY BASED ON CULTURAL HERITAGE?

It is, however, the non-violent past of European traditions in dialogue – the highly diverse yet highly interrelated realm of European arts, literature and science – that provides Morin and other Euro supranationalists with the core of a common European identity. It was in this very field of high culture, Morin notes, that most European dialogue and cross-fertilization took place. Starting with the Gothic cathedrals and continuing to Cubism and abstract painting, European art and painting freely crossed the national and linguistic frontiers to become a common cultural heritage of all Europeans. This shining example of cultural unity in diversity is further buttressed by a catalogue of names – Calderón, Shakespeare, Molière, Dante, Erasmus, Cervantes, Montaigne, Rimbaud, T. S. Eliot, Dostoevsky, Tolstoy, and, of course, Mozart, Beethoven, Mahler, Berg and many others (Morin, 1990, p. 87). The list, naturally, could be extended further, but even in shorter, more perfunctory lists, at least some of the above names are bound to appear. It is at the level of the catalogue of names that we shall find the beginnings of a consensus among the Euro supranationalists: all of them would agree that some such list of names forms the core of the European culture which in turn defines the core of common European identity.

Another related point of consensus is to be found in a list of European intellectual and cultural innovations, which forms another core, that of Europe's contribution to world culture. This list usually starts with Ancient Greece and Rome and with the political philosophy and practice of democracy and individual autonomy. Then, at least in Morin's list, come the achievements of Renaissance humanism and, later, of the Enlightenment, and we end with the triumph of the natural sciences and the technological revolution. This invented tradition of the continuity of European political thought, as Agnes Heller (1992, p. 14) noted, appears to mirror Hegel's philosophy of history in which each stage in this line of progress contributes to the advance of the next. Morin's recapitulation of this uplifting story, in keeping with our own more pessimistic age, omits the element of progress but leaves the traces of continuity.

Out of the somewhat purified European past thus comes a list of famous men (no women, sadly, appear on this list as yet) and a list of cultural achievements which Euro supranationalists claim as a common European heritage. This way of constructing a common European cultural 'community' or 'heritage' is, of course, not the only one. Hugh Seton-Watson (1985, p. 9) bases the concept of this community on the sense of allegiance which transcends the local territorial and social loyalties of European peoples; the origins of this transcending proto-European allegiance he then traces back to early Christendom, 'the first community of Christian peoples'. But, however one constructs this common heritage, one becomes a European by accepting it as one's own: if one identifies with a common European heritage or has a sense of belonging to the European cultural community, one has in effect identified oneself as a European. It is this acceptance of a common European cultural heritage that transforms an individual into a European and gives him a new, inclusive supranational identity.

Let us now examine two major objections to this strategy of supranational identity construction. The first, voiced by Agnes Heller (1992), rejects the notion of a common European heritage based on one or both of these lists. The abstractions called the 'European painting', the 'European novel' and 'European music' are, according to her, nothing but abstractions. There is no European novel but only the English, French and Russian novel and likewise for the rest. To see this, she invites us to look at what the European nations used to export to their colonies: among the goods exported in this way we find no European music, novel and painting. Instead, she argues, European colonial masters exported modernity in the guise of economy, statecraft and technology, the modernity which, in her view, characterizes the fleeting notion of common European identity (Heller, 1992, p. 17). There is only one common European achievement – that of modernity in statecraft, economy and technology which, as it becomes a global export, provides no effective or lasting basis for a European supranational identity. In effect, her argument goes beyond her, possibly ironic, search for a common European culture among the export goods of European capitalists. Her argument turns on a simple demand to prove that a list of great cultural achievements and of their makers reflects the existence of a common cultural heritage. Producing a list of such men and cultural achievements, by itself, is no proof of a common cultural heritage or of anything in common to the men and cultural achievements listed. Such lists prove as little (or as much) as the lists of European exports to their colonies.

But how does one prove the existence of a supranational cultural heritage? A common national heritage, one may want to argue, is simply a particular cultural canon – once again a list – which is widely accepted among the nationally-minded intellectuals and their rank and file, the intelligentsia, as representing their common heritage. Such canons are not meant to prove the existence of national cultures (the existence is more often assumed than proven) but, rather, to vividly illustrate national cultural achievement and to serve as sources of national pride. No doubt the acceptance of such national canons and their role as sources of national pride is much facilitated by the language which the canonized men allegedly share with those who take pride in their achievements. There is, of course, no common language of the European cultural canon. But as this proved no obstacle to the dialogue and cross-fertilization among the members of the canon, it is no obstacle, one may argue, to the acceptance of the canon and its role as a source of European pride.

On this view, Morin and Euro supranationalists are presenting a rather vague canon of supranational heritage for contemplation and acceptance by those searching for the roots of Europeanness and/or a source of European pride. The canon is not a proof intended to convert the unconverted, that is, those who do not believe in the existence of a common European cultural heritage. To demand that the proposed European canon provide a proof of a common European heritage is then to misunderstand the European supranationalist project.

However, Heller's doubts about the existence of the canon suggest another more general problem. National cultural identities, based on accepted cultural canons, presuppose a unity of culture, usually based on a standard (or to-be-standardized) language. The whole purpose of a cultural canon is vividly to illustrate this presumed cultural unity: one canon, one language, one literature, one culture, one nation. In contrast, Morin and other Euro supranationalists argue that the common European identity be based on a cultural diversity: many languages, many literatures, many cultures, many nations, but one all-embracing cultural canon and, consequently, one European supranation. It is this very unity in diversity that makes European cultures or culture unique and therefore a suitable point for cultural and supranational identification. Now Heller in effect casts doubt on the inference from diverse cultures to a unique and transcending European supra-culture: the highly diverse cultures of Europe, she suggests, offer no basis for such an inference.

In defence of such an inference, Morin points to cross-fertilization and to dialogue; the cross-fertilization and dialogue among European cultures make these national cultures much less national than they appear at first sight. In addition, one could argue that the unified national cultures, based on the cherished national cultural canons, are as much products of planned construction as is the new supranational European culture. If we grant that the national cultures are neither predetermined nor primordial but constructed, their continued existence and even flourishing is not, by itself, an insurmountable obstacle to the construction of a supra-culture of Europe. The major question is then not *whether* such a supra-culture can be constructed but *how* this should be done. In this context, one could certainly question the suitability of the standard model of construction of national cultures (via unified cultural canons) for the present task. Is a European supra-culture to be constructed simply by pilfering existing national cultural canons of suitable supranational European cultural achievers and achievements? Isn't there a more effective method of constructing a European supranationality?

It is the effectiveness of this method of construction that Anthony D. Smith seems to question: he doubts that the 'supra-cultural' project contains the right ingredients required for success at least in the foreseeable future. Unlike Heller, he admits the existence of a rather weak cultural heritage – the family of European cultures – but then argues that this family is insufficient to produce a sense of supranational identity comparable to the already established national identities. Smith thus concedes that the 'major cultural and historical traditions' – such as Roman law, Greek philosophy and science, Hebraic ethics and Christian theology, and their Renaissance and Enlightenment successors – have created a European family of cultures, of cultural traditions and discourses 'which have been adapted to the circumstances of each community and state in Europe'. Yet in spite of this, '"Europe" [Smith's quotation marks] lacks a secure ethnic base with a clear-cut set of common historical memories, myths, symbols, values and the like' (Smith, 1993, p. 134). The memories, myths and symbols which it does possess – Smith's example is that of medieval (Catholic?, Orthodox?) Christendom – are flawed or increasingly irrelevant and unusable for many of Europe's peoples. What interest, Smith asks, would Frederick Barbarossa have for English and French citizens, or a Catholic Mass for German or Swede Protestants? And to which of these are the peoples of Europe going to feel a European loyalty? By loyalty, Smith here means the readiness to make sacrifices including that of one's life. To the European family of cultures Smith denies, first, the right mix of common ingredients and, second, sufficient strength to induce the desired loyalty or allegiance.

By raising the question of loyalty and allegiance, Smith appears to conceive the projected supranational European identity as a mobilization tool. But, as we have seen, the present project rejects the possibility of using European identity as such a mobilization tool. Perhaps Smith only wants to argue that unless a new identity can serve as a mobilization tool, it cannot compete with the established ones which are successfully used as such tools: let the drums of war roll and see how quickly European supranationality would disappear: as quickly as the internationalism of the proletariat did in 1914. But once again this is not the arena in which the European supranationality would aim to compete: the aim of European supranationalism is to silence the drums of war by undermining and removing nationalisms which fuel wars and aggression.

If the argument based on the roll of drums misses the point, what about the argument from the absence of the right mixture? The right mixture, in Smith's own words, is a 'secure ethnic base with a clear-cut set of common historical memories, myths, symbols, values, and the like'. A 'secure ethnic base' is based on the belief (whether true or not) of a common ethnic ancestry or 'common blood'. No one believes in a common ethnic ancestry of Americans, Britons and Australians and their present national identity – for better or worse – is not constructed on any 'secure ethnic base' in this sense. Their identity is based on a belief in a common culture, including, most importantly, common political culture and tradition, that is, on a more or less clear-cut set of common historical memories, myths, symbols without any 'secure ethnic base'. Is a 'secure ethnic base', then, necessary for the construction of *every* national identity and, thus, for any supranational identity, capable of competing, successfully, with the existing national identities? The appeal to common ancestry or blood in Europe has been used to instil national pride and a sense of shared destiny to politically and linguistically fragmented populations, such as the populations of nineteenth-century Italy and Germany. In this process, it has proved an effective instrument of 'national unification', that is, for the creation of nation-states and of mobilization for war. In the process of the creation of nation-states out of former Yugoslavia and in the resulting wars, such an appeal to common ancestry and blood has once again proven its effectiveness. Almost all the dominant national ideologies in this region appeal to the common ancestry and blood of their target populations; this is particularly evident in the national ideologies of the ruling Macedonian, Croatian, Bosnian Muslim and Kosovo Albanian political parties which claim that the identity and survival of their target national groups is under threat from their neighbours. The need for a 'secure ethnic base' is thus most evident for purposes of mobilization of the target groups in the process of nation-state building in an allegedly hostile environment.

The present project of European supranationality does not aim at the 'unification' of European nations into a European nation-state (and it denies the existence of any threats to Europeans). In view of this, its need for a 'secure ethnic base' – even if there were such a base – would be doubtful. The project aims at constructing a set of common symbols, myths and values without such an ethnic base. The set which Morin lists – the symbols of shared cultural achievement and achievers, the myths of dialogue and cross-fertilization, and the values of democracy, human rights and individual autonomy – is sufficiently common to Europe to withstand the type of counter-example that Smith advances. The two counter-examples he lists, that of Frederick Barbarossa and of the Catholic Mass, do not appear on Morin's or any other Euro supranationalist's list for the simple reason that they are not regarded as commonly shared European symbols and values.

Morin, for one, intentionally lists only persons and achievements which can safely cross all European national borders.[2]

MASS DISSEMINATION: IS SUPRANATIONAL EUROPEAN IDENTITY POLITICALLY USEFUL?

The problem with Morin's set of European symbols, myths and values is not the absence of a European commonality or of a clear rationale. The principal problem with these symbols and values is that they are not easily accessible or disseminated among the mass of their target populations. Smith (1993, p. 134) is certainly right in observing that:

> for the moment the ethnic and national levels of identification will take priority, and remain much more vivid and accessible to the mass of population, than more abstract, shadowy and higher-level regional identities like that of 'Europe'.

Restricting the base of the Euro identity to the realm of European high culture makes it, if not less vivid, certainly less accessible to those whose interest in and acquaintance with this high culture is limited. The number of people to whom Dante's poetry or Tolstoy's novels evoke the sense of common European identity is limited to those who are in some way or other acquainted with these works. But if the problem here is not that of the absence of commonality of culture but of its mass dissemination, then perhaps the dissemination of the existing national identities could at last provide a model for the dissemination of Euro identity.

The major channels of the dissemination of national identities have been and still are the nation-state school system and its popular media. In the former, it is the teaching of (national) history which is the main instrument of the propagation of national ideas and identities. It is, then, not surprising that the first steps for the dissemination of Euro identity appear to have been made in the school teaching of history: the first Council of Europe's conference on history teaching, entitled 'The European Idea in History Teaching', was held in 1953 (Slater, 1995, p. 25). One of the latest steps in this direction, a secondary school history written by 12 European scholars and translated into 16 languages (Delouche, 1992, 1993), focuses on the same set of themes as Morin does – the shared European historical experiences, dialogue and cross-fertilization as well as common values of Europe – without avoiding the history of inter-European wars and conflicts. However, unlike Duroselle and Morin, its authors make no appeal to the future, ending their work with the question 'The End of a Divided Europe?'

(Delouche, 1993, p. 380). Yet their supranationalist approach is evident not only in their selection of topics but in the volume's avowed aim to serve 'the young Europeans in the course of their studies and may be considered as *the prototype of a textbook of history of Europe: the first Eurotextbook*' (Delouche, 1992, p. 3, emphasis in the text). This aim, as it appears, has not been achieved as yet: no national school administration in any European Union member state has officially approved its use as a textbook. Whether any common school textbook will be approved for use in European state school systems is still an open question, although all members of the European Union have made attempts to 'Europeanize' their school curricula (Shennan, 1991, pp. 146–9).

As for the popular media, in spite of several attempts at the 'Europeanization' of print and television media, the future, according to European media experts, is unlikely to bring about a common European television programming or a European mass-circulation tabloid. This has led some scholars to conclude that the dissemination of European identity through common European media is neither necessary nor desirable (Shelley and Winck, 1993, p. 185). In any case, no national government appears to be ready or able as yet to embark on a campaign of Europeanization of its media or their broadcasts.

These debates and the absence of political commitment to mass dissemination of the Euro identity, one can argue, indicate only that the Euro identity project is still in the state of intellectual fermentation, the first stage in Hroch's three-stage development of national movements (Hroch, 1985). This, of course, is an optimistic view which implies that once the second stage is reached, and Euro identity is accepted both by European intellectuals and their rank and file, the intelligentsia, the third stage, that of systematic mass dissemination of the new identity, would almost naturally follow. One does not need to be a Euro pessimist to see that the European intelligentsia's espousal of European identity does not guarantee its ultimate mass dissemination. As the absence of official approval for common history textbooks suggests, it is the political and bureaucratic masters of Europe who need to be won over, not so much to the idea of a common European identity but to its political usefulness. Once they come to see the idea as politically useful – and not only harmless as it is now – they may allow or direct the existing nation-state apparatuses to disseminate it.

But what would the idea of European identity, as constructed by Morin and other European supranationalists, be useful for? As we have seen, as presently conceived, it has no mobilizational value and it is not even intended to enhance the sense of superiority of Europeans to Others. In short, it is not directed against any Other, either as an enemy or as a potential rival. This not only sharply distinguishes it from the well-established national identities but seriously diminishes its political usefulness. To see this, one only needs to ask what core European values a politician could be asked to defend or, if defence here seems inappropriate, to promote. Well, these are, according to Morin and other Euro supranationalists, the values of tolerance, liberalism, democracy and universal human rights. As Smith had already noted, this is a highly abstract and not all that vivid a set of values. And as all mainstream politicians in the European Union member states promote – or at least endorse – these values, their promotion could bring no particular advantage nor votes to any politician whose political appeal would be based solely on these allegedly European values. As constructed by Morin, the values of Europeanism do not seem to include concrete, non-abstract, values which find their expression in everyday life; there seems to be no European equivalent to the values embodied, for example, in cricket playing or in one's loyalty to one's local pub or soccer team. These abstract European values do not seem to be of any particular use to a European politician nor do they have a role to play in much of the everyday life of his or her constituents.

Commemoration of the gloriously fallen in the national cause nowadays takes only a minute segment of everyday life: each nation-state officially celebrates their memory only a few times a year. And although such mass celebrations do not take much of the ordinary citizens' time, memorials to the gloriously fallen or to the victories of one's nation dot the landscape of all cities and most towns of Europe. They are not only a memento of the glory of, and the sacrifice for, one's nation but offer a fairly ubiquitous, if not always very vivid, testimony of its continuity extending over many generations. Memorials and monuments both of the gloriously fallen and of the worthy national workers – politicians, artists, soldiers, and, in Australia, donkey drivers – thus relate an individual member of a nation to his or her ancestors as well as to posterity. They create a sense of intergenerational bonding and collective agelessness to which an individual member of a nation is entitled simply in virtue of his or her national identity. Belonging to a nation in our secular age thus appears to offer a secular substitute for a sense of (collective) immortality.

The roots of common European identity could be conveniently traced to the Ancient Greek myth of Europa and the mists of time before recorded history. If so, couldn't a European identity, tracing so long a lineage, offer a more attractive if somewhat mythical sense of agelessness than any of the existing relatively young national identities? Could such an identity be constructed around the myth of a united struggle for the freedom of Europe commemorated in a series of suitable monuments and memorials? Any attempt to use Europeanism in a presentation of continuity through a

European-oriented set of monuments and memorials would face, among other problems, the problem of double-representation: the distinguished European predecessors as well as those who fell fighting for the freedom of Europe were, after all, members of particular European nations or proto-nations. Even if we search for the gloriously fallen long before the advent of modern European nations – for example, in the fields of Châlon-sur-Marne where Europe was saved from Attila's hordes – the heroes of this fifth-century battle belonged to some of the proto-nations or *ethne* of Europe. Their memorial would seem to be a memorial to the Burgundians, Gauls, Franks and Visigoths (and to any other group which is reputed to have participated in the battle). Naturally, if meant as a memorial of the fallen Europeans, one could conveniently ignore or, perhaps, only de-emphasize their membership of these separate *ethne*. Any such move to de-emphasize their 'ethnic' membership would, however, be a first step to converting Europeanism from supranationality into a substitute nationality. For we would be effectively arguing that in fighting and dying for Europe and not for their individual homelands, all these Burgundians, Gauls, Franks and Visigoths became Europeans and almost miraculously lost their separate identities. In this way, by making them into Europeans, we may hope to establish an intergenerational bond of all Europeans with those early heroes of the European cause.

But this strategy significantly differs from Morin's supranationalism: not only does it glorify, in a limited sense, war on the European soil, but it also aims at superseding various national identities in Europe by an all-encompassing Euro identity. In short, the new Euro identity here is no longer supranational but of a substitute national European identity. Comparing these two models of constructing a Euro identity, one could ask: Could a supra-nationalist model of the type which Morin promotes, provide an intergenerational bond of this kind? Or does an attempt to construct an intergenerational bond among the dead, living and yet unborn Europeans, have to lead to the construction of a substitute and not a supranational European identity? Does the failure to provide such an intergenerational bond doom the supranationalist project as a project of an enduring and effective European identity?

NOTES

1. '[P]erhaps the most striking difference between Russia and the Eastern Europeans is in the answer to the question "Do you ever consider yourself

European?" ... [M]ore than three-quarters of Russians questioned said "Rarely" or "Never".' Survey conducted by Professor Richard Rose of the Centre for the Study of Public Policy, University of Strathclyde. 'Eastern Europe: Feeling Perkier', *The Economist*, 2 March 1996, pp. 52–3.

2. A similar discussion of the Euro supranationalist project is found in Pavković, 1996.

REFERENCES

Davies, N., *Europe: a History* (Oxford, Oxford University Press, 1996).
Delouche, F. (ed.), *Histoire de l'Europe: une initiative européenne de Frédéric Delouche* (Paris, Hachette, 1992).
Delouche, F. (ed.), *Illustrated History of Europe: a Unique Portrait of Europe's Common History* (London, Weidenfeld and Nicolson, 1993). (A translation, with some changes, of Delouche 1992 into English.)
Duroselle, J.-B., *L'idée de l'Europe dans l'histoire* (Paris, Denoel, 1965).
Duroselle, J.-B., *Europe: a History of its Peoples* (London, Viking, 1990).
Heller, A., 'Europe: an Epilogue', in Nelson B., Roberts, D. and Veit, W. (eds), *The Idea of Europe: Problems of National and Transnational Identity* (New York, Berg, 1992), pp. 11–21.
Hroch, M., *Social Preconditions of National Revival in Europe: a Comparative Analysis* (Cambridge, Cambridge University Press, 1985).
Lipgengs, W. (ed.), *Documents on the History of European Integration*, Vol. 1 (Berlin, Walter de Gruyter, 1985).
Morin, E., *Penser l'Europe* (Paris, Gallimard, 1990).
Pavković, A., 'How to Construct a European Identity: a Few Suggestions', *Contemporary European Studies Association of Australia Newsletter*, No. 17, 1996, pp. 10–21.
Seton-Watson, H., 'What is Europe, Where is Europe?', *Encounter*, Vol. 65, No. 2, 1985, pp. 9–17.
Shelley, M. and Winck, M. (eds), *Aspects of European Cultural Diversity* (London, Routledge, 1993).
Shennan, M., *Teaching about Europe* (London, Cassell, 1991).
Slater, J., *Teaching History in the New Europe* (London, Cassell, 1995).
Smith, A. D., 'National Identity and the Idea of European Unity', *International Affairs*, Vol. 68, No. 1, 1992, pp. 55–76.
Smith, A. D., 'A Europe of Nations – or the Nation of Europe', *Journal of Peace Research*, Vol. 30, No. 2, 1993, pp. 129–35.

10 Europe ... the Creation of a Nation? A Comparative Analysis of Nation-Building[1]

Bego de la Serna-López

Nietzsche predicts that he will be asked, 'What are you really doing, erecting an ideal or knocking one down?' Here he anticipates the most common charge made against him and his followers. 'When you have cleared the work of these false ideals, nothing will be left. You can only destroy and never affirm. You are irresponsible in a destructive way (and hence must be ignored, accused, punished for your adventurism).' Nietzsche responds with a counter-charge:

> But have you ever asked yourselves sufficiently how much the erection of every ideal on earth has cost? How much reality has had to be misunderstood and slandered, how many lies had to be sanctified ...? If a temple is to be erected *a temple must be destroyed*: that is the law – let anyone who can show me a case in which it is not fulfilled!

I take Nietzsche to say here that every ethic is destructive in the act of being constructive and that every ethic subjugates admirable possibilities in the world and the self to maintain itself. Most ethics deny the element of destruction and subjugation within them. They shroud it in a cloud of meta-idealism: the will of God, the telos of history, the dictates of reason, the law of nature, the general will. Nietzsche seeks an ethic which can be adopted while affirming the necessary element of destruction and subjugation in it. He seeks a brave ethic (Connolly, 1988, p. 160).

It is one of the contentions of this chapter that all the terminology currently used around the concept of nation and/or processes of nation-building has specifically contemporary meanings which are historical products. Particularly, they are the product of the socio-political, economic and philosophical events which took place from the end of the eighteenth century through the nineteenth century up to the present time.[2]

The semantic changes in key terms which have taken place through time do not reflect a dramatic shift *per se*, rather, new meanings are incorporated and emphasized against the previous ones. Repetition of the new meanings within the new contexts and the claim that these are the traditional[3] understandings of the terms according to historical records will freeze the new meaning. The new meaning will be thus transformed into the true traditional meaning and projected backwards in time. The interpretation of the past will therefore be bound from this point in time onwards by the 'new' traditional understanding.[4]

The material expression of nationality, of being a national, is the institution of citizenship. The term citizen, in its modern meaning,[5] refers to the individual participating in the community (nation), by taking an active role (for example, voting and standing for elections, paying taxes, getting involved with pressure groups, going to war, etc.) to ensure the viability of the social organization (the nation-state). Citizenship also implies that the community (the nation-state) will fulfil its duties such as ensuring the protection – physical and/or material – and the well-being of its members.

Thus, citizenship seems an unproblematic term. However, citizenship in its modern understanding was first articulated and enforced during and after the French Revolution. It was then that the equivalence of citizen and national took place, and then when this identification of terms and concepts was put in direct relationship with the state – specifically with the newly established nation-state. It was the government of the new French nation-state which established for the first time (and in line with the idea of citizenship derived from Roman Law particularly as interpreted during the Imperial era[6]) a clear criterion for citizenship which was inclusive in as much as it did not account for ethnic, religious, social, economic or linguistic considerations,[7] or as Brubaker states (1992, p. 35):

> Modern national citizenship was an invention of the French Revolution. The formal delimitation of the citizenry; the establishment of civil equality, entailing shared rights; ... the articulation of the doctrine of national sovereignty and of the link between citizenship and nationhood; the substitution of immediate, direct relations between the citizen and the state for the mediated, indirect relations characteristic of the ancien régime. This model of national citizenship ... showed the rest of the world 'the image of its own future'.

Some other Western European states, for example, the United Kingdom of Great Britain and Ireland, Spain or Portugal, although unified states, did not introduce the concept of citizenship until the turn of the century, at the earliest.[8]

At the same time that both terms, that is, citizen and national, were being assimilated, developments were taking place in the study of the natural sciences[9] and particularly within zoology. These developments wrongly appropriated by sociological and political theorists were translated into the identification of nations with specific ethnic groups. Given that ethnic group was synonymous with race, racist discourses and behaviour within society were able to become institutionalized and academically blessed. This development occurred in both Germany and Italy but also certainly in other Western European countries. The homogeneity of populations was being claimed: as a legitimizing element of the *de facto* situation;[10] or as the inevitable progression towards modernity and civilization.

> Nobody can suppose that it is not more beneficial to a Breton, or a Basque of French Navarre, to be brought into the current of the ideas and feelings of a highly civilised and cultivated people – to be a member of the French nationality, admitted on equal terms to all the privileges of French citizenship, sharing the advantages of French protection and the dignity of French power – than to sulk on his own rocks, the half-savage relic of past times, revolving in his own little mental orbit, without participation or interest in the general movement of the world. The same remark applies to the Welshman or the Scottish Highlander as members of the British nation. Whatever really tends to the admixture of nationalities, and the blending of their attributes and peculiarities in a common union, is a benefit to the human race.
>
> (Mill, 1861, p. 44)

This identification of an ethnic group or a race with a nation was heavily criticized by Ernest Renan in 1882 in his lecture 'What is a nation?' He considered it a fictitious exercise for any given individual or society to claim descent from one or another ethnic group. He considered this an abuse and misuse of the term 'race' which he said should be treated as an historical term (today it would be called a social construction) for he understood there was only one race, that is, the human race, thus negating any use whatsoever of the term to biology:[11]

> Ethnographic considerations have had nothing to do with the constitution of modern nations. ... The truth is that there are no pure races and to base politics on ethnographic analysis is to rest it on a chimera. The noblest countries ... are those whose blood is most mixed. Is Germany an exception in this regard? ... What an illusion! ... The primitive Aryan, Semitic and Turanian groups were not of a piece physiologically. These groupings are historical events that took place in a particular era,

let's say fifteen or twenty thousand years ago, whereas the zoological
origins of humanity are lost in impenetrable gloom ... Race, as we historians understand it, is something that is made and unmade.

(Renan, 1882, in Woolf, 1996, pp. 53–4)

The term state and the term nation have been equated ever since the
French Revolution. The state was considered the representative of the
nation. The nation was the last and first recipient of authority. The nation
was the citizens.[12] Contemporary discourses do not offer a single definition of the term nation. In fact, the term has been modified to adjust it to
the different theories constructed around the term nationalism, and thus, it
is being (re)defined accordingly.

The basic mainstream theories could be arranged in four categories,
namely: modernists, primordialists, perennialists, and ethnicists or possibilists. The modernists' basic underlying assumption is that modernity pre-
dates nationalism, therefore the nation, as we understand it today, is also a
modern phenomenon. Primordialists, on the other hand, claim that nationalism pre-dates modernity, therefore nation is a pre-modern entity.
Furthermore, they argue that the nation is the natural unit of history.
Perennialists also argue that nationalism pre-dates modernity and so does
the idea of the nation. However, they do not consider the nation to be a
natural property of human beings but rather the result of social construction deriving from certain socio-economic and/or political factors. Finally,
the possibilists or ethnicists claim that the phenomenon of nationalism is a
modern one while the nation is pre-modern in its character and existence.
The nation is traced back through ideas of ethnicity.[13]

The three cases, that is Germany, Italy and the EU, were (and still are)
confronted with the question of the nation. It is widely accepted that the
EU is not a nation,[14] while Germany and Italy are and were nations. This
debate does not concern itself with whether or not Germany and Italy are
nations today.[15] However, it is an important element in this debate to
assess whether they were nations or not in the nineteenth century.

Anderson (1991) offers a very interesting account in which the nation as
an absolute, outside the perceptions and the imaginations of the people,
does not exist. Taking Anderson's understanding of the imagined community, it could be said that the nation is a construction, the product of socio-
economic and political events which seek legitimization in the past and
which will justify its existence into the future, through the purposefully
directed actions of the present. In other words, although it is assumed
today that Germany and Italy are nations, it seems quite reasonable to

argue that this was not a unanimous or hegemonic position in the nineteenth century. Furthermore, disputes over the representation of the nation were common and constant, even among those who thought in terms of the Italian or the German nation. Once the unification of the state was achieved these disputes did not die away, rather the battle for accessing the sphere of decision-making and having a say in the way the nation was being defined (for example, criteria for citizenship, religious affinity of the state, official language) became fiercer.[16] The same disputes are taking place within the EU. Although it has been widely stated that the EU is not a nation, strong disagreements over the nature, role and shape of the EU arise time and again.[17]

In Germany and Italy the liberal party, specifically in the years prior to unification, became the national symbol. The identification of liberal ideology, industrial capitalism and the idea of the nation and its emancipation became part of one and the same aim. All these elements were understood as inherently related to each other and intrinsically linked to modernization and progress.

In the EU there is not an available or suitable discourse which will bring these elements together. On the contrary the opposition of the different regions (nation-states), as they perceive European policies as clashing with their interests, has created a propitious environment for the brewing of 'new', 'old' nationalisms. This contemporary situation can be compared to the opposition and discontent that individual states were experiencing as they became confronted with the new 'national' parliaments and institutions.[18]

These discourses are in fact shaping and creating the identity which the EU might come to have. This is a very important debate because the process of the construction of identities is a process of exclusion, limitation and demarcation.[19] It is a process of allocation of power as certain definitions[20] become settled and take on the appearance of truth while others vanish from the agenda and, therefore, from public discourses and, borrowing C. W. Mills' terminology (1959),[21] from the social imagination. In a similar fashion but focusing on the aspect of temporality, Bhabha[22] argues (1990, p. 292) that:

> The focus on temporality ... provides a perspective on the disjunctive forms of representation that signify a people, a nation, or a national culture ... It is the mark of the ambivalence of the nation as a narrative strategy – and an apparatus of power – that it produces a continual slippage into analogous, even metonymic, categories, like that of people, minorities, or 'cultural difference' that continually overlap in the act of writing the nation.

This process of delimitation and exclusion is one that can also be traced in the processes of nation-building in Germany and Italy in the nineteenth century.

Therefore, this nineteenth-century debate, which was one of the discourses enmeshing the nationalist claims in Italy and Germany, is similar to the debate which has sprung up in relation to the EU. The ideas and terminology used to explain and analyse processes of nation-building have been transferred to the debate about the EU. Thus primordialists, modernists and ethnicists have all had their say on the feasibility of the EU project. Primordialists, perennialists, or ethnicists, on the one hand, will argue the impossibility of the EU because there is no 'mythomoteur' (Smith, 1986, p. 15) which will give 'sense and cohesion' to the group. On the other hand, they will argue that Germany and Italy (as much as any other nation-state) were impelled to become nation-states, because their ethnicity was the driving force behind their history and destiny.[23]

It is contended here that the Germany and Italy of the nineteenth century were also political, ethnic and linguistic *impossibilities*. The ethnic, religious, social, historical and economic differences within and among the populations of Germany and Italy have been pushed aside in sociohistorical accounts.[24] Overlooking these differences and, therefore, the strategies used to overcome them prevents us from explaining the process and/or understanding it. Thus, the only path left open to us appears to be an examination of the phenomenon of state-formation and nation-building upon the criteria provided by nationalist ideology. This is, for example, what Riall (1994, p. 62) seems to be advocating:

> It is in this way that the revisionist historiography of the past two decades cannot fully explain the process of national unification. In order to understand why Italian liberals, however impractical their programme and however unrepresentative they were of society at large, were still able to create an entirely different impression of themselves, we need to look elsewhere. Paradoxically, this search leads us right back to a discussion of the political, ideological and emotional appeal of unitary nationalism.[25]

The problem with this approach is its tautological character. In other words, because it seems that there is not a rational explanation for an historical event – that is the nation-state, or specifically the unification of Germany and Italy – the rationale is found in the emotional appeal of nationalism. However, as Breuilly (1993, p. 96) has stated:

> Nationalism was more important as a product than as a cause of national unification ... Nationalism had little popular appeal ... These severe

limitations ... have been obscured by the success of unification. Success itself seems to point to the central importance of nationalism.

Cultural nationalism, in both Germany and Italy, is one of the features which preceded the material realization of the nation-state. These cultural nationalisms espoused a particular version of the nation, which did not represent the material reality. They were the combination of idealized visions of bygone days with idealized versions of a 'brighter' future. However, until the national-liberal movement put these cultural images into a context (the material reality of the world of politics and economics) they were dismissed by the established élite groups, and sometimes by the very people which the advocates of nationalism claimed to represent.[26]

In the case of the EU there are also cultural versions and visions of Europe which do not represent the material reality lived by the European citizens. Cultural 'europeism' is a phenomenon which started taking shape as early as the end of the eighteenth century,[27] for example in Kant's 'Towards Eternal Peace'. Furthermore, the nineteenth century in Europe, depicted as the era of nationalism, also saw the birth of the idea of Europe enriched as a federation of nations. In fact, it was in the nineteenth century that the idea of Europe materialized as an historical entity. Romantic ideas about the nation were adding extra impetus to the quest for the development of industrial capitalism and the creation of a rational and efficient macro-social organization. As the nations were condensing into historical entities so, simultaneously, was the idea of Europe[28] materializing as an historical entity.

In our three cases there has never been a unanimous view of what the nation is. In Germany, liberal-nationalist interpretations were divided between *kleindeustch/grossdeustch*, historical constructions – produced as a result of the different political spheres of influence. Interpretations were also divided along religious lines (Jewish/Catholic/Protestant/secular Germany), with the 'ghost' of the 'Holy Roman Empire of the German Nation' ever present in thoughts and minds. They were deeply divided by the different traditions and dialects of the individual states. There was also the highly significant division between rural and urban life,[29] where people had clearly distinct perceptions of their particular environment and of their place within their communities and within the world.[30] Last but not least there was the division between literate and illiterate groups.

In the case of Italy it is evident that there were divisions between individual states. There were not only linguistic distinctions but also differences arising from historical political divisions of the territories between local and distant powers, which also shaped the potential construction of different 'Italies' (Candeloro, 1968). The religious differences in Italy (although considered today a Catholic country) were also evident. The Catholic/Jewish/secular Italy[31] gave another set of parameters within which the national parliament had to function and create definitions. The rural and urban divide was not only highly significant in the nineteenth century but remains so; it has been claimed not only to be a local division but, further than that, it has been turned into a geographical-ethnic division within the newly created nation-state.[32]

The EU presents all of these elements. There are linguistic divisions. There are religious divisions. There is the rural and urban divide, which, although it is not as sharp as in the nineteenth century, has given rise to something similar, namely the distinction between industrialized and backward areas. The division between literate/illiterate is considered of little broad significance today, but a contemporary dichotomy exists between graduates and non-graduates.[33] Furthermore, there are distinctions based upon skin-colour within the EU.

There are similarities in the process of identity formation for the three cases. There are four elements or areas which are going to be examined in some detail. These areas are:

1. The absence of a common institution or: how to construct a common institution.
2. The role of the *state*.[34]
3. The attitude of the individual states.
4. The issue of citizenship.

First, none of the cases could/can rely on a common institution in the form of a unified or centralized *state*, despite claims of historical precedents.[35] The choice of one particular past over another is not based upon the truth of one or upon the falsehood of another, but it rather confirms that one version better serves – or reflects – the needs and interests of 'powerful' groups within the state apparatus.

Second, the centralization of the state offered/offers the possibility for the creation of a common identity either in national or European terms. The state is considered from that point on as the medium through which individuals relate to each other. The semantic change in the word citizen has reflected and embodied the shift in the established relationship between members of a community, usually a city, to a direct link with the state. The state became the only legitimate entity available as the public sphere widened[36] and the churches, guilds, cities, universities and rural communities were forced to move to the rhythm of modern times, into extinction ... or metamorphosis.[37]

Furthermore, there is not a single element or set of elements – cultural or linguistic – strong enough to permeate the whole society across the claimed territory. Regarding the German and Italian cases, dialects have become relegated from the status of 'proper' languages. This aspect could be interpreted as a sign of the awareness displayed by nineteenth-century Italian and German politicians and bureaucrats alike, regarding the importance to be placed on homogeneous characteristics as criteria to define the nation. This can be described as a conscious process of social engineering.

The distinction between dialect and language is very tenuous.[38] Primarily, the distinction results from a combination of socio-political and economic forces, and is not based on some supposed quality of the 'high language' over the dialect. The distinction is historically based and therefore socially constructed. Furthermore, the existence of a centralized or unified state which promotes and adopts a particular dialect as the official language 'smoothes' the path to acceptance of that particular dialect as the *language of the nation.* The choice made will usually advantage (socially, politically, economically, etc.) a particular group within the society. This process will seem to start the shaping of the 'national identity' but will help to create a bond, a link, an identification between the state and this particular group which, although referred to as an emotional or cultural bond, is clearly based in material advantages for some particular group or groups.[39]

When language has been made a priority for the consolidation of the state, it will normally be used to define the category of national, thus national identity will also be defined in terms of the language used. This category – 'language used' – and specifically the way it is applied, links the private and public realms, breaking the distinction between what is the individuals' realm and what is the state's realm.[40] In other words the correlation between a specific dialect and the state links the members of the group(s) speaking that dialect to the state in a particular fashion, different from other groups within that state. Because the state has chosen one particular dialect instead of another, the state (or the dominant group(s) within it) is taking the leading role in the construction of identities, and in this particular case of the national identity. In this sense it is significant that both Germany and Italy have adopted only one language or dialect:

> In one part of Italy, Piedmont, Italian was barely known; either French or the local dialect were used. For the uneducated, Italy and the Italian language meant nothing. They spoke dialects incomprehensible to people from other parts of the peninsula.
>
> (Beales, 1981, p. 24)

Regarding the EU the strategy has been to make official all the 'national languages'. This strategy, while publicly establishing a balance among all the members and offering a formal environment of equality, clearly differs from the strategy used in the German and Italian cases. Furthermore, this strategy does not seem to provide the EU with any single language which could be presented as an element for identity formation.

Third, most of the individual states opposed/oppose the centralization/unification of the *state*. This opposition was/is translated into expressions of nationalism (EU) or patriotism[41] (in the Germany and Italy cases). They each justified and legitimized this opposition as their right to self-defence from interference and meddling with their sovereignty. For example, in the German case, according to John (1990) the debate between *kleindeustch* and *grossdeustch*[42] was widespread and anti-nationalist associations were appearing everywhere. However, Hanover, among the northern states, seemed to be the only one where this type of association had any success at all. The presence of these anti-nationalist associations was apparently related to a feeling of mistrust of Prussia's government and politics. In Hanover, the liberal-nationalists, while arguing for political unity, were strongly opposed to any form of centralization. In other words, it seems that nationalists were, at the 'national level', advocating and supporting the option of a federation of states, while at the level of the individual states they were working towards a centralized state in the modern sense. In the Italian case the resistance of 'local' élite groups to the centralization and unification of the state is notorious, as Riall (1994, p. 60), for example, has noted.[43]

It would be useful to mention that, by this stage, the administrative and territorial structure and organization of an important number of the individual states had adopted the Napoleonic Code and had changed dramatically. The Congress of Vienna did not counteract this development but indirectly supported them instead by the strategic device known as 'nondecision' making (Bachrach and Baratz, 1970, pp. 43–51). In other words, the Congress of Vienna gave a legitimized character to the territorial and political divisions established during the Napoleonic period. In the German case, the weaknesses of the Confederation were readily used by the individual states to strengthen themselves.

> These states ... emerged as relatively strong political units. ... Territorially, ... they were enlarged ... . Rulers enjoyed full sovereignty as well as actual power. Partly as a result of, and partly in response to, the exigencies of the Napoleonic period, in many states the administrative and legal systems had been reformed and made more efficient ... many such

enlarged states ... built up powerful local myths and traditions, inventing and sustaining a strong regional particularism which would by no means be easily submerged in a united Germany.

(Fulbrook, 1996, p. 103)

There is evidence that this was also the case in Italy, although this statement needs to be qualified because, while it is true that the administrative structures and the territorial divisions were hardly modified, the power of the rulers of the individual states in the Italian Peninsula was very much dependent upon external forces and their particular socio-economic and political interests:

> the map of Restoration Italy superficially appeared similar to that of the eighteenth century ... Balance-of-power politics signified strengthening the victorious allies and the small countries ringing France. In Italy, this meant handing over Genoa to Piedmont and Venice to Austria. These changes violated 'legitimacy', one of the Congress of Vienna's vaunted watchwords, since both republics had a centuries-long history. The Congress's other precept, 'compensation', strengthened Austria's control of the peninsula.
>
> (Di Scala, 1995, pp. 44–5)

The EU also provides an example of this situation. The member states are very content to play with and around the political and economic institutions of the EU insofar as they can prioritize their own interests:

> Since the outbreak of the dispute Greece has blocked the flow of European Union funds to Turkey, which it would have been eligible to receive under its customs union with the bloc. Pangalos insinuated that Greece has no intention of lifting its blockade so long as the issue remains open. 'I am waiting to see this progress and I think the EU should also wait before funding Turkey in any way,' he said.[44]

However, they will readily use any collision of interests within the European Commission to make the claim that the principle of sovereignty is being violated:

> The greatest fear of a diminution of (Westminster) parliamentary sovereignty is to be found at or near the political core of the UK: those who feel that they have some input into the power structure fear losing all or part of it ... so it is also true in the debate on 'ever closer union' within the EC ... To try to counteract this image, Harold Macmillan argued that, in time of crisis: 'We British will certainly be prepared to accept merger of sovereignty in practice if not in principle ... Britain might be

united in a fit of absence of mind or by a series of improvisations which would be particularly gratifying to my countrymen.'

(Stephenson, 1993, pp. 239–49)

The problem of how to successfully (re)construct identities in this situation is obvious: how can individuals' expectations, duties and rights be derived from more than one single entity?

Calhoun (1994, p. 12) tries to understand this phenomenon, or give an answer to this situation using Cascardi's work. Thus he argues:

> In the modern era, identity is always constructed and situated in a field and amid a flow of contending cultural discourses. In Cascardi's terms, 'The modern subject is defined by its insertion into a series of separate value-spheres, each one of which tends to exclude or attempts to assert its priority over the rest.' ... And as Cascardi goes on to argue, 'The tension and even incommensurability among the various discourses – at the extreme where they claim autonomy – appears not just as an "external" difficulty for individuals but as a series of contradictions within the "subject-self".'

A process of overlapping spheres takes place and each of these entities asks from the person absolute loyalty and commitment. In the case of Germany and Italy the creation of a common national identity was further stretched by the rapid development of the industrial and agrarian forms of capitalism. The universality of the nationalist claims (based in deep contradictions[45]) have to be broken down into particular terms. In other words, and from a practical point of view, only a narrow definition of the nation could succeed. The successful definition shapes the national identity and thus sets the boundaries. The importance given to the protection of these boundaries varies through time and according to circumstances. It seems that there is a correlation between economic crisis and/or dramatic changes in the socio-economic fabric of any given society(ies) and the emotional appeal to protect *these* boundaries.

The discourses which popularized the term 'Fortress Europe' during a period of great economic crisis and social apprehension exhibit this tendency perfectly. This phrase highlights the defensive character of an organization even before it has been fully accepted; and it also highlights the strong voluntaristic intention to establish an entity clearly defined in territorial, economic, social and political terms.

In the three cases the legal approach to the concept of citizenship has proved highly problematic. In the EU case the first implication of citizenship of the Union has been the acquisition of double nationality. As

Elspeth Guild (1996, pp. 39–46) has noted, it seems very surprising that this fact has not provoked a massive outcry from all the states within the Union given their common position on the issue of double nationality. The EU has been built around four fundamental freedoms; free movement of persons, goods, services and capital. With the establishment of the legal concept of 'citizenship of the Union' these four freedoms have been directly linked to the Union and therefore, this link has established a direct and personal relation between the individuals and the EU. Previously, these rights were granted to the citizens of member states, not to the persons on an individual basis. Today the member states are no longer a mediatory power between the nominal freedoms and the right to exercise them.[46] Maybe the appropriate question here should be: What does it really mean to be a European citizen?

Prior to the French Revolution the link between peasant (not considered individually) and the monarchy (the material representation of the state and the nation) was mediated by the feudal lords. After the Revolution the link became individual and personalized. Each individual became a citizen in a direct connection to the state.

In the German and Italian case the individual states, as action and reaction to the influence of the French Revolution and the Napoleonic period, had in some cases begun and in other cases accelerated the process of construction of a modern centralized state. These states attempted to enforce their claims of sovereignty within the territories upon which they laid their claims. Thus, individual states started the implementation of policies geared toward mass taxation and mass conscription. These elements (or needs, from the point of view of the modern state) imply a pressure (real or imaginary) to comply with the needs of modern times in order to survive, in a highly changeable economic environment, and in an environment of shifting political alliances and unclear social roles. These two elements implied, borrowing Breuilly's terminology, state-wide citizenship. However, 'there was little incentive for states, to define who were their citizens' (Breuilly, 1997).

A case geared to explain this inhibition can be made when it is taken into account that the concept of citizenship was not alien to eighteenth- and nineteenth-century populations. What was alien to them was the establishment of a direct relationship between the individual and the state, in general, and/or the individual and the national-state, in particular. Loyalties were focused upon the communities because privileges, means of living, social prestige and fortune derived from the fact that any given Bürger existed because of the community and the community existed because of the citizens. The 'unification' meant that, on the one hand, every inhabitant of the territory claimed was to become a citizen. On the other hand, previous citizens now held a double citizenship. National citizenship demanded mass conscription and mass taxation. 'National citizenship' did not seem to offer an immediate benefit to the majority of the population, but it rather meant, at least in many cases, the loss of their identities.[47]

However, not all the groups in the society were reluctant to accept the idea of a state-wide citizenship. The advantages for groups such as large merchants and small pedlars, civil servants, intellectuals and free professionals seem quite obvious. These groups did not need the holistic, static understanding of citizenship that home towns (and cities to a certain extent[48]) proffered in order to acquire identity, social prestige or the means of livelihood; in fact their major common characteristic was movement. Social mobility, territorial mobility, economic mobility ... Movement and the ability to deal in, and adapt to, the insecurity of a market, a society or any particular circumstance was a condition upon which these groups counted to help them to adapt to the accelerated environmental changes that industrial capitalism, liberal ideology and the dismantling of the era of the great powers had brought about.

The EU also has shown a great deal of reluctance to define who its citizens are. It is interesting to speculate how and why this situation has come about given the availability of well-documented experience from around the world since the nineteenth century – and before. Besides obvious politico-economic considerations which affect the social legitimization of established power structures at the national level it is interesting to look again at the Italian and German examples from the nineteenth century. Exactly as in the nineteenth century, contemporary individuals are not unfamiliar with the term citizenship – and people are equally unclear about its implications: what does it mean to be a member of Europe?

The capitalist system has created an economic environment which is changeable and unstable. The economic situation together with a general mistrust of, and between, politico-economic élites has fomented an atmosphere in which shifting political alliances and unclear social roles (defined contemporaneously in terms of gender, class, culture, skin colour, etc.) pervade all the societies of the member states of the EU.

As mentioned above the links between each individual, each citizen, and the Union itself have now become forged:

> There is nothing inherently difficult nor indeed particularly uncommon about an expansion of loyalty ... the commonest experience ... has been the growth over time of the level of loyalty by the growth through

accretion of the state. Venetians and Neopolitans have over the generations been transformed into faithful Italians.

(Heater, 1990, p. 196)

And yet, although Italy and Germany achieved a successful political unification, the social unification – the effort to create a common (self-evident) identity – remains a work in progress; the fragility of such arrangements can easily be seen: North/South Italy; East/West Germany (even in other countries with older national traditions: Flemish/Wallonian Belgium; England/Scotland/Great Britain; Gallego/Castellano Spain, etc.) are all examples where the lack of a sense of social unity creates pressure for political redefinition. If the EU becomes a successful political union it is clear that any social unification will demand the passing of more than one generation to become realized.[49]

NOTES

1. I wish to thank both Professor M. Fulbrook and Mr P. Wheadon for their encouragement, advice and support.
2. See, for example, Greenfeld (1992), where in the introduction (pp. 4–9) she explains the semantic change of the term nation as an historical product; Held (1989) especially Chapter 7 in which citizenship is presented as an historical process; Reynolds (1994). See also, van Gunsteren and Dahrendorf both in van Steenbergen (1994). These articles show how terms, so widely used today in academic and popular discourses alike, have changed their semantic meaning. Furthermore the socio-economic and political reality that these semantic changes may reflect go far beyond mere linguisitc games. See finally Brubaker (1992).
3. It would be useful to bear in mind that 'the legal historian T. F. T. Plucknett, once showed that the medieval term, "custom from time immemorial" need only mean 21 years'. Quoted in 'A Critique of Recent Trends in the Social History of "Leisure" ' by Stedman Jones (p. 46) in Cohen and Scull (1985).
4. For more on this debate see for example: Williamson (1978); Fowler (1996); Althusser (1971).
5. In its modern meaning citizenship excluded a wide range of the people. The contemporary understanding continues to ostracize large numbers of the community and/or makes it very difficult for certain groups to acquire the full status of citizenship. Nevertheless, certain groups previously excluded (for example, women, workers) have been included. The liberal/modern meaning of citizenship bears a significant number of contradictions. Nineteenth-century political theorists were not unaware of these problems. Some of them were trying to combat the deep contradictions embedded in

the liberals' demands for equality. Among these I would like to mention Dittmar's work. She worked within the liberal framework and, using the liberal terminology, highlights blatant cases of inequality which could not be sustained if the liberal premises were going to be taken seriously. Her work compared the oppression that Jews and women, alike, were suffering in the name of 'God' and of 'liberalism'. For more on her work see, Herzog (1990); also, Vogel (1994).

6.   See Nicolet (1993) and Hobsbawm (1992).

7.   On this see, for example, Renan (1996).

8.   By way of contrast, the terminology used in the United Kingdom of Great Britain and Ireland was 'subject and crown'. This terminology remained untouched and pervaded the legal and popular discourses until the 1970s. It was the Immigration Act (1971) and the accession of the UK to the EEC and the EAEC (1972) that offered an opportunity for a change in the terminology. Switzerland, regarded as a highly democratic country, did not 'grant' full citizenship to women until 1973.

9.   The development of the natural sciences will not have any value *per se* if the philosophical framework is ignored. Therefore, this development ought to be put into its historical-philosophical context; understood as modernity, enlightenment. This development or, more accurately, this change in the way humans and societies were perceiving and understanding their environment assumes a set of theoretical premises which, although questioned at the time they were formulated, have been accepted as absolutes.

> Hume's epistemological position is ... the distinction between 'impressions' and 'ideas'. ... knowledge about the world as it really 'is' can be gained only from the realm of immediate sense experience or 'impressions'. All other cognitive activity ... is relegated to the retrospective/theoretical realm of 'ideas'. This 'idea' realm does not *correspond* with reality *per se*, simple because as an abstract category it does not correspond with what actually (physically) exists in the universe. ... Hume's scepticism concerning the inherent inadequacies of this approach is also of significance here. This scepticism led Hume to a series of conclusions about all empiricist-based thinking that has immediate relevance for any discussion on the positivist-Realism ... This is primarily because Hume's major conclusion was that empiricist-based claims for real knowledge cannot be defended, *except in metaphysical terms*.
>
> (George, 1994, pp. 51–2) (emphasis in original)

See, also: Bauman (1991); Foucault (1988); Hayek (1994); van Loon (1930); Montalenti (1989).

10.   '*De facto*' situation refers to the combination of several elements such as the political institutions, the socio-economic arrangements, etc.

11.   Thom (1990). Here Thom puts Renan's lecture in its particular historico-political context, that is within the philosophical and political debate that took place in nineteenth-century Europe, in general, and France in particular.

12.   On this see, for example, Smelser and Warner (1982); also Abendroth and Lenk (1971).

13.   I am grateful to T. Malakos for suggesting this classification.

14.   For example Habermas (1994) p. 29.

15. Nevertheless, it could be suggested that Germany and Italy are today more of a nation-state than, let us say, Great Britain, Spain or Portugal ever were or probably will be.

16. For discussions on this, see, for example, Grew (1963); Randeraad (1993); Greenfeld (1992); Blackbourn and Eley (1984); Woolf (1996); Fulbrook (1993); Riall (1994); Dickie (1992); Breuilly (1993); and, by the same author, 'The National Idea in Modern German History', forthcoming in Fulbrook.

17. See, for example, Wederveen Pietersen (1991); Daalder (1990); Wilson and Van der Dussen (1995).

18. See, for example, Randeraad (1993); Riall (1993, 1994).

19. See, for example *Race and Class*, Vol. 32, No. 3, 1991; Hylland Eriksen (1993); Anthias and Yuval-Davis (1992); Castles and Miller (1993); Winkler (1993).

20. See Gordon (1980); Bachrach and Baratz (1970); Lukes (1974, 1986).

21. Here I am making reference to Mills' theory as developed in his work *The Sociological Imagination*. The implication of this theory is that only what is discussed within society by society is real.

22. It should be noted that Bhabha does not talk about the EU; his article concentrates on the nation-state.

23. Jews have been taken as an example of members of an ethnic group who have managed after a long struggle to acquire a state of their own. This statement gives rise to important questions about the way in which Jewish people have been defined and characterized. It is assumed that all the followers of the Jewish faith have had the same experiences, that their myths and symbols are necessarily the same, while ignoring, however, that the Jewish people are divided by, among other things, the interpretation of basic aspects of the faith, in the same way that Christians have different dogmas and lines of interpretation.

> One instance of this transformation of the past occurs in a letter written against Zionism by an orthodox rabbi of Eastern Europe in 1900. In this letter the Dzikover Rebbe contrasts the traditional view which the community of Israel had of itself, and the new nationalist interpretation of the Jews' past ... and this letter thus exhibits in a clear and striking manner the operations of nationalist historiography, as well as the traditional interpretation which it has challenged. 'For our many sins,' writes the Rebbe, 'strangers have risen to pasture the holy flock, men who say that the people of Israel should be clothed in secular nationalism, a nation like all other nations, that Judaism rests on three things, national feeling, the land and the language, and that national feeling is the most praiseworthy element in the brew and the most effective in preserving Judaism, while the observance of the Torah and the commandments is a private matter depending on the inclination of each individual. May the Lord rebuke these evil men and may He who chooseth Jerusalem seal their mouths.' ... In Zionism, Judaism ceases to be the raison d'être of the Jew, and becomes instead, a product of Jewish national consciousness.
>
> (Kedourie, 1994, p. 51)

24. It should be noted that partial constructions of 'Otherness' had happened in both areas under discussion. For example, the North/South discourse in Italy

or the Northern Confederation/Southern states in Germany. However, the fact remains that the Italianness of a Neapolitan or the Germanness of a Bavarian were not in question.

25. I should point out that I may have misunderstood Riall's intention here as, overall, the argument she presents in this work is highly coherent.

26. See, for example, Breuilly (1993); Riall (1993, 1994); James (1990); Applegate (1990); Davis (1991).

27. There is, in fact, evidence that the idea of a unified Europe goes as far back in time as the fourteenth century. See for example, Duroselle (1957). Obviously, as with the historical accounts of the existence of different nations from time immemorial, one should be cautious as to the actual meaning behind the concept of a European alliance. Common sense suggests, as with the concept of nation, that the implications and understanding of the idea of Europe was not the same as contemporary accounts and/or descriptions of the European project in meaning or intention.

28. See, for example Wilson and van der Dussen (1995).

29. Special mention should be made here of the 'home towns' whose particularism shaped their similitudes, namely: all of them conformed to a pattern based on their functionality regarding the citizens' moral, economic, social and political well-being, and this aspect made them into a distinctive polity that separated them from the countryside or the cities. The countryside and the cities held, thus, a few aspects in common, especially when compared to the 'home towns'. For more on this subject see Walker (1971).

30. See for example Jarausch and Jones (1990); Mosse (1995).

31. There were also people of the Islamic faith: see Calisse (1928).

32. 'Revisionist' literature has pointed out that the *latifundi* was in fact the product or the result of the implementation of 'agricultural' capitalism all across the south of the Italian peninsula and not the remains of the 'feudal' system. On these debates see, for example, Riall (1994).

33. This dichotomy is opposite to the literate–illiterate division of the nineteenth century. People excluded from higher education tend to be isolated from the policy-making process and the agenda-setting mechanisms; possibilities for influencing politicians are limited both directly and indirectly, through poor access to networks and, not least, to academic discussions which influence policy decision-making.

34. By *state* should be understood the unified state, in other words, Germany, Italy and the EU. In the case of the EU the work is more hypothetical than factual in the sense that there is not a unified European state – in its contemporary understanding. By individual state should be understood all the political entities existing or, regarding the EU, the independent entities which exist.

35. Fulbrook (1996); Breuilly (1996); Wilson and van der Dussen (1995).

36. The French Revolution transformed the semantic meaning of the term public. The Public was understood as the nation. The Public was not any longer synonymous with the élite groups, that is nobility and high bourgeoisie. The meaning of the term Public shifted from 'what everyone can see' to 'what belongs to everyone'.

37. See for example, Habermas (1989); Meriggi and Schiera (1993).

38. The formal distinction between a 'dialect' and a 'language' is based upon several criteria, such as the production of printed material; the similitude of

grammatical constructions between the language and the dialect; and the possibility of understanding the dialect given the knowledge of the language, etc. My criticism is that all these criteria are fictitious. The difference between language and dialect is a political one with socio-economic implications for the populations. In Spain, for example, four *languages* have been officially recognized (Gallego, Vasco, Catalan and Castellano). Three of them are Latin dialects. The possibility of understanding these three languages through 'knowing' only one is very high. The grammatical differences are predominantly the result of the purposefully directed action of academics and politicians in the late eighteenth century and, in the nineteenth century, trying to legitimize language-based nationalist claims. In Italy only one official language has been recognized, 'Italian' as popularized by Dante; the rest of the languages are considered dialects. The same applies to the German case in which only one dialect has been officially recognized, 'High German' as popularized by Luther with his successful translation of the Bible into this particular 'vernacular dialect'.

39. See the critique by Vazquez-Montalbán (1996, p. 49) regarding the uses and abuses of nationalist ideas and concepts and their relationship to material advantanges.
40. See for example Habermas (1989).
41. These references to patriotism and nationalism should be understood as the material expression of the defence of 'local' interests. In other words, nationalism is used because the contemporary political division of the world is based on what has come to be known as the nation-state. Patriotism is used to express a similar political force, developed within the individual states, which was at work during the nineteenth century but whose aims were opposed to nationalist claims and interests.
42. This dichotomy is a shortcut to express two highly differentiated 'imagined communities'; two visualizations of the 'German nation' to be. Each of them was based upon a set of assumptions and 'ideas' about the role, shape and characteristics of a 'nation-state', in general, and the 'German nation-state' in particular.
43. Riall notes: 'It is clear that in many areas, the benefits of national unification or liberal government offered little incentive for the local elites to co-operate with the central authority'. See also Davis (1991).
44. Quoted from Reuters New Media (1996).
45. The French case offers definitions of nation and nation-state which are basically civic and secular. In that sense it provides the most all-embracing definitions and a broader understanding of both terms. However, even in this case, these definitions are based on exclusion and limited access. The French revolutionaries established the basic right to private property, removed feudal rights (for the nobility) and duties (for the peasants), but maintained the submission of women to men.

> The history of European marriage laws, from the Middle Ages until well into the twentieth century, records the extensive range and the tangible form of those special powers which allowed a husband to control body, property and freedom of his wife. ... The relationship between husband and wife mirrored the bonds between superior and inferior, ruler and

subject. While in the legal order of the medieval period all social relations conformed to principles of hierarchy and ascribed status, modern legal doctrines since the seventeenth century assumed the abstract equality of all individuals as legal agents. By the end of the nineteenth century, marriage alone (if we exempt the special case of paternal power over children) had retained some of the peculiar attributes of feudal bondage. It had remained a status relationship in which a husband, *qua* husband, had certain proprietory rights to the person of his wife. [... she was d]eprived of full property rights in her person and labour, of contractual capacities to the state and its law. Conversely, the husband's rights of command as well as his obligations of protection and representation had a distinctively public dimension. He was citizen and ruler in one person ... The tension between the general principle of equality and the perceived demands of order and stability has ... affected marriage in a particular way ... The predominant motif for committing women to the strictest rules of obedience and submission must be sought in the belief that only the coercive sanctions of the law will enable a husband to ensure the sexual fidelity of his wife. This assumption runs as a persistent theme through legal arguments from the seventeenth to the nineteenth centuries ... What persists ... is the ghost of women's independence and the spectre of anarchy that it evokes ... the preservation of civil society over time with the undisturbed passage of property along family lineages and, hence, the guaranteed certainty of biological fatherhood.

Vogel also quotes a passage from *Democracy in America* in which de Tocqueville clearly states the political and philosophical 'rationale' upon which 'domestic hierarchy' is intended to be legitimized:

Nor have the Americans ever supposed that democratic principles should undermine the husband's authority and make it doubtful who is in charge of the family ... Thus, then, while they have allowed the social inferiority of woman to continue, they have done everything to raise her morally and intellectually to the level of man. In this I think they have wonderfully understood the true conception of democratic progress.

(Vogel, 1994, pp. 80–1)

46. Guild (1996, p. 33): 'Such a division of meaning between the two terms national/citizen would appear to hold true for citizenship of the Union. As every national of a member state is a citizen of the Union, the quality of nationality appears to be the international law relationship of the individual as participant in a member state to the Union ... There is suddenly a direct link between the Union and the individual.'

47. In some instances the loss of 'identity' also meant the loss of livelihood. Examples of this can be found in Walker (1971).

48. Although it seems that cities were more open to external influences and movement than the home towns. In other words, they were more cosmopolitan.

49. Attention must be drawn here to the fact that Italy and Germany did not bestow national citizenship ahead of political unification as has been the case in the EU.

REFERENCES

Abendroth, W. and Lenk, K., *Introducción a la Ciencia Política* (Barcelona, Editorial Anagrama, 1971) (Original title: *Einführung in die politische Wissenschaft*, 1968).

Althusser, L., 'Ideology and Ideological State Apparatuses', in Althusser, L., *Lenin and Philosophy and other Essays* (London, New Left Books, 1971).

Anderson, B., *Imagined Communities: Reflections on the Origin and Spread of Nationalism* (London, Verso, 1991).

Anthias, F. and Yuval-Davis, N., *Racialised Boundaries* (London, Routledge, 1992).

Applegate, C., *A Nation of Provincials* (Berkeley, University of California Press, 1990).

Bachrach, P. and Baratz, M. S., *Power and Poverty: Theory and Practice* (New York, Oxford University Press, 1970).

Bauman, Z., *Modernity and Ambivalence* (Cambridge, Polity Press, 1991).

Beales, D., *The Risorgimento and the Unification of Italy* (London and New York, Longman, 1981) (First published by Allen and Unwin, 1971).

Bhabha, H. K., *Nation and Narration* (London, Routledge, 1990).

Birnbaum, P. and Katznelson, I. (eds), *Paths of Emancipation: Jews, States and Citizenship* (Princeton, Princeton University Press, 1995).

Blackbourn, D. and Eley, G., (eds), *The Peculiarities of German History. Bourgeois Society and Politics in 19th Century Germany* (Oxford, Oxford University Press, 1984).

Blockmans, W. and Genet, J. P. (eds), *Visions sur le développement des états européens: Théories et historiographies de l'état modern* (Actes du colloque, organisé par la fondation de la science et l'Ecole française de Rome, Rome 18–31 mars 1990).

Breuilly, J., *Nationalism and the State* (Manchester, Manchester University Press, 1993).

Breuilly, J., *The Formation of the First German Nation-State* (London, Macmillan, 1996).

Breuilly, J., 'The National Idea in Modern German History', in Fulbrook, M. (ed.), *German History since 1800* (London, Arnold, 1997).

Brubaker, R., *Citizenship and Nationhood in France and Germany* (Harvard, Harvard University Press, 1992).

Calhoun, C. (ed.), *Social Theory and the Politics of Identity* (Cambridge, MA, Blackwell, 1994).

Calisse, C., 'A History of Italian Law', in *Continental Legal History Series*, Vol. 8 (London, Murray, 1928) (Translated by Layton B. Register).

Candeloro, G., *Storia dell'Italia Moderna*, Vol. V (Milan, Feltrinelli, 1968).

Castles, S. and Miller, M. J., *The Age of Migration: International Population Movements in the Modern World* (London, Macmillan, 1993).

Cohen, S. and Scull, A., *Social Control and the State* (Oxford, Basil Blackwell, 1985).

Conolly, W. E., *Political Theory and Modernity* (Ithaca, New York, Basil Blackwell, 1988).

Daalder, H., 'Centres, Bureaucraties et le développement des Gouvernements democratiques éstables', in Blockmans, W. and Genet, J. P. (eds), *Visions sur le développement des états européens: Théories et historiographies de l'état modern* (Actes du colloque, organisé par la fondation de la science et l'Ecole française de Rome, Rome 18–31 mars 1990).

Davis, J. A., '1799: The Santafede and the Crisis of the Ancien Régime', in Davis, J. A. and Ginsborg, P. (eds), *Society and Politics in the Age of Risorgimento* (Cambridge, Cambridge University Press, 1991).

Dickie, J., 'A World at War: the Italian Army and Brigandage 1860–1870', *History Workshop Journal*, No. 33, 1992, pp. 1–25.

Di Scala, S. M., *Italy from Revolution to Republic: 1700 to the Present* (Boulder, Westview Press, 1995).

Duroselle, J. B., 'Europe as an Historical Concept', in Grove Haines, D. and Zeeland, van P. (eds), *European Integration* (Baltimore, The John's Hopkins Press, 1957), pp. 11–21.

Foucault, M., *Madness and Civilisation: a History of Insanity in the Age of Reason* (New York, Random, 1988).

Fowler, R., *Linguistic Criticism* (Oxford, Oxford University Press, 1996, 2nd edition).

Fulbrook, M. (ed.), *National Histories and European History* (London, UCL Press, 1993).

Fulbrook, M., *A Concise History of Germany* (Cambridge, Cambridge University Press, 1996) (updated version).

George, J., *Discourses on Global Politics. Critical (Re)Introduction to International Relations* (Boulder, Lynne Rienner, 1994).

Gordon, C. (ed.), *Foucault, Michel: Power–Knowledge: Selected Interviews and other Writings, 1972–1977* (Brighton, The Harvester Press, 1980).

Greenfeld, L., *Nationalism: Five Roads to Modernity* (Harvard, Harvard University Press, 1992).

Grew, R., *A Sterner Plan for Italian Unity* (Princeton, Princeton University Press, 1963).

Guild, E., 'The Legal Framework of Citizenship of the European Union', in Cesarani, D. and Fulbrook, M. (eds), *Citizenship, Nationality and Migration in Europe* (New York, Routledge, 1996).

Habermas, J., *The Structural Transformation of the Public Sphere: an Inquiry into a Category of Bourgeois Society* (Cambridge, Polity Press, 1989) (Translated by Burger, T. and Lawrence, F., Original title: *Strukturwandel der Öffentlichkeit*, 1962).

Habermas, J., 'Citizenship and National Identity', in Steenbergen, B. van, (ed.), *The Condition of Citizenship* (London, Sage, 1994), pp. 20–36.

Hayek, F. A., *The Road to Serfdom* (London, Routledge, 1994).

Heater, D., *Citizenship: the Civic Ideal in World History, Politics and Education* (London, Longman, 1990).

Held, D., *Political Theory and the Modern State: Essays on State, Power and Democracy* (Cambridge, Polity Press, 1989).

Herzog, D., 'Liberalism, Religious Dissent and Women's Rights', in Jarausch, K. H. and Jones, L. E. (eds), *In Search of a Liberal Germany* (New York, Berg, 1990), pp. 55–87.

Hobsbawm, E. J., *Nations and Nationalism since 1780: Programme, Myth, Reality* (Cambridge, Cambridge University Press, 1992, 2nd edition).

Hutchinson, J. and Smith, A. (eds), *Nationalism. Oxford Readers* (Oxford, Oxford University Press, 1994).

Hylland Eriksen, T., *Ethnicity and Nationalism* (New York, Pluto Press, 1993).

James, H., *A German Identity* (London, Weidenfeld and Nicolson, 1990) (Revised edition).

Jarausch, K. H. and Jones, L. E. (eds), *In Search of a Liberal Germany* (New York, Berg, 1990).

John, M., 'Associational Life and the Development of Liberalism in Hanover, 1848–1866', in Jarausch, K. H. and Jones, L. E. (eds), *In Search of a Liberal Germany* (New York, Berg, 1990), pp. 161–87.

Kay, D. and Miles, R., *Refugees or Migrant Workers?: European Volunteer Workers in Britain 1946–1951* (London, Routledge, 1992).

Kedourie, E., 'Nationalism and Self-determination', in Hutchinson, J. and Smith, A. (eds), *Nationalism. Oxford Readers* (Oxford, Oxford University Press, 1994), pp. 49–55.

Loon, H. van, *The Life and Times of Rembrandt van Rijn* (New York, Garden City Publishing Company, 1930, Originally published as *R. v. R. The Life and Times of Rembrandt van Rijn*, no date available for original publication).

Lukes, S., *Power: a Radical View* (London, Macmillan, 1974).

Lukes, S., *Power* (Oxford, Blackwell, 1986).

Meriggi, M. and Schiera, P. (eds), *Della Città alla Nazione* (Bologna, Il Mulino, 1993).

Mills, C. W., *The Sociological Imagination* (Harmondsworth, Pelican Books, 1959).

Mill, J. S., 'Nationality', in Woolf, S. (ed.), *Nationalism in Europe 1815 to the Present: a Reader* (London, Routledge, 1992 [1861]), pp. 40–8.

Montalenti, G., 'Il Concetto Biologico di Razza e le sua applicazione alla Specie Umana', in *Atti dei Convegni Lincei*, No. 84 (Rome, Accademia Nazionale dei Lincei, 1989), pp. 3–16.

Mosse, W. E. 'From "Schutzjuden to Deutsche Staatsbürger Jüdischen Glauben"': the Long and Bumpy Road of Jewish Emancipation in Germany', in Birnbaum, P. and Karznelson, I. (eds), *Paths of Emancipation: Jews, States and Citizenship* (Princeton, Princeton University Press, 1995), pp. 59–94.

Nicolet, C., 'Rome et les conceptions de l'état en France et en Allemagne au XIX siècle', in Blockmans, W. and Genet, J. P. (eds), *Visions sur le développement des états européens: Théories et historiographies de l'état modern* (Actes du colloque, organisé par la fondation de la science et l'Ecole française de Rome, Rome 18–31 mars 1990), pp. 17–44.

Randeraad, N., *Authority in Search of Liberty* (Amsterdam, Thesis Publishers, 1993).

Renan, E., 'What is a Nation?', in Woolf, S. (ed.), *Nationalism in Europe 1815 to the Present: a Reader* (London, Routledge, 1996), pp. 48–61.

Reuters New Media, *European Poltics* (Yahoo! Headlines through the Internet, 3 May 1996).

Reynolds, S., 'Regnal Sentiments and Medieval Communities', in Hutchinson, J. and Smith, A. (eds), *Nationalism* (Oxford, Oxford University Press, 1994), pp. 137–40.

Riall, L., 'Elite Resistance to State Formation: the Case of Italy', in Fulbrook, M. (ed.), *National Histories and European History* (London, UCL Press, 1993), pp. 46–69.

Riall, L., *The Italian Risorgimento* (London, Routledge, 1994).

Smelser, N. and Warner, R. (eds), *Teoría Sociológica. Análisis histórico y formal* (Madrid, Espasa Universidad, 1982) (Translated from the English by J. L. García-Molina, Original title: *Social Theory, Historical and Formal*, 1976).

Smith, A., *The Ethnic Origins of Nations* (Oxford, Basil Blackwell, 1986).

Soldatos, P., *Le Systéme institutionnel et politique des communautés européenes dans un monde en mutation* (Bruxelles, Bruylant, 1989).

Steenbergen, B. van, (ed.), *The Condition of Citizenship* (London, Sage, 1994).

Stephenson, J., 'Britain and Europe in the Later 20th Century: Identity, Peculiarity and Sovereignty', in Fulbrook, M. (ed.), *National Histories and European History* (London, UCL Press, 1993), pp. 230–55.

Thom, M., 'Tribes within Nations: the Ancient Germans and the History of France', in Bhabha, H. K. (ed.), *Nation and Narration* (London, Routledge, 1990), pp. 23–44.

Vázquez-Montalbán, M., 'Polonesa', *El País*, 18 June 1996, p. 49, Madrid.

Vogel, U., 'Marriage and the Boundaries of Citizenship', in Steenbergen, B. van (ed.), *The Condition of Citizenship* (London, Sage, 1994), pp. 76–90.

Walker, M., *German Home Towns: Community, State and General State 1648–1871* (London, Cornell University Press, 1971).

Wederveen Pietersen, J., 'Fictions of Europe', *Race and Class*, Vol. 32, No. 3, 1991, pp. 3–11.

Williamson, J., *Decoding Advertisements: Ideology and Meaning in Advertising* (London, Marion Boyars, 1978).

Wilson, K. and van der Dussen, J. (eds), *The History of the Idea of Europe: What is Europe?* (London, Routledge, 1995) (First published by the Open University, Milton Keynes, 1993).

Winkler, H. A., 'Nationalism and Nation-State in Germany', in Teich, M. and Porter, R. (eds), *The National Question in Europe in Historical Perspective* (Cambridge, Cambridge University Press, 1993), pp. 181–96.

Woolf, S. (ed.), *Nationalism in Europe 1815 to the Present: a Reader* (London, Routledge, 1996).

Part III
Historical and Cultural Perspectives

11 Poland, Post-Communism and the Nation-State

Edward Acton

The subject of this chapter concerns the prospect of Poland's post-communist transition and the future of the democratic nation-state. I want to set my remarks in the context of the long-term development of the nation-state in Europe. To do so I will begin by referring to a well-known essay on nationalism written by a nineteenth-century British historian, best known for the adage that 'Power tends to corrupt and absolute power corrupts absolutely' (Lord Acton, 1985, II, p. 383).

Lord Acton's essay (Lord Acton, 1985, I, pp. 409–34), published in 1862, provides plenty of food for thought. In it, he portrayed Poland's experience as the very source of modern nationalism. He traced what he called the 'theory of nationality' back to the partition of Poland in the late eighteenth century. This, he said, was the most revolutionary act of *ancien-régime* Europe. For the first time in history monarchs suppressed a great state and divided a whole nation among its enemies. They did so because the elective crown without royal blood meant they could never secure a permanent hold upon it by the conventional means of intermarriage and inheritance. The result of their act, however, was to convert 'a dormant right into an aspiration and a mere sentiment into a political claim'. Thenceforward, Acton continues, there was a nation demanding to be united to a state – a soul, as it were, wandering in search of a body in which to begin life over again. In other words, the Polish cause gave birth to the theory of nationality. The essence of this theory is that the territorial shape, the political frontiers of a state should coincide with the national contours.

Acton was writing before the Polish rebellion of 1863, before the completion of Italian unification, before the process of German unification had even begun. But already he was convinced that the theory of nationality would transform the face of Europe. He saw it as one of three theories which challenged the old order – alongside 'equality' and 'communism' – and he firmly predicted that it was destined to exert greater influence than the other two. Like many after him he traced its spread both to Napoleon, and the manner in which he provoked national reactions in Germany, in Russia and in Spain, and to the Congress of Vienna where it was ignored

157

by the Holy Alliance in 1815 – although he noted that at Vienna the French
statesman, Talleyrand, did declare that the Polish question ought to take
precedence above all others because the partition of Poland had been one
of the first and greatest causes of Europe's destabilization (Lord Acton,
1985, I, p. 419).

Looking back now, it is possible to write much of European history in
the four or five generations since the 1860s in terms precisely of the influence of the theory of nationality, defined as the idea that each nationality
should establish sovereign independence over a national homeland. It
provided the trigger for the outbreak of the First World War as imperial
powers clashed over Serbian and Belgian independence. By the time of the
Treaty of Versailles in 1919, the principle seemed virtual common sense.
The League of Nations was founded upon it. The Second World War, too,
broke out over it. The settlement of 1945 re-established the patchwork of
pre-war nation-states in the West, and the economic recovery of the post-
war years has been persuasively interpreted in terms of their restoration
(Milward, 1992). At the same time, the USSR paid lip-service to it in
Central Europe and even within the frontiers of the Soviet Union itself.
Moreover, the momentous upheaval through which we are still living, the
collapse of Soviet and Communist power, has seen the process go a great
deal further: the smaller Warsaw Pact powers have snapped the ties which
bound them to the USSR while the former Union Republics have broken
away and created independence.[1] Yugoslavia, too, has been dismantled in
the name of the right to national self-determination. Some parts of the
story have been painful, bloody and destructive but others have been
heroic and almost impossible to regard as anything but progressive. And
of none is this more true than the case of Poland. Certainly in British eyes,
there has been no historic European nation more manifestly treated with
injustice and more ruthlessly repressed by its neighbours and let down by
its friends, and thus no more evocative, no more romantic cause. The
restoration of full Polish independence can be seen as the culmination of
the story.

And yet, I want to suggest that the tale turns on an almost painful paradox. For a powerful case can be made, and is being made with increasing
conviction by Western European political, legal, economic and cultural spe-
cialists, that in Europe the democratic nation-state as a political form has
already passed its sell-by date. Just as conditions seem most propitious for
a stable and democratic Polish nation-state to emerge, that formation is
coming under pressure from every direction. The paradox applies across
Central and Eastern Europe, but it is most acute in the case of Poland. Why
so? Because on almost any traditional barometer Poland appears better

equipped to sustain a nation-state than any of its potential competitors. If we review the major currents undermining the nation-state, we find, it seems to me, that Poland is better placed to resist those currents than any other nation in Central or Eastern Europe, and arguably better placed than many in the West, including Britain.

Let me begin by considering three different directions from which the threat to the nation-state in Europe is coming. The first of these is from challenges by ethnic, religious, racial, cultural and regional minorities. In most Western European states the issue of who actually belongs to the nation has become increasingly problematic – be it in Spain, in France, or in Belgium. Cultural and economic developments seem in many respects to be refining and highlighting minority identities. In Britain we are very conscious of this trend – which is visible not only in the ancient minority peoples of Scotland and Wales, but also among immigrant communities originating in Africa, Asia and the Caribbean, and indeed in some regions, notably the West Country. This makes it more and more difficult to find a discourse which unites rather than divides citizens of the nation-state, which succeeds in foregrounding what they have in common rather than what defines their different allegiances. Yet the British case seems relatively modest when set in a Europe-wide context. Consider, for example, the Russian case. Some 25 million Russians find themselves outside the borders of the new Federation, while within those borders about 20 per cent of the population are non-Russian. Moreover, the country's constitutional structure includes 22 autonomous republics, home to about 30 million citizens. Each is based on a nominal national minority. Each has many of the trappings of statehood without sovereignty. We have seen the potential disruption – albeit in extreme form – in the case of the Chechen Republic. Compared to this, Poland represents a near model homogeneity. The proportion describing themselves as Polish and Catholic runs to fully 95 per cent. If one people living within the boundaries of one country and governed by one state is the core of a nation-state, then Poland looks set fair.

This relates to the second development which Western commentators point to as weakening the bonds which hold together the nation-state, and that is the declining potency of the myths and symbols of nationhood. Multiple identities are nothing new; national identity has long coexisted with myriad other elements in self-definition – political, social, ideological as well as ethnic, denominational, local and regional. But what distinguishes the present climate is that at the same time as minority sense of identity is being sharpened, majorities are having their profile blurred and merged at the edges. In part this is because of the internationalization of cultural life, the enormous increase in cross-cultural exchange, both high and low, be it through television, radio, videos, or the written word. Even the French have been all but helpless in the face of post-war Americanization. In part, too, it is because of the dramatic shifts in the relative power and wealth of different nations.

In Britain we have suffered grievously here: we are still caught up in the bewildering process of coming to terms with acute 'downsizing' as a world power. This underlies much of the palpable decline in respect for the monarchy, for parliament, for traditions and pageants which seem increasingly to belong to a bygone age, to be irrelevant and even laughable. There is no dominant church that can appeal across the nation, and the subject matter of our school curriculum – notably in literature – is more and more contentious. The question of what history should be taught to children is hotly disputed. The kind of thing an earlier generation was brought up with, a firm chronology of 'Our Island Story', told from above and moving from one success to another, is for most teachers anathema; while politically-driven efforts to restore kings and queens to centre stage reek of anachronism and illiberalism. A comparable sense of doubt and questioning, it has been widely argued, pervades the sense of identity of almost every major Western European nationality.

Once again, to keep a sense of proportion it is salutary to glance at the post-Soviet Russian predicament, at the blows to national pride involved in supposedly repudiating the entire Soviet era and trying to return to the days of the Duma and the twin-headed eagle. The socio-cultural drama unfolding there, the crisis of national identity, is of another order, coming close to a form of national amnesia. If the history of the great Soviet people, and Russians as elder brothers, is so desolate, if all that the Soviet regime claimed as its achievement is to be repudiated, what then is it to be Russian? Is it not virtually a dirty word, an embarrassment? What is there to take pride in? On what can self-respect be based? What grounds are there for hope? What images, shared memories, common myths are left? And it is not only soul-destroying for the individual but puts at risk any sense of community spirit, of common interest, of social bond, of belonging.[2]

By contrast, turning to Poland, there is a remarkably smooth correlation between the assertion of national identity and the project of building a post-communist society. In fact, the present conjuncture would seem tailor-made to evoke a powerful sense of continuity, of historical consciousness, of pride in the resilience of Polish national identity rooted in Catholicism, tempered by resistance to oppression from east and south and west. Poland would seem ideally placed to pass on to the next generation a revered cultural heritage, a common pride in past greatness and grief for past ordeals, and a common sense of achievement in the re-establishment of independence. On the face of it there would seem relatively little difficulty about the post-1989 recasting of the modern history syllabus, about a national narrative which runs from the partitions of the late eighteenth century, through the heroic rebellions of 1830 and 1863 to the hope and the promise of 1918, before the villainy of 1939, the heroism of 1944, the tragedy and resurgence of 1956, 1970 and 1980, and the final, peaceful triumph of 1989. Of course, even Polish identity is not problem-free: one thinks of the precipitate decline in respect for the Church, the divisions over the communist past, the distinctive features of and tensions between different regions. Yet one can imagine a compelling, if Whiggish, account perfectly designed to underpin a clearly defined sense of national pride and common identity.

A third development which Western European commentators point to when pondering whether there is a crisis of the nation-state concerns the relative insignificance of current threats to national security. Traditionally, the state's prime function has been to guarantee its citizens against external danger. In the era of the Cold War, there was, of course, such a perceived threat to Western European nation-states, but it was met within a supranational framework, an alliance manifestly dependent upon and sponsored not by the nation-states of Western Europe but by the American hegemon. Since the end of the Cold War, that threat has receded, but in a sense the result has been to bring home even more forcefully how little the Western European nation-state on its own can deliver – even when armed with 'independent' nuclear weapons. Disasters such as those in Yugoslavia have brought home how little weight each nation-state carries on its own; the semi-detachment of American foreign policy has underscored how lightweight are Western European states acting in isolation; the dizzying cost of research, development and procurement has forced supposedly independent states to pool their resources; and above all, current external dangers are perceived more in terms of general destabilization and mass migration rather than specific threats to the security of one or another European state.

Here again, the Polish case is different. The urge for a network of alliances to guarantee security is clearly no less great than in the West. But whatever the objective reality, it can come as no surprise given the country's modern history that there should be a powerful sense of very specific threats to Poland as such. Pacific though both Russia and Germany may be at present, it would be positively bizarre were the Polish sense of *potential* danger not to remain acute. As inhabitants of an island not invaded for nearly a thousand years we are in a poor position to appreciate how deep is the impact of having the homeland physically shifted westward in the aftermath of bloody invasion and ruthless repression.

Thus it would seem that Poland is set to effect the transition from Soviet satellite to true nation-state; that she is poised to deliver precisely the promise that has given nationalism so powerful an appeal in the last two centuries: the promise to establish an independent polity in which a democratically controlled government exercises sovereign power in the interests of the national community (Breuilly, 1982). And yet the thesis here is that this is the very moment at which a question-mark hangs over the ability of even the most homogeneous nation-state possessed of the most clearly defined sense of common identity to deliver democratic control over its destiny. The evidence is accumulating of what in Britain is known as a 'democratic deficit'. The common thread is that ever more of the problems the nation-state confronts are insoluble except on international terms. Let me point to a few of the main features.[3]

The first concerns the internationalization of crime, the sheer scale of drugs traffic, fraud, money-laundering and terrorism. Europe has witnessed a long-term increase in each of these but the collapse of the Communist world, and especially the desperate weakness of law, order and policing in most of the Soviet successor states, has injected a qualitatively new element. Exploiting the communications revolution that drives so much of the current shift in the world order, the international networks involved in each branch of crime confront isolated states with problems they cannot handle.

Very much the same may be said of the exacerbation of pollution. The scale and implications of environmental degradation confront each state with problems with which it is ill-equipped to cope. The rhetoric and promise of sovereign power and government responsibility belie the reality of dwindling finite resources, acid rain and massive climatic shifts. Each of these problems is by its very nature international in its causes and its effects. On its own no state can arrest the process or halt its impact at the national frontier. What each of these problems seems to demand is co-operation between states, collective action on an international scale. To assert this is not to assume that even global co-operation will stop the pressure on the environment. What is plain, however, is that in isolation Western European nation-states can make no substantial impact at all.

Best documented and most dramatic is the internationalization or globalization of economic life.[4] We are in the midst of an explosion in the growth of international links and economic interdependence. At one level, it may be seen in the massive increase over the past three decades in foreign travel – be it driven by tourism, business or student exchange, be it by rail, motorway or jet. At another, in terms of the phenomenal expansion of international communication networks from the telephone to fax, e-mail and the Web. At a third, in terms of the sheer scale and power of international companies, capital movements and currency volatility. This decade has seen the governments of once proud 'great powers' helpless when caught in the path of tidal waves in the international economy. The humiliation meted out to both the British and French governments over the value of the pound and franc respectively has left a powerful impression. But politicians in even the most advanced industrial states suffer from a growing sense of the sheer impotence of pursuing a merely national strategy within an integrated world market. Fiscal, legislative and tariff intervention appear ever less effective in the face of deregulated financial markets and mighty multinational companies free to respond by simple withdrawal of capital. The result has been to induce an insecurity of employment, a shift from full-time and permanent to part-time and fixed-term jobs, a work-related level of stress that had no equivalent in the first post-war decades. In a very real sense, supposed European nation-states no longer govern their own national economies.

Related to this is the growing question-mark over the nation-state's ability to sustain social welfare at the level expected by its citizens. It is this problem which is widely regarded as the supreme threat to the legitimacy of the nation-state. Yet it is now everywhere finding increasing difficulty in coping with it. The welfare bill is under pressure from numerous directions: the demographic profile of Western Europe steadily increasing the pensions bill, the sustained level of historically high unemployment and related benefit payments, reflecting the nation-state's fading capacity to take effective counter-cyclical measures as well as competition from newly-industrialized countries; the steep rise in the cost of delivering medical care. Post-war welfare provision has by no means crumbled. Even governments which yearn to cut costs are having the greatest difficulty in doing so, so important does this provision remain in shoring up their legitimacy. But should current trends continue, and substantial failure follow, the pressure for political action at either the sub-national or the supra-national level is likely to grow inexorably.

It is in this context that the ever-thickening network of international political and institutional links across Western Europe should be viewed. The supreme, though by no means the only, expression of this is the European Union. Integration between member states has already invaded territory long regarded as inseparable from the claim of national sovereignty through the removal of customs barriers, standardization of commercial regulations and the creation of a single market; the steady decline in border and passport controls; the joint co-operation between intelligence agencies and police to tackle drug-trafficking, international fraud, money-laundering and terrorism; the adoption of a common flag and common citizenship; and the marked extension of European law and of the authority of international courts over national ones in all areas of European Union competence under the treaties. The Maastricht Treaty of 1992, as William Wallace points out, touches on almost all the core functions of the European nation-state – control of territory, and borders, police, citizenship, immigration, currency, tax, financial transfers, economic management, political representation, accountability, foreign policy and defence.[5] The Social Chapter represents a partial intervention in the sphere of welfare. It is by no means a foregone conclusion that the aspirations of Maastricht will be fulfilled. The ructions caused by moves to hasten monetary union may well be a foretaste of things to come. But there could scarcely be more forceful evidence of a crisis of confidence in the capacity of the autonomous nation-state.

The steps taken towards pooling sovereignty have in no sense overcome the democratic deficit referred to above. The effect has merely been to make glaringly obvious what might otherwise have continued to be obscured. For minimal measures have been taken there to entrench democratic control over the emerging legislative process at the European Union level. In Britain, it has long been possible to uphold the myth of parliamentary sovereignty despite the increasing impact of global socio-economic forces over which Westminster exercises no control at all. But the fact that there is a higher level of law which can override the will of Parliament is rapidly being brought home to us. Yet the democratic deficit cannot be overcome unless the nation-state openly acknowledges its limitations, its incapacity, its inability. And this is where the traditional appeal of nationalism and the traditional discourse and rhetoric associated with the nation-state are so dangerous. However strong the logic demanding collective action at a multinational level, no international organization has made significant headway in displacing national identities and allegiance with supranational ones.[6] And yet as long as the pretence continues that the nation-state can deliver what it plainly cannot deliver, electorates are encouraged to live in a make-believe world where they are doomed to disappointment by successive governments while exercising no control over the institutions that are best placed to deliver.

Of course there are those who see resignation in the face of the relative decline of the nation-state as tantamount to accepting a reduction in liberty.

For some, what puts liberty at risk is the sheer size of the European Union, rendering the citizen helpless in the face of it; for some, it is the remoteness of the bureaucratic apparatus, of 'Brussels'; for a third group, it is the lack of democratic control over the European Commission, the impotence of the European Parliament that is at fault; for yet others, it is the very fact of once sovereign nations being reduced to marginal minorities and deprived of sovereignty. Among British nineteenth-century liberals, John Stuart Mill (1946, p. 294) for one, saw it as a general principle that liberty depended on the application of the theory of nationality: 'It is in general a necessary condition of free institutions that the boundaries of governments should coincide in the main with those of nationalities.' But on this liberals were not unanimous.

By way of conclusion, let us return to Lord Acton. He was convinced that almost the reverse was true, that the principle of nationality aimed at a settlement that was impossible, and that once this is finally recognized the outcome must be a system which the theory condemns – the liberty of different nationalities as members of one sovereign community. He was entirely sympathetic to the demands for national liberty when the state tried to impose uniformity and centralization. But in his view, the greatest bulwark against oppression is precisely the presence of different nations under the same government. This, it seemed to him, is the most powerful way to balance interests, to multiply associations, to promote independence by forming coherent groups of public opinion. National diversity in the same state, he argued, is a firm barrier against the excessive intrusion of government. Indeed, he concluded that 'The co-existence of several nations under the same state is a test, as well as the best security of freedom.' But this was on the understanding that the only kind of multinational state that will not provoke a reawakening of nationalism is one which abides by the principle of subsidiarity, one where the federal parliament will be limited and many functions will be performed by a hierarchy of provincial and local representative bodies. And finally, like an early forerunner of the European idea, he predicted that 'When different races inhabit the different territories of one Empire composed of several smaller States, it is of all possible combinations the most favourable to the establishment of a highly developed system of freedom' (Lord Acton, I, pp. 425, 430).

We in Britain, who claim to have enjoyed the pleasures of the nation-state for hundreds of years, are wrestling with this conundrum. Poland approaches it, from the other end. There is much we can learn from each other.

NOTES

1. For a useful collection of essays on the process, see Lapidus *et al.* (1992).
2. See Acton (1995), pp. 343–56.
3. For two influential works, see Hutton (1995) and Dunn (1995).
4. For two useful articles, see Cable (1995), pp. 23–53; Schmidt (1995), pp. 75–106.
5. See Wallace (1995), pp. 52–76. This section of my article draws heavily on Wallace's fine overview.
6. On the resilience of national identity and the appeal of the nation-state, see Smith (1995) and Mann (1993), pp. 115–40.

REFERENCES

Acton, E., *Russia: the Tsarist and Soviet Legacy* (London, Longman, 1995).
Lord Acton, *Selected Writings of Lord Acton* (Fears, J. R. (ed.), 3 vols, Indianapolis, Liberty Classics, 1985).
Breuilly, J., *Nationalism and the State* (Manchester, Manchester University Press, 1982).
Cable, V., 'The Diminished State: a Study in the Loss of Economic Power', *Daedalus*, No. 2, 1995, pp. 23–53.
Dunn, J. (ed.), *Contemporary Crisis of the Nation State?* (Oxford, Blackwell, 1995).
Hutton, W., *The State We're In* (London, Jonathan Cape, 1995).
Lapidus, G. W. *et al.* (eds), *From Union to Commonwealth: Nationalism and Separatism in the Soviet Republics* (Cambridge, Cambridge University Press, 1992).
Mann, M., 'Nation-States in Europe and Other Continents. Diversifying, Developing, Not Dying', *Daedalus*, No. 3, 1993, pp. 115–40.
Mill, J. S., *Considerations on Representative Government* (McCallum, R. B. (ed.), Oxford, Blackwell, 1946).
Milward, A. S., *The European Rescue of the Nation-State* (London, Routledge, 1992).
Schmidt, V. G., 'The New World Order, Incorporated: the Rise of Business and the Decline of the Nation-State', *Daedalus*, No. 2, 1995, pp. 75–106.
Smith, A. D., *Nations and Nationalism in a Global Era* (Cambridge, Cambridge University Press, 1995).
Wallace, W., 'Rescue or Retreat? The Nation State in Western Europe, 1945–1993', in Dunn, J. (ed.), *Contemporary Crisis of the Nation State?* (Oxford, Blackwell, 1995).

12 Songs of Love and Hate:[1] the Role of the Intelligentsia, Music and Poetry in Forging Serbian Ethnic National Identity

Robert Hudson

> *Ima jedna zemlja stara što sa nebu ima cara,*
> *Ima Cara, oj Lazara što suncem razgova,*
> *Srbija, naša majka mila, Srbija sve nas je rodila,*
> *Živela Srbija.*[2]

> *Le ciel serbe est couleur d'azur*
> *Au dedans est assis un vrai dieu serbe*
> *Entouré, des anges serbes aux voix pures*
> *Qui chantent la gloire de leur race superbe.*[3]

The Serbian ethnologist, Ivan Čolović commented in his recent publication, *Bordel Ratnika*[4] (1994, p. 23) that: '*Naša politika puna je folklorika ...*' ('Our politics is full of folklore'). Given the rise of ethnic nationalism during this last decade of the twentieth century, any conference, or edited collection of papers, engaging the question 'Why Europe?' which focuses upon problems of culture and identity should, at some point, address the process, nature and impact of ethnic national identity upon the European scene. It is the aim of this chapter to explore further the link between politics and folklore with special reference to the music and poetry of Serbia in the formation and maintenance of ethnic national identity.

National identity has often been forged, or manipulated through the work of awakeners and intellectuals, rather than coming directly from the people. The process, as described by Gellner (1993, pp. 58–62), has involved the gathering together and interpretation of demotic culture, such as folk music and dance, folk costume and oral literature to formalize a nascent national culture. This process of ethnification has been common throughout the region of Eastern and Central Europe since the 1820s.[5]

Responsibility for the process of ethnification, which lays emphasis upon identity and belonging to an 'in group' by demonizing, in turn, an 'out group', and emphasizing perceived differences between an 'us' and a 'them' may be laid at the feet of the folklorists, poets, ethno-musicologists and amateur local historians of the late nineteenth and early twentieth centuries who placed too much emphasis upon folk music, dance, songs, poetry, costume and tradition.[6] It is the process of ethnification and the creation of ethnic national identity which has resulted in the songs of love and hate, which in themselves reaffirm hatreds between different peoples. Yet this criticism is not simply an issue long since buried in the past, but a process which continues and is flourishing in parts of Europe at the end of the millennium.

Whereas Vuk Karadžić (1787–1844) and Petar Petrović Njegoš (1813–51) are two outstanding examples of this process in nineteenth-century Serbia, it could be argued that contemporary Serbian intellectuals, such as Dobrica Ćosić (b. 1921) and Veselin Djuretić are continuing this tradition today through their academic and media output.

I contend in this chapter that the role of intellectuals in forging national identity, based upon demotic culture, is not just a phenomenon of the nineteenth and early twentieth centuries, but that it remains an important phenomenon at the end of the millennium, aided by the media, especially radio and television. This has particularly applied in recent years to Serbia and the Republika Srpska as, until August 1995, it had applied to the Krajina Serb Republic, with a revival of attempts to create a 'Greater Serbia' and the concomitant aim of establishing the unity of Serbian ethnic space, or Serbian *Lebensraum*.[7]

One of the vehicles in the creation of a 'Greater Serbia' is the intertwining thread sewn between *poetry, patria and purity* that carries the myth of community and common culture,[8] since poetry expresses historical memories, myths, symbols and traditions (Smith, 1991, p. 11). These concepts and themes are expressed in elevated imagery, usually highly symbolic, which may be found particularly in early tribal songs, epic folk poetry and popular national musical varieties. These themes often concern either the myth of the community itself, or are about 'heroic' individuals who represent that community. Such individuals become the mythical ancestors of communities that have been transmogrified into 'super families' (ibid.). In the Serbian case there are two roots: the traditional liturgical literature of churchmen, which has been secularized for a historically self-conscious bourgeoisie (Holton and Mihailovich, 1988, p. xxviii); and a peasant tradition of folk singing and recitation of oral narratives in verse by illiterate and sometimes blind singers (*guslari*) who become the composers and the keepers of the people's history. These two roots then became complexly intertwined.

In this chapter I will consider briefly some selected literary examples gleaned from Serbian poetry/songs (*pesme*) and national music since the beginning of the eighteenth century[9] and compare these with extracts of popular music from the 1990s. However, I will take as my starting point reports of the Second Congress of Serbia in order to contextualize further current intellectual attitudes in Serbia concerning Serbian ethnic national identity.

THE VECTORS OF GREATER SERBIAN ETHNIC NATIONAL IDENTITY

At the outset, one needs to establish that respect for education and educated élites is deeply rooted in Serbian society. Writing in 1949, the historian Severin K. Turosienski (pp. 230–1) commented that:

> Where ability to obtain an education has long been associated with freedom from the oppressive rule of a foreign tyranny, attending school and learning to read and write have been regarded as privileges to be cherished, not obligations to be endured. Writers, teachers, and professors (in Serbia) have enjoyed a prestige not always bestowed on their colleagues in other countries. ... Professors have been leaders in the political and economic life of the country.

The issue of this process was raised again in a recent conversation with former BBC correspondent and Independent MP, Martin Bell who drew attention to the considerable number of academics who play a leading role in the Republika Srpska government based in Pale, such as Dr Karadžić and Professors Koljević and Ekmečić, to name but a few.[10]

In his article, reporting on the Second Congress of Serbian Intellectuals, held in Belgrade in April 1994, Stan Markotich (1994, pp. 18–23) explained that throughout its evolution, the ideological underpinning and aims of Serbian nationalism were the property of Serbian intellectuals and political leaders, and he added, citing Ivo Lederer (1969), that the overwhelming majority of the Serbian population in the nineteenth century, which consisted largely of illiterate peasants, was isolated from the emerging political and intellectual trends and contributed little to the development of Serbian nationalism. This has been borne out again more recently by Richard and Ben Crampton (1996, pp. 130–1) who have commented that: 'Of the four Balkan states, Albania excluded, [at 81 per cent] Yugoslavia in 1921, had the largest proportion of its population engaged in agriculture and fishing.'[11]

The importance attached to the role of Serbian intellectuals in forming policy and opinion continues today, and President Slobodan Milošević has used nationalist academics and their theories to justify his policies, in winning the support of intellectuals for his regime. Three years after the publication of the *Memorandum* of the Serbian Academy of Arts and Science (Akademia Srpska Umjetnoste i Nauka), Milošević himself said of the Academy:

> I don't really see why it should not have an influence upon politics in Serbia. What people, what state in the world, that claims to be intelligent, would be ashamed of its academy?[12]

The Congress itself demonstrated the continuity of the role of intellectuals as national awakeners in developing the 'Greater Serbia' idea. Here they looked at pragmatic issues, such as linguistic policy and economic plans that could serve as a foundation for the integration of Serb-populated areas outside Yugoslavia (Serbia and Montenegro) proper.

The linguist Pavle Ivić offered an appraisal of the current status of the Serbian 'literary language', arguing that it needed standardization and that this could be effected by the imposition of *ekavsko* (once referred to as the eastern variant of 'Serbo-Croat'). Such policies of language planning have already taken place in the Republika Srpska, in an attempt to identify more closely with Serbia, so that *ekavsko* is employed by the administration, the media and in schools instead of *jekavsko* which is the linguistic variety normally employed throughout Bosnia and Herzegovina.[13]

Meanwhile the Bosnian Serb historian, Miodrag Ekmečić, formerly of the University of Sarajevo, and author of *Stvaranje Jugoslavija* (The Making of Yugoslavia) went to a great effort in propounding the idea that the Serbs today are the victims of a conspiracy devised by the United States and the Vatican. This reflects Republika Srpska propaganda materials, faxed to the University of Derby from Pale in the summer of 1993 with comments reflecting Ekmečić's work, such as: 'Black and Yellow Monarchy', 'Italian Trickery' and 'the kitchens of the Vatican', expressions that are similarly employed by Veselin Djuretić, historian at the University of Belgrade and a member of the Academy, who has advocated using the river Naretva as the Serb frontier so that Serbia would have access to the Adriatic coastline.[14]

The 1400 delegates who attended the Second Congress of Serbian Intellectuals endorsed the concept of a 'Greater Serbia', a *Serbia irredenta* or *Serbia reconquista*, which had first been propounded by Ilija Garašinin in his *Nacertanije* (Outline) of 1844, in which he laid the groundwork for future efforts to unite under Belgrade's authority all Serb populated lands and that those lands, especially Kosovo, were regarded as belonging to Serbia by historic rights.[15] This idea was fully endorsed in the writings of Vaso Čubrilović (1897–1990).[16] Čubrilović's ideal was for a return to the medieval empire of Tsar Stjepan Dušan (1331–55), when the Serbian Empire was at the pinnacle of its power and authority.

The unification of Serbian ethnic space, or 'Greater Serbianism', whereby the *prečani* (those Serbs living beyond the rivers Danube, Sava and Drina, in Vojvodina, Slavonia and Bosnia) were to be united with the Serbs of Old Serbia, was therefore based upon shared cultural, linguistic and religious factors: that is a sense of community, shared linguistic variety, Orthodoxy and a common history and literature. Because of a history of constant movement and migration (*seobe*),[17] there developed a need to push to the north and the west; to develop Serbian space or Serbian *Lebensraum*.

Again in 1991, Dobrica Ćosić, reputed to have been one of the leading academicians who had signed the *Memorandum* of 1986, as well as being President of Yugoslavia (Serbia and Montenegro) and author of *Vreme Smrti* (*The Time of Death*)[18] which recounted Serbian suffering during the First World War, has commented that:

> One should never forget that we Serbs, through our great migrations, finally left for the north and the west. I am certain that it will always be in these directions that we will find our objectives.[19]

This, and the ideas of Garašinin and Ćubrilović, leads us into the politics of ethnic cleansing (*etničko čisćenje*). The expression 'ethnic cleansing' had first been employed during the reign of Djordje Petrović, otherwise known as Karađorđe (1762–1817), founder of the Serbian royal dynasty, by the celebrated Serbian writer and language reformer Vuk Stefanović Karadžić (1787–1864) (Grmek *et al.*, 1993, p. 40).

Stojan Protić (1857–1923), a leading member of the Serbian Radical Party, once stated that:

> As soon as our army crosses the Drina, it will give the Turks twenty-four – perhaps forty-eight hours – to return to the faith of their forefathers and then slay those who resist, as we did in Serbia in the past.

Of course the expression 'Turks' employed here, refers to the Bosnian Muslims, since 'the faith of the forefathers' is Orthodoxy and this text both pressages the 'ethnic cleansing' of the early 1990s as well as being a reflection of Njegoš' *Gorski Vijenac* (*Mountain Wreath*) which I will consider later in this chapter. Suffice it to say that Serbian ethnic identity is closely linked with the Serbian Orthodox faith, which, since the foundation of the Nemanjić dynasty in the twelfth century and the time of Saint Sava (1175–1235) has been seen as a vital prerequisite for membership of the Serbian state.

The extracts which follow are a representative sample taken from key Serbian writers from the late seventeenth century to the present day: Petar Petrović Njegoš (1813–51), Arsenije Čarnojević (1633–1706) and Zaharije Orfelin (1726–85). I have decided not to include work by the otherwise oft-cited Vuk Stefanović Karadžić, who was responsible for collecting together the canon of Kosovo ballads in his *Narodne Pesme* (Peoples' Songs) and the tales of Marko Kraljević, though I will make reference to them in passing.

First something of the writers themselves. Arsenije Čarnojević was a celebrated Serbian writer who:

> organised a mass migration of over thirty thousand families from the Old Serbian lands ... in 1691 ... (to) the flat lands north of the Sava river (Slavonija) and across the Danube and into the regions known as the Srem, Bačka and the Banat (generally referred to as Vojvodina), deep into Hungary.
>
> (Holton and Mihailovich, 1988, p. 35)

Zaharija Orfelin is recognized as one of the most distinguished Serbian writers of the mid-eighteenth century (ibid.); whereas the Montenegrin Prince Bishop, Petar Petrović Njegoš, writing in the mid-nineteenth century, has been described in the introduction to the 1930 English translation of his work *Gorski Vijenac*, as the 'Serbian Shakespeare'.[20] His work is crucial for understanding the ethnic hatred of Orthodox Serbs for their Muslim brethren, as is demonstrated by these short extracts taken from Bishop Danilo's soliloquy:

> From out of Asia where they have their nest,
> This devil's brood doth gulp nations up. (ll. 19–20)

> Is half a world so small, to thee so small –
> A half-world filled with horror of thy deeds
> That pois'nous stenches from thy demon soul
> Thou now must bring to spue upon our Rock? (ll. 50–3)

The 'Rock' refers to Montenegro which at the time was under the hegemony of the:

> ... faithless Turk, with Koran ...
> Behind him hordes of that accursed breed,
> As locusts pestilent lay waste the fields. (ll. 3–6)

And although he claims not to fear this 'Devil's spawn,/Though they be thick as autumn leaves', Bishop Danilo then asks himself the question:

> What will this Dragon in our Christian land?
> Why nourish we a snake within our breast?
> What 'brothers' these? (ll. 704–6)

In the Serbian literary canon, made up from a tradition of liturgical literature, national epics and the peasant tradition of folk song to the accompaniment of the one-stringed instrument, the *gusle*, there are several key themes. Serbia is alone, hated and misunderstood by all non-Serbs. Serbia is a victimized and 'satanized' people, defeated in battle and abandoned by God. Biblical themes abound. The evening meal before the battle of Kosovo is the Serbian 'Last Supper', brought about by betrayal and internecine strife between princes: no wonder the expression *Samo Sloga Srbina Spasava* ('Only Unity Saves the Serbs'), first created in the twelfth century by St Sava, the founder of the independent Serbian Church, became the national motto of Serbia. Equally, the Migrations of 1691 and 1705, which led to the settlement of Serbs in Vojvodina and the Slavonijas, are treated almost on the level of the Babylonian captivity, and the Serbs as a people in bondage and slavery, forced out of necessity to fight or work for other powers.

> How has Serbia fallen, glorious once and gracious
> with the flowering of my people, in former days so
> plenteous with my mighty Emperors, and all my valiant soldiers
> bounden now to yield themselves in slavery to others.
> … Left alone to make my way, to other Emperor-lieges,
> shedding bitter tears to woe, I place myself in bondage.
> All now but revile me, slander me nost foully …
> … All my Serbian frontiers and my lands weep loudly
> that no more my valiant knights ride amongst them proudly.
> (Zaharija Orfelin, *Plač Srbiji*, 1761 [Trans., Bernard Johnson]:
> Holton and Mihailovich, 1988, p. 63)

With reference to the *Seobe* or 'Migrations' of the late seventeenth and early eighteenth centuries, which have had a deep influence upon the pathology of Serbian ethnic national identity, Arsenije Čarnojević provides us with his *Prayer to the Sleeping Lord* in 1705:

> By day and night I flee with my impoverished people
> from one place to the next
> like a ship on a great ocean.
> We give ourselves to flight

and wait for the sun to set,
the day to end,
and the dark night to pass,
and the misery of winter is above us.

(Arsenije Čarnojević: Holton and Mihailovich,
1988, p. 38)

Of course the 'winter' and 'night' referred to here are metaphors for the 'Dark Age of Turkish occupation', highlighted again in Njegoš' *Gorski Vijenac*, with the deeply emotional lines: 'Oh, dark, dark Day! Oh, outlook ever black!/My fearing folk held underfoot' ('Crni dne, a crna sudbino!/ O kukavno Srpstvo ugašeno' [ll. 43–4]).

Always lingering in the background is a strong sense of atavism and the memory of greater days, of the lost past and golden age of empire and of Stijepan Dušan 'Silni' ('The Strong') and of Serbian heroes, Miloš, Lazar and Vuk Branković. These heroes abound in Karadžić's collected poems, but will be found elsewhere, such as in Orfelin's Serbian Lament:

... The flower of my bravery at Kosovo lay fallen;
who is left to comfort me ...?

(Zaharija Orfelin, *Plač Srbiji*, 1761
[Trans., Bernard Johnson]:
Holton and Mihailovich, 1988, p. 64).

Similarly from Njegoš we find:

Our hope it was all buried long ago,
In one great grave on Kosovo's broad field. (ll. 135–6)

There therefore exists a Serbian *Sonderweg* and collective solipsism whereby, in the Serbian collective conscience, the Serbs 'turn in on themselves'. The Serbs have been abandoned by God. Čarnojević develops this in his *Plač Srbiji* (Serbian Lament) against the background of the Great Migration of 1705:

Our troubles double in strength,
and I say through my tears:
How long, O Lord will you completely forget us?
How long must we strengthen ourselves, in order
that we may deserve you?

(Holton and Mihailovich, 1988, p. 38)

Njegoš, in *Gorski Vijenac*, again shows how God has deserted the Serbs, in this case for their disunity and the betrayal of Serbian leaders at the battle of Kosovo, with the plea '*Pomoz', Bože, jadinijem Srbima*' ('Help us Serbs, oh God, in all our misery') and again in Bishop Danilo's soliloquy:

> Our God hath pour'd His wrath upon the Serbs,
> For deadly sins withdrawn His favour from us:
> Our rulers trampled underfoot all law
> With bloody hatred fought each other down ...
> ... Our God hath pour'd his wrath upon the Serbs
> A seven-headed monster He sent forth
> To plague and extirpate the Serbian Name.
>
> (Wiles translation, 1930)

Likewise with Orfelin:

> All my elders shun me now, turn away their faces,
> all walking in darkness, me alone and piteous,
> abandoned to my torments, ah how great my sadness!
> Ah most wretched Serbia, where can now my hope rest ...?
>
> (Trans. Bernard Johnson: Holton and Mihailovich, 1988, p. 64)

For a people which was subjected to Ottoman hegemony for a period of over 500 years, it can be said that epic poetry provided the main vehicle of 'inspiration to those who needed reassurance that the nation would eventually rise against its oppressors' (Singleton, 1985, p. 45). In the words of Dobrica Ćosić: 'The Serbian people [are] humiliated, maligned, fooled, surrounded by a lack of understanding and hate.' By this exclusion from the European mainstream they have forged their own identity. They have been transmogrified, in Ćosić's own words, into the 'vampire of history'.[21]

More recently, academician Antonije Isaković has commented that:

> Our myths give us greater strength and we must live with them. Each time that we have been faced with difficulties, we have returned to Kosovo, to Karađorđe and to popular poetry. These myths and all our mythology, which affect our intellectuals as much as our Church, take us down a fairly narrow corridor.[22]

What is that narrow corridor? Is it the geopolitical space which links Serbia with the *Prečani*, or Serbs beyond the Drina, Danube and Sava, the result of the earlier flow of migration? Or is it the vector of Greater Serbia or *Serbia irredenta*?

Later an ethnic identity that expressed a sense of uniqueness, and of collective solipsism, tinged with triumphalism would echo again after the Balkan Wars and the First World War. Patriotic songs celebrating Serbia's trials, tribulations and victories experienced in these wars have taken on an almost sacred aura. Key examples are provided by the songs: *Tamo Daleko*, *Marš na Drinu* and *Ko to kaže, ko to laže*. Since the breakup of the former Yugoslavia, these songs, banned during the Tito period, have become popular again, and can be bought in cassette and CD form on markets in all the towns throughout Serbia, or ordered on the Internet.[23]

Tamo Daleko celebrated a deep love for the country, which, as the title suggests, had become so distant to the minds of Serbian soldiers retreating with the Serbian army into Albania in 1915:

> Tamo daleko, daleko od mora,
> Tamo je selo moje,
> Tamo je Srbija.
> (Over there and far away, far from the seashore,
> There lies my village,
> There lies Serbia.)[24]

Marš na Drinu ('March on the Drina') was composed in 1915 by Stanislav Beniški, and, with its jaunty melody, a Serbian *kolo* or round dance, became extremely popular in a recent recording by Gordana Lazarević:

The heart of the Serb people
overflows with courage
Come all you captains, officers and trumpeters,
All you musicians and play the March on the Drina.
(Chorus, a Kolo)

Sviraj te Marš na Drinu to je pesma stara
Kad je čujem zapevami srca iz nedara.
Tri su cara pobelili, ratnici i seljaci,
Pevali su Marš na Drini za cela junaci.

(Play the March on the Drina this is an old song
Whenever I hear you my heart sings with joy.
Three empires have been defeated by warriors and peasants,
Who sang the March on the Drina for all the heroes. [My translation])

These songs have been described as: 'the embodiment of (Serbian) heroism, proudness, aggressiveness, stubbornness, victimization and ultimate victory' (Radivojević, 1997).

The third example, *Ko to kaže, ko to laže, Srbija je mala*, states that whoever claims that Serbia is small is a liar, since she has won three successive wars against the Turks, Bulgars and the Austrians. This is a theme taken up by Dobrica Ćosić, in his claim that Serbia always wins the wars but loses the peace, a reference to 1912, 1913, 1918 and 1945.

In the wake of these nationalist songs, new musical developments have taken place in Serbia since the breakup of the former Yugoslavia. According to Čolović (1994, p. 99) the first cassette of new political folk songs appeared on the label *Beograd Top* in 1989. Similar developments took place on Serbian Radio in 1992; a new popular folk music that took the name *Poselo* ('folk party') from the programme of that name broadcast on Radio Televizija Srbija's 'Belgrade 202'. At the same time *Ponos Radio* ('Radio Pride') began broadcasting nationalist songs 24 hours a day, with new interpretations of *Četnik* songs from the Second World War and contemporary songs from the current wars that celebrated new heroes, such as Arkan and the fictitious warrior, Kapitan Dragan, who accompanies himself to the sound of the guitar rather than that of the *gusle* of the more traditional singers (Čolović, 1994, p. 99). Kapitan Dragan has become the new folklore image of the epic heroes of Serbian national culture.

I have selected three examples from *Poselo* on 'Belgrade 202' which both demonstrate the continuity of themes to be found in the canon of Serbian demotic culture and demonstrate how these are interpreted in the current climate. Atavism, continuity and the reminiscence of past golden ages are shown in the following song:

> Wherever I go, I think of Serbia
> and her glorious past,
> defended by my father and his father,
> let everyone know, Serbia will last!
> While the sky is blue and the sun does shine,
> Serbia will forever be mine!
> Oh, Serbia my mother, do not fear the war,
> You'll always have two sisters
> when your brother is no more,
> these two sisters the world has not yet seen,
> the Bosnian Serb Republic
> and the Serb Krajina!
> Those who threaten, let them come!
> Serbs are not Turks to pray to Allah!
> The Serb nation is defended,
> Serb lands are protected,
> by Arkan's heroes, warriors without fear,
> These are valiant boys, Serb volunteers!
> (Branko Milinković , *Hate Speech*, Belgrade, 1994, p. 63)

Again the metaphor of Serbia as a mother and of the Greater Serbian project as an extended family is demonstrated here, reflecting the text of

Živela Srbija, cited above, with its '*Srbija, naša majka mila*'. The hatred
of Islam that may be found in Njegoš is also reflected here, along with the
concept of Serbian bravery, although the heroes are new: Arkan's tigers,
rather than Marko Kraljević, Miloš or Prince Lazar. There is also the
theme of sunshine and sunny skies, that is so common in the myth of the
Serbian homeland. In the spring of 1995, the slogan, *Proleće je i mi smo u
Srbiji!* ('It's spring and we're in Serbia!') could be found everywhere on
the streets of Belgrade.

Pan-Slavism and Orthodox unity are conjured up in the text of the next
song, which recalls to some extent the yearning of Tsrnianski's hero, Vuk
Isaković in his epic novel, *Seobe (Migrations)*,[25] to leave Austrian con-
trolled Vojvodina after years of military service to the Empress Maria
Theresa, to eventually settle in Russia, seen as a promised land for the
Serbs, while fellow Serbs continued to be ruled by the Ottoman Turks.

> From Kosovo, Dinaric mountains
> and Mt Lovčen
> to the quiet-flowing Don,
> Only Orthodox bells toll as one.
> Toll, toll, Orthodox bells toll
> Us and Russians three hundred million souls!
>
> (Branko Milinković, *Hate Speech*, Belgrade, 1994)

The final example, which also reflects the title of this chapter, and the
two verses cited at the beginning of this text, sum up the Serbian belief in
themselves as God's chosen people:

> They can hate us, they can love us,
> but nobody can touch Serbs!
> This nation will live even after Ustashe,
> Because God himself is a Serb,
> the heavens are our realm!
>
> (Branko Milinković, *Hate Speech*, Belgrade, 1994;
> slightly amended)

NOTES

1.   The reference is, of course to the song-writer and poet, Leonard Cohen,
      whose album *Songs of Love and Hate* had a considerable influence upon
      this writer at the tender age of 17. At the conference 'Why Europe?' I was

particularly amused by Malcolm Crook's reference to Cohen's *Beautiful Losers* as an alternative title, although I felt that another suggestion by one of our Macedonian colleagues, that of 'Songs of Hate and Self-pity' might be taking the theme a little too far!

2. *Serbia, our darling mother* ... Line from national folk song *Živela Srbija*. Translated as: There is a country of old,/Which has a tsar in the heavens/She has a Tsar, Oh Lazar,/Who speaks with the sun/Serbia our dear mother,/ Serbia you bore all of us,/Long live Serbia. (My translation.)

3. Cited in Rebecca West, *Black Lamb and Grey Falcon* (London, Canongate, 1995), p. 464.

4. Čolović (1994) (the title may be literally translated as 'The Warrior's Brothel').

5. In the case of Serbia examples are provided by Vuk Karadžić's *Najstarije pjesme junacke* (*The Oldest Heroic Songs*) and his *Srpske narodne pripovijetke* (*Serbian Folktales*) of 1821, as well as the historical fiction of Jovan Sterija Popović (1806–56), *Boj na Kosovu* (*Battle of Kosovo*).

6. This theme has been developed by Professor Wolfgang Kaschuba of the University of Berlin, in his paper 'European Discourses on National and Ethnic Identities: Old Topics and New Tasks for Historians and Social Anthropologists', delivered at the German Historical Institute, London on 17 October 1995.

7. The term *Lebensraum* has actually been employed in propaganda materials emanating from Pale (Republika Srpska) with reference to the Greater Serbian Project.

8. The concept of 'poetry, patria and purity', or in its original form *Poesía, patria y pureza* has been more fully developed and explored by my colleague Mercedes Carbayo Abengozar in her PhD thesis at the University of Durham, 'La novelistica de Carmen Martin Gaite: una lectura con partida', 1998.

9. It should be noted that the term *pesme* in Serbian can be translated as both poem and song. It is interesting to note that the expression *narodna muzika*, meaning national folk music, used in the former Yugoslavia has been replaced more recently by *izvorna muzika*, meaning authentic music.

10. Conversation with Martin Bell at the University of Derby, on Friday 26 January 1996. It might be added that this author was taught by both Ekmečić and Koljević as a postgraduate fellowship student at the University of Sarajevo in 1977–8.

11. For a general, albeit somewhat critical, review of this book, see Hudson and Haddelsey (1997).

12. *Politika*, 22 December 1989, p. 7. Cited in Grmek *et al.* (1993), p. 233. (My translation.)

13. See the report on BBC Radio 4, *From Our Own Correspondent*, Saturday, 31 August1996, to the effect that the new president of the Republika Srpska, Biljena Plavisć had started using *ekavsko* rather than *jekavso* and that she kept making mistakes: so much for trying to 'out-Serb' the Serbs!

14. With the position of Vukovar more or less settled by the Dayton Accords, this remains the key area of contention between Serbia and Croatia (see *Le Monde*, 23 August 1996).

15. It should be noted that most of the delegates at this conference were over the age of 55 and had been drawn in from the countryside. It would be truer to

describe them as members of the 'intelligentsia' rather than as 'intellectuals' *per se*. Pressure was placed upon the conferees to vote for the concept of a Greater Serbia out of a spirit of patriotism, within the context of inclusion/ exclusion and 'Good Serb/bad Serb'. I am very grateful to Dr Aleksandar Pavković for this information, which is based on his own eye-witness account of the proceedings of the Second Congress of Serbian Intellectuals.

16. One of the members of *Mlada Bosna* in Sarajevo in 1914, Vaso Čubrilović has been described by Mark Almond (1994, p. 89) as a 'theoretician of ethnic cleansing', following his publication of *Iselvanje Arnauta* in 1937, in which he advocated the expulsion of Albanians from Kosovo. He later became a member of the Serbian Academy, and his ideas influenced the drafting of the *Memorandum* in 1986.

17. Of particular interest here are the two volumes of *Migrations* (*Seobe*) by the Serbian author Miloš Crnjanski (1893–1977).

18. Dobrica Ćosić, *The Time of Death* (Muriel Heppell trans., New York, Harcourt Brace Janovich, 1978). This has also been translated more recently into French by Dejan Babić as Dobrica Tchossitch, *Le Temps de la Mort*, Lausanne, 1991.

19. My translation from the French version, p. 74.

20. Petar Petrović Njegoš, *Mountain Wreath* (Wiles Translation), London, 1930, Introduction, p. i. Wiles has provided a very loose translation of the Serbian original, mainly because of difficulties confronted in trying to translate from the Serbian trochaic pentameter to an iambic tetrameter in the English. However, at this stage of my research I have decided to continue using the Wiles version.

21. *Politika*, 16 June 1992, also cited in Grmek *et al.* 1993, p. 294. (My translation.)

22. Antonije Isaković (1992). (My translation.)

23. One example is a Serbian-American group called Frula. Serbianism is reflected in other art styles. For example, in Belgrade today there is a new realist, neo-classical style of painting which seeks to glorify Serbia's medieval past. This is a popular yet official art form. Similarly, in Yugoslav cinema there are examples such as *Seobe* (1994), starring Isabelle Huppert, and the *Time of Dreams* (1990) which is highly critical of partisan activities in the aftermath of the Second World War when 'Christ' returns to Serbia in the form of a vagrant and is hounded by the authorities.

24. A contemporary example of the importance of this song, which nearly became the national anthem of Serbia following the breakup of Yugoslavia (actually *Boža pravda* was eventually chosen), is provided by an evening rock/pop concert from Belgrade on RTS (Radio Television Serbia) on 25 January 1995. At the end of the programme a girl, aged about 12, took the microphone and broke into *Tamo Daleko*. The crowd in the stadium, mostly made up of youngsters, was euphoric in its accompaniment of the young singer.

25. Miloš Tsrnianski (1994).

REFERENCES

Almond, M., *Europe's Backyard War* (London, Mandarin, 1994).

Carbayo Abengozar, M., *Buscando un Lugar Entre Mujeres: Buceo en la España de Carmen Martin* (Malaga, University of Malaga, 1998).

Čolović, I., *Bordel Ratnika* (Belgrade, Biblioteka XX Vek, 1994).

Ćosić, D., *The Time of Death* (Trans. Heppell, M., New York, Harcourt Brace Janovich, 1978). (French translation by Dejan Babić: Dobrica Tchossitch, *Le Temps de la Mort* (Lausanne, L'Age d'Homme, 1991).)

Crampton, R. and Crampton B., *An Atlas of Eastern Europe* (London, Routledge, 1996).

Gellner, E., *Nations and Nationalism* (Oxford, Blackwell, 1993).

Grmek, M., Gjidara, M. and Šimac, N., *Le Nettoyage Ethnique* (Paris, Fayard, 1993).

Holton, M. and Mihailovich, V. D., *Serbian Poetry from the Beginnings to the Present* (New Haven, Yale Centre for International and Area Studies/ Slavica, 1988).

Hudson, R. and Haddelsey, S., 'Signal Failure on Central Line', *The Times Higher Education Supplement*, 2 May 1997, p. 24.

Isaković, A., *Srbi u tesnom hodniku* (Belgrade, NIN, 8 May 1992), p. 31.

Lederer, I. J., 'Nationalism and the Yugoslavs', in Sugar, P. and Lederer, I. (eds), *Nationalism in Eastern Europe* (Seattle, University of Washington Press, 1969), pp. 396–438.

Markotich S., 'Serbian Intellectuals Promote Concept of "Greater Serbia"', *RFE/RL Research Report*, 10 June 1994, pp. 18–23.

Negoš, P. P., *The Mountain Wreath* (Trans. Wiles, J. W., London, Dent, 1930). (Nygegosh, P. P. Prince Bishop of Montenegro, 1830–51.)

Radivojević, M., 'The Nature and Culture of Serbian Nationalism' (unpublished dissertation, University of Derby, 1997).

Singleton, F., *A Short History of the Yugoslav Peoples* (Cambridge, Cambridge University Press, 1985).

Smith, A., *National Identity* (Harmondsworth, Penguin, 1991).

Tsrnianski, M., *Migrations* (Trans. Heim, H., London, Harvill, 1994: Originally published as *Seobe* [Belgrade, Nolit, 1978]).

Turosienski, S. K., 'Education', in Kerneer, R. J. (ed.), *Yugoslavia* (Berkeley, University of California Press, 1949).

13 Ethnotope and Imperium in Nineteenth-Century Russian Literature
Robert Reid

1 ETHNOTOPE AND RUSSIAN LITERATURE

Like the British, the Russians have historically experienced problems in wholeheartedly defining themselves as European, partly for religio-cultural reasons and partly through the ambiguities of geographical position which invite conflicting affiliations with both east and west. My interest is in the way these concerns manifested themselves in the nineteenth century through the medium of Russian literature, an art form which, owing to the restraints of official censorship, traditionally bore the weight of creating and influencing public opinion.

National awareness in the literary context is difficult to typologize, for virtually any discrete formal component of a literary work has the potential for realizing national or ethnic concerns: character, setting, plot and theme nationalize respectively into foreigner, abroad, exotic adventure, xenophobia or patriotism; these are only a few instances. Ethnotope is a structural concept the permutations of which enable us to impose some classification on manifestations of nationality and ethnicity in literary works.[1] Ethnotope has two conceptual progenitors. The first is chronotope as formulated by the Russian critic Mikhail Bakhtin (1978). The Bakhtinian chronotope offers a method of defining the uniqueness of both individual literary works and genres in terms of the two coordinates of chronos and topos, time and place (or space). As a discriminative tool it works well, for either of its coordinates can act as genus or differentia: the chronotope of Gogol's St Petersburg distinguishes itself from that of Dostoevsky through chronos (Gogol was writing earlier) and from that of Lermontov by topos (Lermontov describes different locations in St Petersburg though at roughly the same time as Gogol).

However, although chronotope provides a kind of latitude and longitude for the literary critic, it leaves vast areas uncharted. Psychology and characterization for instance can only be accommodated by reductive means in what is in essence an approach based on setting. Another disadvantage is that while topos as physical setting is a ubiquitous and crucial component in, for instance, nineteenth-century Russian novels and short stories, chronos is a more elusive concept and not necessarily the one which springs to mind most readily as the second defining component of a work or genre. Thus where a work revolves chiefly around a local religious conflict it might be more useful to define it thematically as a religiotope or to style works which deal with a specific social class in its own environment as a sociotope.[2] By doing this we fashion a more precise thematic instrument out of the structural raw material of the chronotope. For present purposes, then, ethnotope will offer us two coordinates by which to locate and define national themes in works of fiction: topos and ethnos. However, for a precise account of the origin of ethnos and topos in this context and in order to establish the quality of the relationship between both coordinates we must refer to a second theoretical source.

The 1830s was a period when questions of national identity began to be discussed particularly earnestly in Russia. The best known form which these discussions took was the debate between Slavophiles and Westerners which set the agenda for arguments about Russia's relationship to Europe for a century to come and the repercussions of which continue to be felt today. However, this debate was merely one strand of a complex of ideas relating to national self-awareness ushered in by a general enthusiasm for romantic aesthetics and ideology in Russia during the first three decades of the last century. Another, gleaned particularly from the writings of Herder and Madame de Staël, was the notion of autochthony developed in Russia by the writer and journalist Orest Somov. As with many other ideas imported during the romantic period the lexical estrangement wrought by translation, as well as subsequent refinements by Russian thinkers, meant that the version which took root in Russia was a distinctly Russian formulation of a European idea.

For Somov (1997, p. 24) the key requirements of literature were *narodnost* and *mestnost*. *Narodnost* meant a sense of the Folk, of nationality, in short of ethnic specificity. Its matrix was clearly romantic nationalism and, in the first instance, *narodnost* implied *our people*. For the romantic writer the Folk was encountered both as other and own, the former hypostatizing the latter in an authentic ethnic identity. Equally, *narodnost* could imply an interest in nationalities other than one's own. Indeed orientalism was by this time a recognized aesthetic end in itself; in practice, though, as Yury Lotman (1985, pp. 10–11) points out, the exotic South provided a vital bearing in the triangulation with the West by which Russia sought to locate itself in the nineteenth century. Under these conditions one's own *narod* or people is encountered comparatively or contrastively, and is literally *de-fined*, for the aesthetic role of the ethnic Other is to show where and what one's own is not. For this reason there is always likely to be an anthropological constant of cultural solipsism in the reception of this Other by the observer.

Mestnost may be regarded as the geographical or topographical equivalent of *narodnost*. As *narodnost* is ideologized ethnos, so *mestnost* is the romantic ideologization of topos, which is constructed or landscaped to yield a particular symbolism, one generally in accord with the corresponding ethnos. Such a romantic aesthetics therefore requires that authentic literature should be about a specific people in its specific place, and adapting the Bakhtinian concept we might refer to the complex of relationships between the people/place coordinates as an ethnotope. The truly ethnotopic character would be an autochthon: a person living among his or her own people in his or her own place. The concepts of ethnos and topos formulated by Russian thinkers on the basis of existing romantic ideas were themselves both symptomatic of and influential on the development of national and international themes in Russian fiction during the nineteenth century. They are thus peculiarly adapted to analysing this fiction and the fiction itself is correspondingly amenable to such analysis.

The full implications of ethnotope emerge only when it is viewed in the binary context of national identity already inherent in the autochthonous formulation: 'one's own people in its own place' – the Russian in Russia. For this primary situation implies a corresponding heterochthonous ethnotope 'The Russian in not-Russia' or, where the binary is Russia/Europe, 'The Russian in Europe'. Thus from a binary ethnic interface a fourfold model can be derived consisting of two autochthonous and two heterochthonous ethnotopes: 1. the Russian in Russia; 2. the Russian in Europe; 3. the European in Europe; 4. the European in Russia. It is theoretically possible for a narrative to contain each of these four thematic moments; in practice, however, only one or two are likely to be dominant, the rest functioning subtextually or inferentially. Of the ethnic binaries capable of providing this model for Russian writers in the nineteenth century there are two which correspond to the principal directions for which the search for Russian identity was concentrated: Russia/Europe on an east–west axis and Russia/Caucasus on a north–south axis.

Before considering individual examples of ethnotope in Russian literature we should clarify some details relating to the specific contexts in which elements of ethnos and topos can interact. The model as formulated may be termed an individual ethnotope in that it lends itself to the analysis of literary situations involving the physical location or dislocation of an individual representative of a given ethnos. For instance, stages one and two of the model taken consecutively and culminating with a return to stage one describe the experience of many young Russians aristocrats, like the poet Lensky in Pushkin's *Eugene Onegin* (1830), who were sent to Germany to complete their education. The emplotment of their experiences can be represented as a series of shifting ethnotopes. However, there are clearly more subtle ways in which ethnotope can manifest itself in literature. Individual ethnotopes need not relate simply to the subjective experience of location or dislocation. Lensky's sojourn in Germany is not described directly in the novel. It is a stored experience, the importance of which is the influence it exerts on his behaviour once back in Russia: a mnemonic rather than an experiential ethnotope – Germany remembered in Russia by a returned Russian.

The other important complex of ethnotopes relates not to personal experience but to foreign culture and cultural imports. These are cultural ethnotopes. It is true that, from a certain theoretical perspective, it may be possible to regard the popularity in Russia of both French texts and French governesses as different aspects of a single cultural phenomenon, but in the interests of critical perspective we need to be able to distinguish sharply between, for example, the presence of Napoleon in Russia as historical fact in 1812, as historical fiction (in Tolstoy's *War and Peace* [1869]) and as a fatal ideological influence (on the hero of Dostoevsky's *Crime and Punishment* [1866]). In the latter instance we are dealing with a mimetic ethnotope, the emulation of an idealized individual from another culture. A related manifestation of mimetic ethnotope recorded in nineteenth-century Russian literature is the affectation of the lifestyle and habits of an idealized European culture by (usually aristocratic) individuals who may nevertheless have had little or no significant contact with that culture. Pavel Kirsanov, the Anglophile in Turgenev's *Fathers and Children* (1862) is an extreme example. In its most diluted and neutral form the cultural ethnotope resolves itself into the manifold stereotypes, exaggerations and downright fictions by which the foreigner is designated in the home culture, in Baconian terms *idola fori*, in ours popular ethnotopes.

There is no doubt that some nineteenth-century Russian writers show particularly marked tendencies towards cultural rather than personal ethnotope. Among these are Pushkin and Dostoevsky, who in their major works deal very effectively with the Russia/Europe ethnotope without troubling themselves to dispatch their Russians to Europe. The dominant ethnotope for both Pushkin and Dostoevsky is therefore the European in Russia, but this European presence is for the most part figurative, metonymic or symbolic. The only foreigners who appear in *Eugene Onegin* are the succession of French tutors who are responsible for the

Russian hero's erratic education, but these lowly figures are merely a small part of the complex system by which European culture takes root in Russia. On the other hand, mimetic ethnotopes play a substantial part in Pushkin's novel. When Tatyana finds a bust of Napoleon and a portrait of Byron in Eugene's study she locates the two keys to his strange and distressing behaviour towards her. Pushkin was fascinated by this ability of iconized or monumentalized personalities to both be and not be present and yet to exert influence. All the major characters in *Eugene Onegin* demonstrate the presence of the foreigner in Russia by means of mimetic ethnotopes; to different degrees and out of various cultural repertoires they effectively enact specific French, German or English stereotypes in Russia while paradoxically remaining Russian.

2 PUSHKIN: RUSSIANNESS AND IMPERIUM

Ethnotope in Pushkin is characteristically diverse, given the ambitious experimentalism of this writer. *The Bronze Horseman* (1837), however, is probably his most significant achievement in this regard: himself not allowed abroad, the author peers with the visionary Peter the Great into the Europe he never visited and into the origins of the 'European' St Petersburg of which he was so characteristic a product. In many ways this work crystallizes the crisis of ethnic identity which beset Russian intellectuals in the 1830s, embodying in its theme, structure and setting the complex of ethnotopic perspectives which come together during this period.

   The Bronze Horseman opens with Peter the Great standing on the shores of the Baltic, dreaming of the city he will found there. Superficially it might seem that a king, at least, if we were to extrapolate from our own Germanic deep structure – *kin*-ing – must quintessentialize his own ethnos. However, this context of ethnic belonging and embodying is utterly abolished by Pushkin's exposition. There is no ethnic or personal orientation by way of prologue; indeed Peter is not even named. Instead, we have a jussive prediction of cityhood; Peter's royal identity is revealed by his decision to build a metropolis: he is a commander in the literal sense, an *imperator*, the efficaciousness of whom is materially borne out by the city of which Pushkin is writing, and, quite probably, in which his reader is reading. By abolishing an initial Russian context, Pushkin allows two resonances to be clearly heard. One suggests both Genesis and St John's Gospel in which, respectively, the 'Spirit of God moved upon the face of the waters', heralding the diachronic process of creation; and the prochronic word of God (*verbum* or *logos*) connoting divine kingship through its identification with Christ, without which 'was not anything made that was made'. Peter, then, is the God-man whose will is unfettered, there being no power above him. He is also, and this is the second resonance, made present to us only by his thought, which thought, becoming resolve brings all into being: poem, setting, city, history, the poet himself, the reader. Both of these elements (the only initial elements) in Pushkin's characterization, represent quite clearly a turn of thought identified by Russian thinkers as essentially (and dangerously) western.[3] We have here both the Cartesian proof of self via individual thought (the *cogito*) and the concept, soon to be elaborated by Feuerbach (and to find full expression in Nietszche) of the god-man (for if there is no higher power to restrain him, man is God).[4] Viewed from this point of view the prologic Peter in *The Bronze Horseman* is a profoundly western and non-Russian figure. The historical Peter is, of course, another matter. What is interesting about contemporary descriptions of him is the ease with which, when abroad, he embraced the role of the (literally) larger than life Russian, and indeed, perhaps the impact of his grand tour helped to set the parameters for the heterochthonous ethnotope by which Russians abroad would be defined ('the Russian in Europe').[5] In the present case, by contrast, we have an unusual characterization entirely by means of stratagems which can only signify for the reader if they are interpreted in the context of the known ideological stereotype; moreover a western stereotype.

What is it, then, which preserves Peter's Russianness in such a poem? Clearly it is topos which ensures this identity. 'From here' says Peter 'we shall threaten the Swede. Here a city shall be founded to spite our haughty neighbour' (Pushkin, 1968, p. 452).[6] War is arguably the most extreme instance of ethnic differentiation and Peter is here standing only a little way short of it. Moving as far as he can to the western boundary of his empire without physically overstepping it, Peter asserts his autochthony by threatening the ethnic Other. If the heterochthonous ethnotope suggests ethnicity affirmed in an alien environment, the autochthonous ethnotope attains to clearest articulation at national frontiers where autochthonies impinge on one another. By this potent means alone Pushkin ensures that the Peter whom he has Europeanized to an extreme degree remains simultaneously Russian. But, on closer examination, the 'nation' which, by logical inference, must be Russian, is a problematic entity. The ground on which Peter stands is not Russian, or, put another way, the ground is only Russian because Peter is standing on it. The topos which is *ante urbem conditam* and with which the poem opens is in fact Finnish. Indeed, it is the Finn alone who provides the only explicitly articulated ethnotope in the poem: 'Before him [Peter] coursed the river's broad expanse on which there sped a lonely, wretched coracle. Here and there on banks of marsh and moss stood blackened huts, shelters of the hapless Finn ...' (Pushkin, 1968, p. 452). So, in one sense, the standing Peter embodies a hete-rochthonous ethnotope – the Russian in Finland – though by the time Pushkin is writing, this place, St Petersburg, is not only no longer Finland, it is metropolitan Russia. Peter, of course, as Russian, effectively autochthonizes this Finnish ethnotope the moment he steps upon Finnish soil. If he can threaten Sweden from here then the source of this threat is already Russia and no longer Finland. However, the ethnotopes implied here – 'Russian in Finland' and, potentially, 'Russian in Sweden' – are ethnotopes of occupation and aggression. It is not the Russian abroad which is envisaged, but the Russian 'at home' thanks to violent appropria-tion. And yet: Finns, Swedes, Cartesian cogitos and philosophies of pure will ... there is nothing here which is characteristic of the Russian ethnos per se. The paradigm is essentially an imperial one, exhibiting the trans-ethnicity common to empires by definition, underpinned by a *pax Faustiana* whereby the nucleus of power retains imperium at the price of diluting its own ethnic identity.

This means that, since imperium is essentially non-ethno-specific, dis-placing the Finnish ethnos and threatening the Swedes ('... where once the Finnish fisherman ... cast his ancient net ... now ... palaces and towers crowd the lively banks ...' [Pushkin, 1968, p. 453]) Russianness proper is thematically decentred in a work which appears to celebrate the founda-tion of the modern capital of Russia by one of Russia's greatest tsars. Thus it turns out that the Russian autochthonous ethnotope in this work is embodied not in kingship but in the humble Eugene, the 'Russian in Russia' of the poem.[7] There are obviously no grounds for doubting the ethnic affiliation of Eugene (even the Greek etymology seems to under-write his credentials in this respect). The topological coordinate is, how-ever, more problematic. Is St Petersburg Russia? Time, it seems, has made this area Russia ('and before the younger capital ancient Moscow has faded like a purple clad widow before a new empress' [Pushkin, 1968, p. 453]) but the autochthony of the Russians who inhabit the city, is, to say the least, but a refracted version of the full-blooded autochthony idealized by romantic aesthetics.[8] Citizenship is, indeed, a kind of displacement of the ethnotope in which the urban affiliation interposes itself between eth-nos and primal topos operating by a kind of logical *a fortiori*: a Petersburger therefore a Russian. Although Eugene is a Russian, he is not truly an autochthon in St Petersburg: he is not representative of a people *in its own place*, since he, like the city itself, and all its inhabitants, is, in historical terms, a comparatively recent import. The sympathy which Eugene attracts to himself in the poem, and this applies to the other so-called 'little men' of Pushkin, Gogol and, later, Dostoevsky, is based upon civic, rather than ethnic considerations; the little man is an appeal to Russians' democratic rather than ethnic sentiments and he is, moreover, a metropolitan phenomenon par excellence, or, at least, like Samson Vyrin in *The Stationmaster* (1830), a provincial servant of the metropolitan centre.

St Petersburg and its citizens, then, constitute, in effect, a heterochthonous ethnotope disguised as autochthonous: the autochthony is illusory. Ethnos has appropriated topos by force and the peace between the two is uneasy. From this point of view, then, the flood which destroys Eugene's hope of a better life, driving him to madness and ultimate death from grief and self-neglect, is reappropriation by topos of its rightful space.[9] It literally occupies the abode of the interloper who is helpless before it: whereas the aboriginal Finn sped along it in his 'lonely wretched coracle' in autochthonal harmony with his surroundings, Eugene is left stranded in the flood astride a monumental lion, a stark symbol of alien artificiality. Essentially, of course, all subject ethne are alike challenged by imperium and this applies as much to Russians in the Russian empire as to other nationalities. The Russian intelligentsia's preoccupation with the *narod*, the peasant masses, as the source of genuine Russianness, has therefore to be seen in this light. It implies equally the functional deracination of other significant social groupings in imperial Russia: the bureaucracy, the aristocracy and the intelligentsia itself. There is also, moreover, a clear similarity of approach to the portrayal of the Russian peasant in nineteenth-century literature and that of the native inhabitants of the South who are discussed below.

The logic of this argument would suggest that in the context of Russian literature, autochthonous ethnotopes are not a self-evident phenomenon for either reader or author but have to be asserted as authentic over against insistent instances of non-authentic autochthony enforced by the imperial condition. Pushkin, for instance, has to assert before the reader his right to present a genuinely Russian heroine in the form of Tatyana in *Eugene Onegin*, and defend the homeliness of her name (II, 24). If she is a true autochthon – a Russian woman in Russia – the hero, with his refracted St Petersburg Russianness, is certainly not. It is, to be sure, unrealistic to argue that Tatyana is Russian, while Onegin is not, but the metropolitan, and therefore ultimately imperial, nature of Onegin's identity militates against ethnic specificity. From an ethnotopic point of view, the Europeanization of Russians like Onegin, a legacy of Peter's reforms, is not so much an ethnic phenomenon as an imperial one: the encouragement of foreign (mostly French) culture in all aspects of the life of a certain stratum of society is a vital aesthetico-ideological expression of imperium, its superstructure, in effect. It is true, of course, that the Russianness of Tatyana is itself conditional and relative; that she is also steeped in western literature and that both her parents, nurse and the few peasants we are allowed to glimpse in the novel exhibit certain traits which are more ethnically authentic than Tatyana. Indeed Tatyana's Russianness, and the degree of its adulteration, are merely elements in the whole complex of ethnotopic phenomena whereby the novel problematizes the question of national identity. Though this question is, moreover, at root one with an ethnotopic basis, I have elsewhere argued that, in *Eugene Onegin*, for instance, it can be approached by replacing the ethnic coordinate with a social one (sociotope), thus attributing to the topological location and dislocation of characters a primarily social rather than ethnic coloration.[10] This, however, is only to suggest that there may be other complementary ways of formulating intra-ethnic social division and affiliation, since both ethnotope and sociotope relate to the point of contact between group identity and physical location.

3   IMPERIAL TYPES IN GOGOL, TURGENEV AND DOSTOEVSKY

Both Gogol and Turgenev exploit similar estrangement techniques to Pushkin in delineating Russian autochthonicity. In *Dead Souls* (1842) and *The Government Inspector* (1836) a stereoscopic point of view operates whereby the Folk is seen through the eyes of a visitor from the metropolis and vice versa. These points of view are complementary; the visitor sees the ethnos only in terms of (financial, sometimes sexual) exploitation; the ethnos relates to the incomer as the incarnation of imperial power (*The Government Inspector*) or (*Dead Souls*) as an alien being of unfathomable motivation. Though superior in intelligence and cunning, a bearer of sophisticated metropolitan knowledge, the imperial figure is radically depersonalized in Gogol: Khlestakov is invested with a fraudulent official personality while the official for whom he has been mistaken, the real government inspector who is announced at the end of the play, has necessarily no personality at all (being uncharacterized), and is, like Peter in *The Bronze Horseman*, pure power. Likewise, Chichikov in *Dead Souls* is deliberately depersonalized by Gogol ('a gentleman not handsome, but also not bad-looking, not too fat and not too thin; you couldn't say he was old, neither that he was too young': Gogol, 1960, V, p. 9). The peripatetic nature of these characters further adds to this depersonalization: they are the antithesis of the real, rooted, topologically located populations among whom they find themselves. The exploitative model here is essentially imperial and, apart from its intra-ethnicity, has broad affinities with the inter-ethnic instances of exploitation which we find, for instance, in literary treatments of the Caucasus around the same time (1830s–40s).

The relationship between psychological authenticity and ethnicity is crucial in Russian literature in this period: to be real is to be ethnically rooted. The deracinated figures of Dostoevsky, whether they originate in St Petersburg or not, tend to be associated with ideas relating broadly to imperium. Thus the theoretical premise of Raskolnikov's murderous acts in *Crime and Punishment* is that humanity is divided between a servile majority and a tiny élite who are destined to rule: most recently exemplified by Napoleon. Ivan Karamazov is associated with the Legend of the Grand Inquisitor which represents the Catholic Church as a religious imperium in which the paradigm of earthly political power has entirely supplanted the divine law of its founder. It does not do enough justice to the significance of these characters to regard the intellectual constructs they produce as merely evidence of western influence in its more pernicious aspects. What is clearly more important in such cases is an imperial concept of power, shared equally by Russia and the West. In each of the above cases, however, this imperial paradigm is an introjected *idée fixe* which has ousted individual identity. Raskolnikov and Ivan Karamazov are as much victims of the imperial model as is Peter's Eugene in *The Bronze Horseman*.

Turgenev's *Sketches from a Hunter's Album* (1847–51) use the same peripatetic device as Gogol's works but the protagonist's imposture is of a more subtle nature. Turgenev's hero is a hunter only in the most tokenistic of senses. It is a sham occupation in that the evidence for its pursuit in the *Sketches* is far outweighed by preoccupations of a different order. Since Turgenev was an avowed Westernizer it is not surprising that the received interpretation of the hunter device is that it is part of a rhetorical strategy whereby Turgenev expresses his progressive views on the humanity of the peasant and his disgust at the abuses meted out to them by brutal landowners and their bailiffs. Yet, as a reformer, Turgenev merely locates himself as a modified or progressive imperialist. Turgenev's reformist politics is clearly felt in his attitudes and characterizations. Ironically it is this ideological coloration which marks him out as non-autochthonous among the peasantry.[11] In a sense the hunter comports himself like a spy in enemy territory: eavesdropping to obtain the peasants' true views on situations makes him a benign intelligence gatherer and, except for this moral nuancing, one engaged in similar reconnaissance activities to Maxim Maximych in his eavesdroppings in *A Hero of Our Time* (1840). Indeed, the travelogic style of Turgenev's hunter in the heart of Russia is not so very far removed from the Baedekerism of the Narrator in *A Hero of Our Time*.[12] The first person narration of the *Sketches* reinforces the solipsistic isolation of the narrator with respect to the Folk. With his venatic alibi and his judgemental exposé of abuses in the countryside he is not too remote from the official government inspector whose total congruence with officialdom is underlined by his being announced but not witnessed at the end of the eponymous play. In Turgenev's hunter a liberal democratic inspectorate comes to judge, condemn and defend.

4   THE EUROPEAN IN RUSSIA AND THE RUSSIAN IN EUROPE

Russian literature of the nineteenth century provides significant, if problematic, instances of the 'European in Russia' ethnotope in individual, experiential form. Stolz in Goncharov's *Oblomov* (1859) and Insarov in Turgenev's *On the Eve* (1860) are important examples, though on close inspection they prove to have features which prevent them functioning as full representatives of the European Other in the Russian social context. Stolz, for instance, is only half German and was born in Russia. He only appears foreign when his dynamism and hard work, popularly thought of as Germanic traits, are contrasted with the extreme slothfulness of his friend Oblomov, a Russian landowner. Stolz is so drawn that it is not his Germanness that matters but his manifestation of 'Germanic' traits. Insarov the Bulgarian revolutionary in Turgenev's *On the Eve* likewise brings into Russia supposedly un-Russian qualities of selfless patriotism, commitment to a cause and decisiveness. He too, however, is effectively compromised by his nationality: as a Bulgarian among Russians he is a fellow Slav and co-religionist, almost an honorary Russian. His experience as a foreigner in Russia is less important than his galvanizing influence on the Russian heroine of the novel who espouses his political cause and ultimately eclipses him as the novel's protagonist.

For heterochthonous ethnotopes of a genuinely experiential kind we must turn to two quite different sources: Russian works specifically set in Europe and works based on the long-running conflict between the Russian army and the Muslim tribes of the Caucasus. Turgenev offers some striking examples of the Russian in Europe ethnotope. His novel *Smoke* (1867) and two of his short stories, *Asya* (1858) and *Spring Torrents* (1870), are set in Germany. These works draw upon the ethnotope instanced by Lensky in *Eugene Onegin* – the Russian in Germany – and revolve around the romantic experiences of young men engaged on the European grand tour or variations thereof. The German setting in *Asya* is largely introductory: the isolated Russian hero finds himself in a small town on the Rhine during a student festival. While watching the celebrations he encounters two other travelling Russians, a man and a woman, with whom he ultimately forms the intense relationship which supplies the story's plot. Although there are some disparaging initial remarks about the undesirability of encountering one's fellow Russians abroad, the German setting serves here mainly to promote the intimacy and collective isolation of the three Russian characters within a necessarily finite time-span, and more subtly, to allow their respective Russian backgrounds to be reviewed with an objectivity imparted by distance. Structural, rather than thematic, considerations such as these also seem to underlie the German setting of *Smoke*. The events in *Asya* are relayed retrospectively by a participative first person narrator, now in middle-age. We may assume that the action was meant to take place in the 1830s during the heyday of romanticism in Russia. The Germany described is therefore literally the place of the narrator's youth, a kind of topological evocation of youthful idealism.

Spring Torrents uses remarkably similar raw material to *Asya* but from an ethnotopic point of view is a far more interesting work. The narrator is again a middle-aged man recollecting events in Germany some thirty years before and therefore at a somewhat later period than in the first story: 1840. The 23-year-old hero, returning from Italy to Russia, has broken his journey in Frankfurt. Here he falls in love with the daughter of an Italian sweetshop owner and stays on in the city with the intention of marrying her and taking her to Russia.

The ethnotope in this story is complex: the Russian in Europe ethnotope occurs in two symbolic variants: the Russian in Italy and the Russian in Germany. The first of these is only an inferential presence in the text, since the Russian hero, Sanin, has already left Italy by the time that the story begins, but it is sustained by the social and emotional contact which he makes, quite by chance, with the exiled Italian family in Frankfurt.

Gemma, the young woman of Italian parentage with whom Sanin falls in love, is partly Germanized: she speaks German fluently and reads German literature. Her Italian-in-Germany ethnotope is perceived by her Russian lover in ambiguous terms: her love of Schiller, for instance, is used to reinforce her romantic temperament which, however, is presented in the story as symptomatic of her Italian heritage. The rest of her family are parodic Italians: an old retainer who is a retired opera singer and a mother who is a fervent republican.

The Russian traveller has a rival for Gemma in the person of a respectable German businessman to whom she is already engaged. He is portrayed as staid, sensible and boring and is finally cast aside by Gemma when he fails to avenge an insult to her honour; this duty is performed by Sanin who challenges the German army officer responsible for the insult to a duel.

Two national stereotypes emerge in the story: the Italians are portrayed as passionate and artistically sensitive; the Germans are solidly entrepreneurial and absorbed with questions of national unity. However, the story also uses popular ethnotope to produce a correspondingly conventional view of Russians: Sanin's presence in the Italian household elicits from its members vague speculations about Russian life:

> Her picture of Russia had been of a country where snow lay permanently and everyone went round in a fur coat and served in the army – but that the hospitality was quite extraordinary and all the peasants were very obedient.
>
> (Turgenev, 1972, p. 25)

Sanin's willingness to engage the less than enthusiastic German officer in a duel is interpreted by the Italians both as a romantic act and one characteristic of the Russian martial ethos: Russian and Italian romantic values for a moment allied against German civic virtue and bourgeois prudence. All this is undone by the story's unexpected dénouement: In order to raise money for his marriage Sanin decides to sell his family estate to a rich Russian woman who, together with her husband, is taking the waters in Wiesbaden. The woman seduces Sanin who, too ashamed to return to his Italians, slinks home to Russia where he lives out his life in protracted regret for his conduct.

Sanin's 'return to Russia' effectively takes place the moment he meets and consorts with the expatriate Russians in Wiesbaden. His jettisoning of the Italians marks the limit of the wholesome affinity between the two sets of cultural values and the start of an exploration of the negative side of the Russian character. The story seeks to define Russianness first through foreign eyes (the Russian in non-Russia) then through Russian eyes (the Russian in Russia). The structures of both *Asya* and *Spring Torrents* ensure that the foreign episode will have only a component role in what is essentially a Russian experience: the stories are framed by a mnemonic ethnotope: the detailed recollection by the hero of a period abroad up to the point where he returns to Russia and the embalming of this primal European experience begins.

5   RUSSIA AND THE CAUCASUS

The other important ethnotope which the present chapter will address is the Caucasian-Russian interface. In this explicitly imperialist context, movement is largely in one direction – Russians into the Caucasus – and there is very little of the reverse ethnotope: the Caucasian in Russia. Equally because the Russo-Caucasian ethnotope is based on the military occupation of the Caucasus by the Russians the autochthonous Caucasian ethnotope is contrastively obtrusive. In the works of Lermontov 'Caucasian in the Caucasus' is a theme equally important as Russians in the Caucasus, and some of his verse narratives deal exclusively with intra- as opposed to inter-ethnic conflicts. Lermontov's narrative poems treat such supposedly primitive themes as murder, abduction and vengeance among the mountain tribes. Inevitably, however, the autochthonous ethnotopes produced by Lermontov and other Russian writers on the Caucasus are coloured both by imperialist preconceptions about the aboriginals and by a romantic taste for exoticism.

Pushkin set the experimental parameters for the Caucasian ethnotope with two works: *The Prisoner in the Caucasus* (1822) and *The Gipsies* (1824). The latter, though not itself set in the Caucasus, nevertheless translates the imperial theme into the south with Pushkin's characteristic symbolic economy. The hero, Aleko, is a fugitive, possibly from political persecution, who finds refuge with a group of gypsies wandering through Moldavia. On one level it is the orthodox romantic project of the civilized hero seeking refuge among simple children of nature. However, typically for Pushkin, the schematic nature of the work's structure leaves room for the emergence of broader connotations. The hero, Aleko, is not obviously Russian by his name: he is a kind of everyman exile. The gypsies also present an interesting ethnotopic category. They are described as wandering 'in a clamorous throng through Bessarabia' (Pushkin, 1968, p. 381) and so are, from one point of view, an ethnos in a given topos. On the other hand, there is within this topos a settled population which the gypsies entertain on their travels and the members of this must logically be their rivals for autochthonous status. Moreover, the gypsy ethnos cannot be said to be coincident with topos, in that, by their wanderings and presence in various geographical areas, gypsies may be said to belong both everywhere and nowhere. The gypsies' moral code is also as fluid as their movement (indeed the latter becomes a metaphor for the former). Aleko is finally expelled from the company of the gypsies because he murders his lover for her infidelity; the gypsy ethos demands tolerance of others' freedom to act. In this way we may infer that the civilized, probably northern Aleko, has, paradoxically, more in common with the settled ethne of the south, such as, for instance, the Circassians, who would be equally intolerant of such behaviour.

The gypsies are used by Pushkin in a choral role with respect to other settled peoples. Empires come and go but the moral fluidity and physical mobility of the gypsies ensure that they will adapt and endure. The old gypsy who is the father of Aleko's lover compares Aleko's fate among the gypsies to that of Ovid. This classical paradigm of exile is made to emerge as folk memory from the lips of the old man who uses it as an illustration of failure to adapt rather than of the cruelty of absolute power. It is Aleko himself who affirms the conventional view of Ovid as essentially a victim of imperial whim:

> So this is the fate of your sons,
> O Rome, O mighty power!...
> Singer of love, singer of the gods,
> Tell me, what is glory?
> A sound from the grave, the voice of praise,
> Heard from generation to generation?
> Or the tale of a wild gypsy
> Beneath his smoky tent?
>
> (Pushkin, 1968, p. 387)

The conversion of Ovid's biography into a piece of gypsy myth embeds it into the action of the narrative far more effectively than if it had simply been introduced by digressive instantiation. Like the Latin poet's own mythical history of Rome in *Metamorphoses* the plot leaps from one significant event to the next across the lacunae of centuries. The empire which exiled Ovid has fallen; others have replaced it. Only the poet's tragic fate is remembered by the gypsy bard, a metonymic fragment of an imperial past. But it is a fragment returned to its significant context by the fate of Aleko. Pushkin has turned the imperial perspective upside-down: here it is not (as in his *Bronze Horseman*) creators of empires who are remembered, but exiles from empire, exile being the reverse (or obverse) of the centripetal tendency on which the formation and maintenance of empire depends. The stone which the empire-builders have rejected, to paraphrase St Matthew and the Psalms, is now all that remains. For this temporal perspective to achieve full rhetorical effect the gypsies themselves have to be immune to conventional ethnic definition, by which would be implied a settled autochthony with a history, with the vicissitudes of conquest and enslavement as well as perhaps absorption into empire itself.

If *The Gipsies* succeeds in transcending the preoccupations of fixed ethnotope in favour of more generalized musings on the nature of empire, Pushkin's *Prisoner in the Caucasus* represents a quite specific aspect of Russian imperial expansion. It is the first of a number of works by Russian writers which deal with Russia's encroachment on the free tribes of the Caucasus which intensified in violence during the early part of the last century. These works effect a blend of romantic exoticism with real and often anthropologically accurate observations on life in the Caucasus (both for natives and occupiers) during the period when this area was gradually absorbed into the Russian empire.

The Prisoner in the Caucasus describes the capture of a Russian officer by Caucasian tribesmen who intend to hold him for ransom, a common practice during the early nineteenth century. In the course of his captivity he is befriended by a young Caucasian woman; they fall in love and she helps him to make his escape, she however drowning as they try to cross the treacherous waters of a mountain river. Pushkin's hillsmen have admirable qualities of martial ferocity and untamed virtues, while the captured Russian is a typical young (possibly 'superfluous') man of his time, disillusioned with life's pleasures and embittered by past misfortunes in love and therefore unable to reciprocate that of the native girl. The power of this story (which was imitated or reproduced by several later Russian writers) lies in the inversion of the roles of captor and captive, normally enforced by the imperial experience: the conqueror of the Caucasus himself conquered. Although the heroine's ability to physically liberate the captive is the defining feature of the plot, the theme itself is underpinned by the more figurative notion of romantic liberation through love.[13] The autochthonous identity of the heroine of *The Prisoner in the Caucasus* is underlined by the fact that she dies in her own country (probably willingly, in despair for the loss of her Russian lover). The emotional impoverishment of the hero identifies him as an imperial type. Incapacity for love is a central feature of the hero's inauthenticity; it means that, unlike the Circassian warriors, the Russian carries out his warlike duties with melancholic fatalism and without authentic personal commitment. Here are the philosophical credentials of the imperial functionary as evinced by the classical prototypes of Marcus Aurelius and Pontius Pilate. There is no proper development of the 'Caucasian in the Caucasus' ethnotope in *The Prisoner in the Caucasus* because the Russianness of the hero is swamped by his captivity and a mere abstract otherness. Equally, however, the Caucasian ethnotope is not allowed to proceed beyond highly romanticized reflections on and portraits of the noble warriors of the highlands. Their warlike appetites take them frequently out of the village where the Russian is held captive and this prevents their participation in any plot involving him, a void which is filled by the heroine and the romantic plot.

This is the limit of Pushkin's exploitation of the Caucasian ethnotope. It is left to Lermontov, with vastly more experience of the region and active service in the army, to enrich both the constituent terms of the ethnotope by means of realistic descriptions both of the occupying Russians and the native tribes. Much of his narrative poetry (*The Fugitive* [1838], *Kally* [1830–1], and *Hadzhi Abrek* [1833–4]) is devoted to the latter and although it is formulated in a conventional romantic idiom, its central themes are anthropologically accurate instances of intra-ethnic conflict: ethical crises such as abduction, revenge, punishment for cowardice, etc. Lermontov's relish in describing the warlike and uncompromising attitudes of the tribesmen typifies the respect of the imperial conqueror for the conquered. We find the same, albeit grudging, respect for Caucasian prowess expressed by Maxim Maxymich in *A Hero of Our Time*. This myth of mutual respect by conqueror and conquered is one of the validating political premises of empire.

Lermontov's novel, *A Hero of Our Time*, unlike his verse, provides instances of both autochthonous and heterochthonous ethnotopes. It is a collection of five stories bound together by the experiences of Pechorin, a young Russian officer in the Caucasus. The brash newcomer is eager to interfere in the delicate balance between native and Russian occupier and his abduction of a young Chechen princess nearly causes a serious incident. While the newly posted or newly exiled Russian cavalry officer is a stereotype of the Russian occupation, another perhaps more interesting type is that of the naturalized Caucasian. Pechorin's commanding officer in Chechenia Maxim Maximych, is a Russian who has spent so many years in the Caucasus that he has gone partially native. This causes him to be singled out in the novel as a paragon of Russian adaptability but his asiatic acculturation has been at the price of isolation from a rapidly developing Russian metropolitan culture; his successful image in the novel is tarnished by his failure to appreciate the actions and motivations of the sophisticated Russian incomers with whom he comes into contact. Acculturation is therefore not a solution to the problem of the interaction between Russians and the ethnic Other and the ethnotopic progression for the Russian in the Caucasus is essentially the same as it is for Europe: Russian in Russia – Russian in the Caucasus – Russian in Russia.

Tolstoy explored the question of acculturation in the Caucasus from a different point of view and with different results. Olenin, the hero of his novel *The Cossacks* (1863), takes the conventional military route to the Caucasus but, unlike his forbears in Lermontov's works, does not reach the front line where there is the possibility of real contact and conflict between Russian and Caucasian. Instead he is billeted in a Cossack settlement on the edge of Russian-held territory. The Cossacks constitute a distinct collective ethnotope. They exemplify the results of mass acculturation and considerably problematize the question of Russian ethno-cultural identity. Descendants of runaway serfs who fled to the margins of the Empire, they have adopted many of the habits of their Muslim neighbours, are tribally inclined and have a macho military culture. On the other hand, they are fanatically Orthodox, eager to defend the interests of Christian Russia against the infidel, drink alcohol and have a far more liberal attitude to their women than their Muslim neighbours. Never having been enserfed, they do not flatter the incoming Russian officers with the sort of servility accorded to the latter at home on their estates or by their own batmen who travel with them. They have preserved archaic speech patterns and Russian traditions now lost in their country of origin and abhor the modern Russian's taste for tobacco. For the Russian incomer, then, the Cossack ethnotope is both autochthonous and heterochthonous. The Cossack both belongs and does not belong to the Caucasus and in his preservation of traditions now lost in Russia is paradoxically more Russian than the Russians. (Cecil Sharpe, incidentally, offers a similar portrayal of the Appalachian mountaineers he encountered early in this century.)

Tolstoy's hero returns to Russia enriched by his experience among a free people who, though in one sense alien, are for Tolstoy's purposes real Russians who will serve to reinforce his belief in a genuine Russian peasant culture and values.

On the whole both Europe and the Caucasus are used by nineteenth-century Russian writers to further the greater project of a search for Russian identity. Of the four basic ethnotopes: Russian in Russia; Russian in non-Russia; non-Russian in non-Russia; the non-Russian in Russia, we will find that it is a sequential combination of the first two which predominates: Russian abroad: Russian in Russia. The narrative supersession of this final state – a permanent return to Russia after a temporary experience abroad – implies the valorization of Russian over foreign culture, and of recollection over what is recollected. This transformation of the experiential into the mnemonic facilitates the integration of the Other into the autochthonous ethnotope of national self-identity: the Russian in Russia.

NOTES

1.   For a full explication of the concept see my 'Ethnotope in Lermontov's Caucasian Poemy', in Reid (1992).
2.   I have in fact developed the sociotope in the context of the Russian society tale in Reid (1998).
3.   On this Russian anti-rational philosophical tradition see my 'Russian Intuitivism', in Reid (1980).

4. See, in particular, Feuerbach's *The Essence of Christianity* (1841). In Russia Vladimir Solovyov was most closely associated with alerting to the dangers of this phenomenon and his influence on Dostoevsky in this area is particularly marked. On Dostoevsky's fictional elaboration of this question see Walicki (1980, pp. 315–26).

5. For details of his excesses in England, see, for instance, Kochan (1982, p. 98).

6. This and subsequent Pushkin quotations are from: Pushkin, A. S., 1968, I. Hereafter 'Pushkin'.

7. It is true that *Rossiia* is used twice in the latter stages of the prologue of the poem but in terms designed to heighten the imperial connotations: 'When Russia once again celebrates a victory over the enemy ... unshakable as Russia' (Pushkin, 1968, p. 454). Besides this, we must note the use of the more ethnically coloured *Rus* when an explicit autochthonous ethnotope is intended – Chapter 2 of *Eugene Onegin* – where a punning epigraph heralds the arrival of the metropolitan Onegin in authentic rural Russia: O rus! (Hor.) O Rus!

8. Under these conditions Moscow comes increasingly to symbolize the genuine old Russia, and from the 1830s becomes the focus for Slavophile nationalism.

9. Clearly, conflictual ethonotopes are of two principal kinds: (1) those in which the invader or occupier is in conflict with the autochtonous ethnos; (2) those in which the invader or occupier is in conflict with the topos. In artistic practice the two often occur side by side, as, for instance, in the Hollywood western tradition, in which typically settlers must contend not only with hostile natives but with a metaphorically hostile environment.

10. See Note 2.

11. Turgenev's memoir on the Russian peasantry written during his period in the Ministry of Internal Affairs (1842) is very instructive in this context. Opening with the dubious anthropological contention that Russia is the only major European state in which the ruling class are of the same ethnic origin as the ruled, it moves on to lament the lack of 'civic' consciousness in the peasant who is thereby excluded from participation in the sort of modern state which Turgenev clearly wants to see. Inevitably then, Turgenev, himself a landowner, is forced to look in on the peasant from the outside: 'on closer acquaintance' he has admirable 'resourcefulness', although '... it recalls the resourcefulness and mental agility of a fox, and is therefore unworthy of a man living in a well-ordered society'. See Turgenev (1960, I, pp. 459–72).

12. I borrow this term from Layton (1994).

13. Indeed Lermontov's *Bela* shares this theme with *The Prisoner in the Caucasus* despite the fact that its Russian hero imprisons the native heroine.

REFERENCES

Bakhtin, M. M., 'The Forms of Time and the Chronotopos in the Novel', in *PTL*, Vol. III, 1978, pp. 493–528.

Gogol, N. V., *Sobranie khudozhestvennykh proizvedenii v piati tomakh* (ed. Bazanov, V. G., Moscow, Izdatelstvo Akademiya Nauk SSSR, 1960).

Kochan, L., *The Making of Modern Russia* (Harmondsworth, Penguin, 1982).

Layton, S., *Russian Literature and Empire: Conquest of the Caucasus from Pushkin to Tolstoy* (Cambridge, Cambridge University Press, 1994).

Lotman, Yu. M., 'Problema vostoka i zapada v tvorchestve pozdnego Lermontova', in Chistova, I. S. (ed.), *Lermontovskii sbornik* (Leningrad, Nauka, 1985), pp. 5–22.

Pushkin, A. S., *Izbrannye proizvedeniia v dvukh tomakh* (eds Volina, V. *et al.*, Moscow, Khudozhestvennaia literatura, 1968).

Reid, R. E., 'Russian Intuitivism', *Irish Slavonic Studies*, Vol. 1, 1980, pp. 43–59.

Reid, R. E., 'Ethnotope in Lermontov's Caucasian Poemy', *Russian Literature*, XXXI, 1992, pp. 555–73.

Reid, R. E., '*Princess Ligovskaya* and *Princess Mary*: the Society Tale Goes to the Caucasus', in Cornwell, N. (ed.), *The Society Tale in Russian Literature from Odoevski to Tolstoy* (Amsterdam, Rodopi, 1998), pp. 41–57.

Somov, O., 'On Romantic Poetry', in Leighton, L. (ed.), *Russian Romantic Criticism: an Anthology* (Connecticut, Greenwood Press, 1997), pp. 21–45.

Turgenev, I. S., *Polnoe sobranie sochinenii i pisem v dvadtsati vosmi tomakh* (ed. Alekseev, M. P. *et al.*, Moscow-Leningrad, Nauka, 1960).

Turgenev, I., *Spring Torrents* (Harmondsworth, Penguin, 1972).

Walicki, A., *A History of Russian Thought from the Enlightenment to Marxism* (Oxford, Oxford University Press, 1980).

Index